LEGAL STUDIES SERIES

BASIC LAW OFFICE MANAGEMENT

Vena Garrett
Saddleback College
Mission Viejo, CA

GLENCOE

Macmillan/McGraw–Hill

Lake Forest, Illinois
Columbus, Ohio
Mission Hills, California
Peoria, Illinois

Library of Congress Cataloging-in-Publication Data

Garrett, Vena, date.
    Basic law office management / Vena Garrett.
       p.   cm. — (Legal studies series)
    Includes index.
    ISBN 0-02-800282-2 (paperback) :
    1. Law offices—United States.   I. Title.   II. Series.
    KF318.G37   1991
    340′.068—dc20   91-26760

Send all inquiries to:
GLENCOE DIVISION
Macmillan/McGraw-Hill
936 Eastwind Drive
Westerville, OH 43081

ISBN 0-02-800282-2

Printed in the United States of America.

1 2 3 4 5 6 7 8 9   POH   99 98 97 96 95 94 93 92 91

This book is dedicated to all secretaries and paralegals, the unsung heroes who make the rest of us look good in our endeavors, and to my mother, who knows how to do this especially well.

ABOUT THE AUTHOR

After holding positions as legal secretary, paralegal, and law office manager, Vena Garrett opened the first personnel agency in Orange County, California, to specialize in placing temporary and full-time law office personnel. Simultaneously, she became a partner in Ruzzuti-Garrett Corporate Training, one the nation's first training companies to develop secretarial training programs and boss-secretary team building for Fortune 500 companies.

Consulting assignments have included long-range planning for personnel and training, developing train-the-trainer programs and materials, conducting in-house needs assessments, designing program evaluation instruments, and presenting firm-specific programs to all levels of personnel.

As an adjunct instructor in paralegal programs at Saddleback College in Mission Viejo, California, and the University of California at Riverside, Vena Garrett has authored curricula, classroom materials, and evaluation instruments.

Writing projects include her work as author, contributing author, and reviewer of textbooks for various publishers within the paralegal discipline. She is a contributing author to New Business Opportunities magazine. Her educational background includes receiving an M.B.A. (emphasis in human behavior) from National University and a B.S. (management) from Pepperdine University.

CONTENTS

Preface ——————————————————————————— xiii

PART ONE

LAW OFFICE MANAGEMENT CONCEPTS

CHAPTER 1 Functions of the Law Office Manager ———— 2

1–1 Introduction to Law Office Management ——————— 3

Who Becomes a Law Office Manager? ———— 3
Management Terms Defined —————— 4
Practice Management and Operations
Management ——————————— 5

1–2 The Tangible Law Office Management Skills ———— 5

The Planning Function —————— 6
The Organizing Function —————— 10
The Staffing Function —————— 11
The Directing Function —————— 12
The Controlling Function —————— 15

1–3 The Intangible Law Office Management Skills ———— 17

Interpersonal Roles —————— 17
Informational Roles —————— 19
Decisional Roles —————— 19

1–4 The Need for Law Office Management ——————— 20

Today's Law Firms —————— 21

CHAPTER 2   Tracking Revenue and Expenses —— **24**

2–1   Types of Legal Fees and Costs —————— 25

Retainer Fees —————— 25
Contingent Fees —————— 25
Fixed Fees —————— 26
Statutory Fees —————— 26
Hourly Fees —————— 26
Legal Costs and Overhead Expenses ———— 26

2–2   Practice Management Concepts —————— 27

How Fees Are Determined —————— 27
Formula for Setting Hourly Fees ———— 27
The Leveraging Concept —————— 28
The Mix of Business (Practice
Management) —————— 28

2–3   Keeping Track of Time —————————— 29

Why Timekeeping Is Important ———— 30
Timekeeping Systems —————— 30

2–4   Keeping Track of Costs and Expenses ———— 35

Telephone Charges —————— 35
Facsimile Charges —————— 37
Photocopy Expenses —————— 37
Messenger and Courier Service Expenses ——— 37
Ethical Considerations —————— 38

2–5   Client Billing Procedures —————————— 38

Manual Billing —————— 38
Computerized Billing —————— 38
Billing Dos and Don'ts —————— 39

PART TWO

THE TANGIBLE LAW OFFICE MANAGEMENT SKILLS

CHAPTER 3   Administrative Effectiveness in the Law Office —————————— **44**

3–1   Making Good Impressions —————————— 45

Choosing a Telephone System —————— 45
Voice Mail —————— 47
Managing the Reception Staff —————— 48

3–2 Records Management _____ 50

    Creating Files _____ 50
    Filing Systems _____ 53
    Selecting Filing Equipment _____ 56
    Organizing Active Files _____ 59
    Managing Inactive Files _____ 59

3–3 Managing the Law Library _____ 62

    Function of the Library _____ 64
    Automating the Library _____ 64

3–4 Managing Office Equipment and Consumables _____ 65

    Purchasing Equipment _____ 66
    Renting and Leasing Equipment _____ 67
    Tax Considerations _____ 68
    Managing Office Consumables _____ 68

CHAPTER 4 Law Office Facilities Management _____ 73

4–1 When to Consider a Move _____ 74

    Expansion _____ 74
    Consolidation _____ 74
    Image Enhancement _____ 75

4–2 How to Assess an Office Building _____ 75

    Area and Accessibility _____ 75
    The Building Itself _____ 75
    Standard Workletter _____ 80
    The Lease _____ 83
    Lease Checklist _____ 85
    Services of a Commercial Real Estate
    Broker _____ 85

4–3 Getting the Most Usage from Your Office Space _____ 86

    Conducting a Needs Assessment _____ 87
    The Space Plan _____ 87
    Fighting the Space War _____ 88

4–4 Moving the Law Office _____ 91

    Select a Moving Company _____ 91
    Get Estimates of Moving Costs _____ 92
    Take Care of Details _____ 92

4–5 Planning for a Law Office Disaster _____ 93

    How to Prepare for a Disaster _____ 93

CHAPTER 5 Information Management in the Law Office _____ **98**

5–1 Inside the Microcomputer _____ **99**

The Microchip _____ *99*
The Central Processing Unit _____ *100*
Memory _____ *100*
Storage Capacity _____ *100*
Auxiliary Storage _____ *101*
Peripherals _____ *101*
The Operating System _____ *102*
Power Protection Devices _____ *103*

5–2 Five Steps to Cost-Effective Information Management _____ **103**

Step One: Determine Need _____ *103*
Step Two: Choose Software _____ *106*
Step Three: Choose Hardware _____ *109*
Step Four: Select Vendors _____ *109*
Step Five: Networking and Other Options _____ *110*

5–3 Law Office Management Support Software _____ **115**

Document Management Software _____ *115*
Litigation Management Software _____ *116*
Calendar Software _____ *116*

5–4 Preventing Computer-Related Management Problems _____ **118**

Computer Viruses and Bugs _____ *118*
Legal and Ethical Considerations of Software Usage _____ *119*
The Impact of Computers on Management of Support Staff _____ *119*
Coping with the Industrial Injury of the Information Age _____ *120*
Eight Problems a Computer Cannot Solve _____ *121*

CHAPTER 6 Basic Finance for the Law Office Manager _____ **125**

6–1 Basic Accounting Principles _____ **126**

Principle One: Entity _____ *127*
Principle Two: Profit _____ *128*
Principle Three: Time _____ *128*
Principle Four: Profits, Property, Owners' Interest, and Debt (PPOD) _____ *129*
Principle Five: Income _____ *130*
Principle Six: Expense _____ *131*
The Accounting Cycle _____ *132*

6–2   How to Read Financial Statements _____ 134

    *What Kind of Information Should
      You Track?* _____ 134
    How Do You Organize the Information? _____ 135
    *How to Interpret the Basic Financial
      Statements* _____ 135

6–3   How to Develop Budgets _____ 137

    Partner Compensation _____ 138
    Partner Capital _____ 138
    Billing Rates _____ 138
    Steps in Preparing Budgets _____ 138

6–4   Cash Flow Management _____ 143

    Recognizing Cash Flow Problems _____ 143
    Typical Responses to Cash Flow Problems _____ 144
    Components of Cash Flow Management _____ 144

CHAPTER 7   Personnel Management _____ **148**

7–1   How the Times Have Changed _____ 149

    Culture Defined _____ 149
    Cultural Changes and Employees _____ 150
    Employment at Will _____ 150
    Federal Legislation _____ 151
    History of EEO Legislation _____ 151
    *Creating a Safe and Healthful Work
      Environment* _____ 155

7–2   Creating Personnel Policies _____ 158

    The Need for Policies _____ 159
    How to Write Personnel Policies _____ 159

7–3   Factors in Employee Compensation _____ 160

    Factor 1: Compensation Objectives _____ 160
    Factor 2: External Economic Conditions _____ 160
    Factor 3: Internal Considerations _____ 161

7–4   Guidelines for Hiring Personnel _____ 163

    How to Define the Job and the Position _____ 163
    How to Find Qualified Applicants _____ 164
    How to Conduct an Interview _____ 165

7–5   Methods of Evaluating Employee Performance _____ 167

    Management by Objectives _____ 168
    Coworker Evaluation of Performance _____ 169
    Management Performance Evaluation _____ 169

7–6 How to Increase Employee Job Satisfaction _____ 169

    Find Ways to Enrich Each Job and Position ____ 173
    Try the Team Approach _____ 173
    Consider Adjustments in Work Schedules _____ 175

PART THREE

THE INTANGIBLE LAW OFFICE MANAGEMENT SKILLS

CHAPTER 8 Communication Skills and the Law
    Office Manager _____ 180

8–1 How Communication Breaks Down _____ 181

    Elements of Effective Communication _____ 181
    Barriers in Effective Communication _____ 182

8–2 Communicating without Words _____ 185

    Body Language _____ 185
    Decoding Nonverbal Communication _____ 187

8–3 How to Become an Effective Listener _____ 188

    Effective Listening Techniques _____ 188

8–4 How to Give Constructive Feedback _____ 191

    Positive Feedback _____ 191
    Negative Feedback _____ 192

8–5 How Communication Flows within the Firm _____ 194

    The Formal Networks _____ 195
    The Informal Networks _____ 196

CHAPTER 9 How to Be a Leader _____ 200

9–1 Leadership Styles _____ 201

    Autocratic Leadership _____ 201
    Developmental Leadership _____ 202
    Situational Leadership _____ 204

9–2 Leadership Attitudes _____ 205

    Theory X Attitude _____ 205
    Theory Y Attitude _____ 206
    Derived X Attitude _____ 206

9–3   Motivation ———————————————— 208

    Maslow's Need Theory ——————————— 208
    Herzberg's Two-Factor Motivation Theory ——— 211
    Modern Motivation Problems ——————— 212

9–4   Power and Its Impact ————————— 214

    Position Power ————————————— 215
    Personal Power ————————————— 215
    Office Politics —————————————— 215

CHAPTER 10   Managing Groups ——————— 219

10–1   The Nature of Groups ————————— 220

    The Reason for Groups ————————— 220
    Types of Groups ————————————— 221
    Group Characteristics ————————— 222

10–2   Group Conflicts ——————————— 223

    Group Goals and Individual Goals ————— 223
    Agendas ——————————————— 223
    Groupthink —————————————— 224

10–3   Resolving Conflicts ————————— 225

    Managing Controversy —————————— 226
    Managing Conflict of Interest ——————— 229

10–4   Solving Problems and Making Decisions ——— 230

    Problem-Solving Steps ————————— 230

10–5   Negotiating Effective Solutions ————— 233

    Negotiation Styles and Their Outcomes ——— 233
    Choosing a Negotiating Style ——————— 235

Glossary —————————————————— 239

Index ——————————————————— 249

PREFACE

The practice of law is not limited to providing legal services to clients. To survive in today's highly competitive legal services market, all law firms, from the megafirm to the sole practitioner, must apply the basic principles of management. In the smaller firms, the duties and responsibilities of law office manager are often passed on to a paralegal or legal secretary, or to someone who has little or no experience with the basic concepts of sound management principles.

The goal of *Basic Law Office Management* is to provide an overview of general management principles as they apply to managing today's law office. The text is appropriate for students who have no experience in a law firm environment as well as for those currently on a career track leading to managing a law office.

Organization of the Text

The text is composed of three parts. Part One, "Law Office Management Concepts," includes two chapters that introduce the generally recognized operations functions of management and provide a comprehensive overview of practice management concepts.

The five chapters in Part Two, "The Tangible Law Office Management Skills," focus on the tangible, or measurable, management skills, including basic administrative procedures, facilities management, information management, financial management, and personnel management. The basics of finance, explained in Chapter 6, are presented in a nonthreatening, easy-to-understand, experiential format. Students will find a hand-held calculator to be useful throughout this course, particularly for completing the activities in Chapter 6. Some activities will require the students to possess simple mathematical skills (addition, subtraction, multiplication, division, and calculating percentages). Instructors and students are urged to check the laws in their own states regarding specific labor and personnel management questions, as discussed in Chapter 7, since these laws do vary from state to state.

Part Three, "The Intangible Law Office Management Skills," is composed of three chapters that address the hard-to-measure but essential intangible management skills of communication, leadership, and managing groups.

Text Design

Each chapter begins with a topic outline followed by a Commentary section that chronicles a fictitious law firm, Dunn & Sweeney, which was created solely for the purpose of illustrating the application of general management concepts to the practice of law. Any reference to a law firm of the same name existing in either the past or present is purely coincidental.

This text was designed to be user-friendly. The lined margins provide ample space for both instructors and students to make notes within each chapter. Key terms are boldfaced and defined at first use, with an alphabetical list of these terms at the end of each chapter.

Further, each chapter contains assessments and other activities to amplify the management concepts as they are presented, thus enhancing the learning process. Students are encouraged to write in these books, to complete all assessments and activities, and to keep this text at home or in the office as a handy desk reference guide.

Other Learning and Teaching Resources

The accompanying *Study Guide* is designed as student support in the study of law office management. Performing its numerous exercises will help the student achieve the objectives of this course.

Each chapter begins with a fill-in chapter outline followed by a Before and After section, a Management Concepts activity, a Language of Law Office Management vocabulary review, an Applying Principles section, Yes/No statements, and a Case Study. Each activity reinforces the information presented in the text and relates it to real-life situations. In addition, systematic review and use of the *Study Guide* may help the student improve test scores and develop critical thinking skills.

To facilitate the teaching and learning processes, an *Instructor's Manual* accompanies this text. Included are model course syllabi for classes that meet on the quarter system and for those on semester schedules. In addition, there are answer keys to all review and discussion questions contained in the text, along with tests and answers for each chapter including true/false, multiple choice, and short-answer problems.

Acknowledgments

The author wishes to gratefully acknowledge the contributions of the following reviewers, without whose considerable efforts, suggestions, ideas, and insights this text would not be the valuable tool it is.

Vicki Brittain, Esq., Associate Professor, Political Science Department, Southwest Texas State University, San Marcos, Texas

Deborah A. Carlson, Personnel Administrator, Snell and Wilmer, Phoenix, Arizona

Ellen Hall, Program Coordinator, Legal Assistant Program, Utah Valley Community College, Orem, Utah

Judy Long, Paralegal Coordinator, Rio Hondo College, Whittier, California

Kathleen Mercer Reed, Instructor, Legal Assisting Technology Program, University of Toledo Community and Technical College, Toledo, Ohio

Pamela A. Linquist, CLA, Adjunct Faculty, Hillsborough Community College, Tampa, Florida

In addition, the author gratefully acknowledges the support, friendship, and guidance received throughout this project from Marly Bergerud, Robert Nirkind, Rick Adams, Wallace Eater, Nancy Helmer, and Doris Jenner.

PART ONE

LAW OFFICE

MANAGEMENT CONCEPTS

Chapter 1
Functions of the Law Office Manager

Chapter 2
Tracking Revenue and Expenses

CHAPTER 1   Functions of the Law Office Manager

OUTLINE

1-1   Introduction to Law Office Management
    Who Becomes a Law Office Manager?
    Management Terms Defined
    Practice Management and Operations Management
1-2   The Tangible Law Office Management Skills
    The Planning Function
    The Organizing Function
    The Staffing Function
    The Directing Function
    The Controlling Function
1-3   The Intangible Law Office Management Skills
    Interpersonal Roles
    Informational Roles
    Decisional Roles
1-4   The Need for Law Office Management
    Today's Law Firms

COMMENTARY

WANTED: LAW OFFICE MANAGER

Dunn & Sweeney, a prestigious downtown law firm, currently has an excellent career opportunity available for an Office Manager. The individual will be responsible for the administrative operations, as well as recruiting, hiring, training, and supervising all nonattorney staff. The Office Manager will also be responsible for long-term planning for support and space needs, effective use of resources, and control and dissemination of all financial and other information. This vital position requires a degreed individual with experience in office management. Submit resume and salary history to R. J. Sweeney, Managing Partner.

OBJECTIVES

After studying the information in this chapter, you will be able to:

1. Define common management terms.
2. Discuss the differences between practice management and operations management.
3. List the law office manager's typical areas of responsibility.
4. Name and define the tangible and intangible management skills.
5. List the steps to successful planning.

6. Differentiate between efficient and effective management.
7. Identify the resources in a law firm requiring management.
8. List and discuss the steps for getting control of your time.
9. Discuss when to delegate work to others.
10. List the steps involved in delegating.
11. Discuss the purpose for the controlling function and considerations in establishing controls.

1-1   Introduction to Law Office Management

Without doubt the law office manager, or legal administrator as he or she is more often called in large law firms, has become an important and accepted part of the law office management team. The Association of Legal Administrators (ALA), an international educational and networking organization for law office managers, has watched its membership grow from about 600 members in the 1970s to nearly 8,000 members today. Both large and small firms are hiring managers to take care of administrative and personnel matters, thus freeing the lawyers to practice law.

Who Becomes a Law Office Manager?

In 1986 Altman & Weil, a Pennsylvania-based legal consulting firm, conducted a national survey of legal administrators. With 650 responses, the survey revealed that law office managers/administrators come from a variety of occupational backgrounds, with the smaller and medium-sized firms often turning to legal secretaries or paralegals to provide managerial support. Nearly 40 percent of law firms with fewer than 40 attorneys find their office managers right in their own offices. (See Figure 1-1.)

Figure 1-1   Who Becomes a Law Office Manager?

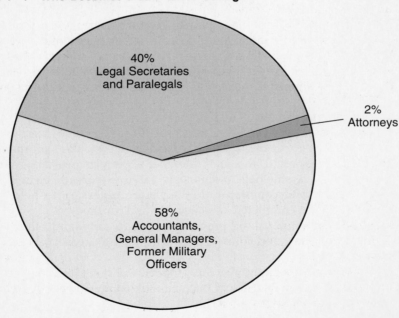

40%
Legal Secretaries
and Paralegals

2%
Attorneys

58%
Accountants,
General Managers,
Former Military
Officers

In the larger firms, legal administrators often have had previous careers in accounting, general management, or the military. Less than 2 percent of administrators were previously lawyers. Thus, law office management appears to be a relatively common career transition for many people who possess expertise in other areas, but may not be familiar with some of the management concepts required to manage a law office.

This book will give you a basic understanding of what you should know to be an effective law office manager.

Management Terms Defined

Management may be the most commonly used word in law offices today. But what is management, and specifically, what is law office management? As used in this text, *management* has two major meanings.

Management is the carefully planned use of an organization's resources to achieve that organization's goals. Management of *organizational resources* in the law office means the carefully planned use of time, people, information, equipment, and money to achieve goals.

Management also refers collectively to the people who establish the goals of the organization and who are responsible for achieving them. In a small law firm, just a few people may make up its management—perhaps only one person is required in the smallest of firms. But large law firms can have numerous attorneys who become partners or co-owners of the practice; or shareholders, attorneys who own shares of stock in an incorporated law firm—all of whom may take an active part in the firm's management.

Management thus refers to both (1) the supervision and running of the law office and (2) the people who supervise and run the firm. Whether you are looking at the people or at the tasks they perform, every organization needs to have its goals carefully planned and carefully implemented—including law firms.

Other terms, such as *accountability*, *responsibility*, and *authority*, are often associated with management concepts. But what do they really mean? **Accountability** is a system for assessing blame or credit for performance. For example, an office manager can be "held accountable" for financial reports not completed on time. Likewise, a manager is also accountable for exceptional staff performance. Accountability provides an incentive to perform tasks competently and diligently. When accountability is not clear, work assignments will suffer.

Responsibility can be used to refer to a specific task and implies a duty to see that the task is performed (i.e., "Sam is responsible for completing the firm's quarterly report"). Responsibility can also refer to overseeing a broader range of activities (i.e., "Jane is responsible for Accounts Receivable").

How can one person be held responsible for the work of others? A staff member usually has responsibility for completing a specific task, while a manager is responsible for seeing that the work delegated to the staff member is done properly. Therefore, if the staff member's performance slips for any reason, the manager is still held responsible for the work delegated. Good planning, delegating, and communication skills are necessary to help ensure that delegated tasks are completed satisfactorily and on time.

Authority can be defined as the power to act or to command others to act. Without authority to make decisions or use the firm's resources, there can be no holding or delegating of responsibility. One duty faced by managers when delegating responsibility is assigning the proper level of authority. If too little authority is given, work completion may be slowed by having to return to management for authorization on matters related to the task. On the other hand, if too much authority is given, subordinates may be tempted to make decisions that they are not equipped to make.

Practice Management and Operations Management

Law firms are divided into two distinct, yet overlapping management areas— practice management and operations management. **Practice management** refers to the mix of the number of cases and types of cases the firm will take. Practice management is a strategic management decision controlled by the firm's top management. In a large firm several attorneys may form a planning committee to shape the future course of the firm and to monitor cases coming into the firm as a way of controlling the direction of growth. In a small firm this management function is likely to be monitored by the senior partner, a paralegal, or the firm's office manager.

The primary purpose of practice management is to ensure that there will be a steady stream of cash flowing into the law firm. For example, if the majority of the firm's cases are in litigation, which often take several years to resolve, the firm will need a source of revenue from fixed fee cases or hourly fee clients to provide cash flow.

To alleviate cash flow problems, firms will diversify the practice. One strategy for the firm that concentrates its practice in the business area might be to diversify to create a corporate division, a tax division, a litigation section, and perhaps a transactional group—specialists in contracts and other routine business matters. Another firm that focuses on family practice could diversify to handle marriage dissolution matters, provide financial and estate planning services, and probate estates.

The law office manager/administrator is the firm's **operations management,** which may, in small and medium-sized firms, include responsibility for all nonlawyer-related activities such as the firm's accounting functions, facilities management, the hiring and firing of support staff personnel, and implementing information technology. Large law firms may have individual managers of human resources, information systems, and paralegals, all of whom might report to the administrator.

There are many ways to structure the management of a law firm. In most cases, operations is at the center of attention today because that is where the bulk of the firm's overhead expenses is concentrated. Soaring office rents, high salaries, and runaway equipment costs require sound management decisions. Working closely with the firm's managing partners, office managers guide and monitor the business operations of the firm.

1–2 The Tangible Law Office Management Skills

When Altman & Weil conducted their survey of law office managers/administrators, they found the functional areas of responsibility of this position to be myriad and diverse. Law office managers may be responsible for all accounting, bookkeeping, and billing functions, including preparing budgets and, in some cases, investing the firm's money and securing loans; recruiting and hiring all nonlawyer staff, and handling all personnel matters, including scheduling, discipline, and discharge, and managing the firm's benefits program; opening new offices, including leasing space, office design, and relocation; purchasing office equipment and supplies, retaining messenger and copy services, and maintaining outside vendor relations; and library maintenance. The law office manager's **tangible,** or visible, law office management skills, then, consist of:

- Planning.
- Organizing.
- Staffing.
- Directing.
- Controlling.

The Planning Function

Planning is the process of establishing future goals and objectives and then figuring out how to achieve them. Planning is a complex process further complicated by the fact that not only do several of the components interrelate and overlap, but plans and the people who make them are in a constant state of flux. The most important justification for planning, however, is that it improves both the individual's and the firm's performance and productivity, which often lead to an improved financial status. One method of evaluating your planning skills is to conduct a self-assessment. A guide is produced for this purpose in Figure 1–2.

Steps to Successful Planning Planning is a skill that can be developed by following logical, sequential steps. The following steps represent one way to formulate plans.

Step 1: Define goals. A **goal** is a specific target that you work toward achieving in the future. Goals that have the best chance of success are briefly stated in writing, contain specific objectives, and can be measured. For example, let's say you are a paralegal working on a complex litigation matter. Your goal is to coordinate the deposition process involving twenty or more deponents currently being represented by ten different law firms with new parties to the lawsuit being added every week. You will first need to determine the date by which all depositions must be taken. This will give you one way of measuring success. Another way to measure success is to stay within your proposed budget. Next, you must figure out the sequence of events leading up to the scheduling of the depositions, and determine how you will keep all parties notified of any schedule changes.

Specifically, your goal statement might read: "To coordinate, schedule, and communicate with all relevant parties to the action in the most efficient, economical, and timely manner to ensure that all depositions are completed no later than June 15."

Step 2: Collect relevant data. This means that you look for the best way to achieve your goal by taking an inventory of the firm's resources as well as looking for circumstances or conditions that could change and possibly pose problems for you.

In assessing internal resources you are looking at both the strengths and weaknesses of the firm in terms of meeting your goals. Do you have secretarial or word processing support available to help you in producing the required legal documents? Are your conference room facilities adequate in which to hold the depositions? Will there be people available to provide coffee service during the depositions and to make photocopies if necessary? How will reception handle

Figure 1–2 Planning Skills Assessment

To evaluate your planning skills, complete this skills assessment by scoring each statement in the blank provided based on the following scale:

Always	Usually	Most of the time	Some of the time	Never
10–9	8–7	6–5	4–2	1–0

1. I am able to spot problems in the regular workflow and start corrective action. _____

2. I have established deadlines for checking on work in progress. _____

3. I am prepared to give answers regarding work for which I am accountable. _____

4. I have an understanding of problems that are involved in making procedural changes and changes in routines. _____

5. I can work out and stick to deadlines. _____

6. I know how to coordinate shared work responsibilities. _____

7. Excessive overtime or trouble with meeting deadlines is not a problem for me or for my group. _____

8. Neither I nor members of my group have frequent unexplainable crises.

9. I have trained others so that work would continue if I were absent. _____

10. I can accurately evaluate the strengths and weaknesses of the people with whom I work. _____

If your total score is:
90–100	Planning is a definite strength.
70–89	You have moderately effective planning skills.
50–69	Your planning skills are average.
20–49	Planning does not give you the desired results.
0–19	Your planning skills need further developing.

the extra burden of telephone calls coming in to the attorneys who are involved in taking the depositions?

You would also be concerned about scheduling around holidays or vacations, the timetable imposed by the court for completion of discovery, the cooperation of deponents and their attorneys, and the availability of court reporters. Any one of these factors could change the circumstances or conditions and interfere with reaching your goal.

Step 3: Select the best method. Once you have gathered all the relevant data, inventoried the firm's internal support available to you, and considered all the possible circumstances or conditions that might cause a change of plans, the next step in the planning process is to create a couple of alternative methods for achieving your goals. For example, one method might be to go off-site to a hotel for the depositions rather than overtax your own facilities. Another might be to hold the depositions in the offices of one of the other law firms involved in the case. Or using your own facilities might be the best alternative.

In selecting the best method for reaching your goal, you want to eliminate unnecessary steps, simplify the process as much as possible, and rate each method according to which will contribute most positively to achieving your stated goal.

Step 4: Develop an action plan. **Action plans** are specific steps in the planning process to get you to your goals. Without these steps you are just engaging in wishful thinking. Of all the steps in the planning process, this is the one where most people get stuck. It is easy to state a goal. It is not so easy to set down in writing the steps to achievement. Your action plan might include:

1. Developing a list of the attorneys with their addresses, phone numbers, and the clients they represent. Deadline: _____.
2. Developing a list of deponents, including addresses and phone numbers (daytime and evening numbers). Deadline: _____.
3. Establishing some alternative dates with your attorney and the court reporter(s); notifying all counsel of these dates and asking for their preferences. Deadline: _____.

Obviously, this list is only a beginning. As you outline the specific steps in your action plan, be sure to include deadline dates for completion. And, while you are developing your action plan, formulate some ideas about alternative actions. Remember—plans are dynamic, not static!

Step 5: Prepare a budget. Some action plans will require money in order to implement them. For instance, if you do not have support staff to help with the paperwork, you might have to hire temporary help. Or, if your conference room facilities are not large enough, you might have to go off-site and rent space in a hotel. Perhaps overtime will be required for some secretarial staff. Any number of expenses could come up when implementing an action plan. Good decision making requires that you know the cost of your actions in advance of implementation.

Step 6: Implement the plan. Planning is justified only if the plans are implemented. Too many people develop elaborate plans and then put them in a drawer. In defense of those people, in the process of developing their plans they have had to think through in detail all the relevant parts required to reach a goal. In a few instances, that process alone is progress enough.

The purpose for the action steps, of course, is to facilitate implementation of the plan. Action steps provide the roadmap to goal achievement. When you have completed the first five steps in the process, implementing the plan is much easier.

Step 7: Follow up. The follow-up process measures progress and provides an opportunity to make adjustments, as required, along the way. For example, in your action steps you will most certainly have set a deadline for receiving information on the attorneys' preferred dates for scheduling depositions. This allows you to control the flow of communication and stay on target with your original goals. Periodic review and evaluation will keep you in control and allow you to fine-tune as you go along. You will also have set down an alternative way to follow up in the event some did not respond by the deadline.

Step 8: Develop a contingency plan. Experienced planners always have a set of contingency, or backup, plans to use if things do not proceed as expected. They know that Murphy's Law (if anything can go wrong, it will) is in operation, particularly when coordinating the schedules of many busy people. For example, a good idea would be to make arrangements with a neighboring firm to use their fax or photocopy machines in the event your equipment is overloaded or not working on the days of the depositions. Likewise, a plan should be in place to notify everyone in the event a deposition is postponed at the last minute. Without being pessimistic, try to think of all the things that could go wrong and plan for them.

Successful planners do not look for shortcuts. Planning does take time. Yet most of us know intuitively that those who take time to plan in the beginning save time in the end. One final thought on planning—*it is essential that plans be written down rather than carried around in your head.* (Figure 1–3 illustrates one such method.) The reason is simple: You have too many other things to think

Figure 1-3 Planning Worksheet

Select a goal you want to work on and complete the planning worksheet.

Goal Statement

To _____

_____ by _____

Data Needed: 1. _____ 2. _____

3. _____ 4. _____ .

Methods

Assessment of Strengths	Assessment of Weaknesses
_____	_____
_____	_____
_____	_____

Action Plan

Activities	Deadline
_____	_____
_____	_____
_____	_____

Proposed Budget

Associated Expenses		Expected Income	
Item	Amount	Item	Amount
_____	_____	_____	_____
_____	_____	_____	_____
_____	_____	_____	_____
_____	_____	_____	_____

Implementation

Action Required	Deadline
_____	_____
_____	_____
_____	_____

Follow-up Schedule

Activity	Date
_____	_____
_____	_____
_____	_____

Contingency Plans

If	Then
_____	_____
_____	_____

about to remember the details of your various plans; and, in the event you need to delegate some tasks to others, they can look at your plan and know exactly your intentions. That factor alone can save hundreds of dollars in duplicated effort.

To summarize, here are the eight steps to good planning:

1. Define goals.
2. Collect relevant data.
3. Select the best method.
4. Develop an action plan.
5. Prepare a budget.
6. Implement the plan.
7. Follow up.
8. Develop a contingency plan.

The Organizing Function

Organizing is the process of coordinating the firm's resources to achieve established goals with the maximum amount of efficiency and effectiveness. In management, being *efficient* means that you have produced the desired results at minimum cost. Being *effective* means that you know how to use the firm's resources to get things done.

More specifically, organizing is an effective way to prevent the costly duplication of activities and is a means for ensuring that all necessary activities are performed. Since the principle resources of a law firm are time, people, money, information, and technology, the office manager is often responsible for deciding who is going to do what, and how the people and activities will be related. This requires skills in time management.

How to Get Control of Your Time Law office managers never have enough time, yet they have all the time in the world. Effective time management is a learned skill. Here are some steps to follow to help you use your daily time allotment efficiently.

Step 1: Focus on one task at a time. Even when you are faced with accomplishing several tasks within a given time frame, you can still train yourself to concentrate only on the task at hand. Use your planning skills to make a step-by-step plan for each project requiring your attention. Delegate as much of the work as you can effectively and set a follow-up schedule for each task. Then, you can focus on your immediate priority without worrying about forgetting something.

Step 2: Use awareness of peak energy time. Your energy level has a great impact on the pace at which you are able to accomplish tasks as well as on your attitude toward your work. When possible, schedule activities that require the most concentration, creativity, analysis, and decision making during your high energy hours. For some, this peak energy time is early morning; for others it may be midday, late afternoon, or early evening. If your high energy hours do not coincide with the busiest part of your workday, you may be able to change your peaks by changing your sleeping or eating habits, or, if possible, by working on a flexible hours schedule.

Step 3: Be neat. You will find that an uncluttered desk and office will improve your efficiency as well as your mood and will be a great stress reducer. Work toward getting papers off your desk and onto someone else's, organized in files, or even into the wastebasket when warranted. The mounds of paper generated and received in a law office are reason enough to adhere to Alan Lakein's famous time management principle—handle a piece of paper only once—as discussed in his book, *How to Get Control of Your Time and Your Life* (New York: Peter H. Wyden, 1973).

Step 4: Learn to say no. You must learn to say no to some tasks, meetings, lunches, and other time-consuming activities in which you are asked to participate or you will end up managing your time in accordance with other people's priorities instead of your own. You may even need to say no to the attorneys—tactfully, of course—or at least to discuss with them how the requested activity fits in with your other priorities.

Step 5: Use a To Do list. If you don't plan your day, your day will be planned by others. Other people's actions will determine your priorities to a great extent. But the real secret of the To Do list is to actually *use* it. Refer to it first thing in the morning, check it regularly during the day to make sure you are using your time wisely, and prepare a new one for the next day before going home at night. Be sure to reward yourself frequently for completing tasks. There are printed forms available or you can develop one of your own. Figure 1–4 represents one format that you might try.

Step 6: Use dead time effectively. Every day you have a certain amount of "dead time" when you are not doing anything that leads directly to accomplishing a top-priority goal—time spent commuting, waiting for someone or something, lunch, coffee breaks, or early morning inertia. You can liven up this dead time, if you *want* to, by reading low priority mail, tackling some quick tasks, making out or checking your To Do list, or catching up on journal and magazine articles. Or you can use this time to relax and renew yourself for the tasks ahead. Dead time periods are actually little windows of free time during your day to be used as you prefer. Use them wisely.

Step 7: Minimize interruptions. Controlling your telephone calls and drop-in visitors can help you control your life. Finding large blocks (one hour or more) of uninterrupted time can be a real time-saver. One way to do this is to establish a daily quiet hour during which you do not take calls or receive visitors. Having your calls screened or recorded on an answering machine (remember to turn off the bell on your phone so you won't be tempted to answer it) gives you time to concentrate on your work. It is still possible to have an open door policy while getting some much-needed time for yourself simply by putting a Do Not Disturb sign on your office door during your quiet hour.

Step 8: Delegate. Whenever possible, delegate tasks or portions of projects to others. A busy law office manager cannot complete daily routine tasks, let alone take on special project assignments, without help.

To summarize, here are the eight steps to getting control of your time:

1. Focus on one task at a time.
2. Use awareness of peak energy time.
3. Be neat.
4. Learn to say no.
5. Use a To Do list.
6. Use dead time effectively.
7. Minimize interruptions.
8. Delegate.

The Staffing Function

Staffing is the process of recruiting, placing, training, evaluating, and developing the law firm's human resources.

No law firm will exist for long without a qualified, well-trained, stable staff of attorneys and support personnel. Because of the need to focus particular attention on this important management function, Chapter 7 of this text is

Figure 1–4 Daily Action Sheet

DAILY ACTION SHEET

PRIORITY CODES

A. Urgent & Important
B. Important
C. Urgent
D. Low Priority
E. Routine

CONVERSION OF TIME INTO DECIMALS

6 Minutes = .1 Hour	36 Minutes = .6 Hour
12 Minutes = .2 Hour	42 Minutes = .7 Hour
15 Minutes = .25 Hour	45 Minutes = .75 Hour
18 Minutes = .3 Hour	48 Minutes = .8 Hour
24 Minutes = .4 Hour	54 Minutes = .9 Hour
30 Minutes = .5 Hour	60 Minutes = 1.0 Hour

INSTRUCTIONS: List all items to be done today, prioritize items according to importance, and number them in the order in which you will perform them.

Date: _____

Priority Order	Code	To Be Done	Time Estimate Hrs.	1/10s

Source: Law Publications, Inc., Los Angeles, CA (1980). Reprinted with permission.

devoted to staffing the law office, evaluating employee performance, and related issues of personnel management.

The Directing Function

Directing is the process of exchanging ideas, motivating, and then leading people toward goals by **delegating,** or assigning, work to others. The critical communication skills required to direct the work of others are presented in

Chapter 8. In this chapter, attention is focused on the equally critical directing skills of delegating.

Why Managers Fail to Delegate To some people, delegating can be a truly frightening situation because they fear losing control. Here are some other reasons why managers fail to delegate:

- *Lack of patience.* "It takes longer to explain than to do it myself."
- *Insecurity.* New managers might feel uncomfortable asking others to do work for them.
- *Anxiety.* Managers may be so anxious to prove themselves that they refuse to delegate.
- *Inflated ego and lack of confidence in others.* "No one can do this job better than I."
- *Inadequacy.* "What if Jim *can* do it better than I can?"
- *Occupational hobby.* Managers are so attached to the job that they just don't want to delegate.

Do you have other reasons for not delegating? If so, bring them to the surface and face them head on. Or are you delegating too much? The short assessment in Figure 1–5 is designed to help you discover whether you have a tendency to delegate too little or too much.

Figure 1–5   How Well Do You Delegate?

Yes	No	
___	___	I often put in overtime hours.
___	___	I usually take work home in the evenings and on weekends.
___	___	My unfinished work pile is getting larger.
___	___	I spend so much time putting out fires there is none left for planning and other important matters requiring my attention.
___	___	I control all the details so that a job is done right.
___	___	Long-range projects are frequently postponed.
___	___	Unexpected emergencies constantly interrupt my work.
___	___	There is no one else who could take on more responsibility.
___	___	I am upset and irritable when the work performed by others does not live up to my expectations.
___	___	High tension and low morale describes our office atmosphere.
___	___	I make most office management decisions.
___	___	When giving instructions to others, I focus on the activities involved, not on accomplishing goals.
___	___	Lately other people have stopped presenting ideas or suggestions to me.
___	___	When I am away from the office, work slows down.
___	___	I think that the office manager should not ask others for help.
___	___	Being a law office manager automatically means being overworked.

If the majority of your answers to the above statements are yes, chances are you are not delegating enough.

When to Delegate   Obviously, some tasks never should be delegated. Likewise, others usually should be given to someone else. Learning to distinguish between the two is a management skill. Situations in which you should consider delegating include:

- When delegating will help develop someone's skills.
- When the delegated tasks will be motivating.
- When problems or projects require research or when recommendations from others will help in decision making.
- When the tasks are routine and could be handled by others.
- When you are continually under too much time pressure.
- When you are willing to take the time and effort to turn over the job skillfully.

What Not to Delegate   Although many tasks can be delegated, some should be handled personally by the law office manager. These include:

- Planning activities associated with achieving the firm's goals.
- Morale problems of nonlawyer staff.
- Assisting in reconciling the differences between lawyers and staff.
- Coaching and directing members of your direct staff.
- Reviewing performance of nonlawyer staff.
- Any direct assignments given to you by upper management.
- Confidential or significant parts of an upper management committee assignment.
- When only a part of a problem is identified without explaining the whole problem.
- Your own pet projects and your own personal errands.
- When there is no qualified talent available.

How to Delegate Effectively   The following steps can be used as a guide to reduce your own anxiety about delegating work to others, to ensure that the work is done correctly, and to make the experience positive for everyone.

Step 1: When possible, match the task to the person. Choose the best person for the job based on skills, speed of work, accuracy, or training opportunities. If the person who receives your assignment does not have the technical skills, motivation, creativity, and dependability to carry out the task, you will not feel comfortable in relinquishing responsibility.

Step 2: Explain why the assignment is important. The person to whom you give the assignment is more likely to take an interest in the outcome if it is clear how the delegated task fits into the big picture and why the individual has been chosen for the work. It is not wise to delegate to get rid of your unwanted chores, such as filing, on a regular basis. Properly delegated work is a growth experience, not an opportunity to dump work on others.

Step 3: Establish goals and objectives. Spell out the degree of thoroughness, accuracy, deadlines, and quality of the finished product you expect. If you want to be explicit, make the assignment in writing.

Step 4: Encourage independence. One reason to delegate is to create opportunities for others to use initiative and creativity in their work. Yet clearly defined and agreed upon performance standards are a must to ensure that both parties know what is expected. Remember that significant growth often occurs from failing. Individuals must be allowed the opportunity to be innovative and to fail occasionally without fear of punishment if they are to be motivated to high levels of performance.

Step 5: Agree on areas of authority and responsibility. Clearly establish the boundaries of authority, responsibility, and accountability for the delegated task. Doing so at the beginning of the project will save time later on and will also make the individual a fully participating party to the process.

Step 6: Get feedback and commitment. To be sure that the individual has a correct understanding of the delegated work, ask that person to give you their version of what has been delegated, why it was delegated, when the project is due, and for what they will be held accountable. Also, establish times for interim meetings for follow-up questions and feedback on progress. If you feel there is a lack of commitment to the delegated task, ask the individual how committed he or she is to seeing the task through to completion.

Step 7: Show interest and offer guidance. When you delegate work to others, one way of keeping control is to show interest and offer guidance or training as required without giving the appearance of looking over their shoulders. Periodic questions about progress will keep you informed and give you the opportunity to step in to make corrections or decisions, if necessary.

To summarize, here are the seven steps to delegating effectively:

1. When possible, match the person to the task.
2. Explain why the assignment is important.
3. Establish goals and objectives.
4. Encourage independence.
5. Agree on areas of authority and responsibility.
6. Get feedback and commitment.
7. Show interest and offer guidance.

By following these steps, directing the work of others should be a rewarding work experience. But remember—be explicit in your instructions, diligent in following up, and willing to offer praise or constructive criticism when merited.

The Controlling Function

Controlling is the process of commanding and directing the firm's resources to achieve planned goals. The purpose of the control function is to check periodically to see if the law firm and the people in it are proceeding according to plan. In order to monitor progress, there must be some evaluation method against which to measure performance. The four logical steps involved in the control process are (1) setting standards; (2) measuring actual performance; (3) comparing actual performance to standards; and (4) taking corrective action.

Taking Control   Managers, by definition, achieve goals through others. Also by definition, managers are responsible and accountable for the work performed by others. Here are the steps managers follow to maintain control of delegated projects.

Step 1: Set standards. Meaningful standards, or a basis for comparison, are required for any control system. Therefore, a considerable amount of time and effort should go into establishing these standards. A question that causes continual debate among office managers is: Does every activity require a standard? For example, should performance standards be required for support staff? Some think this is necessary. Others think that standards are necessary for only those activities that are critical to achieving the firm's objectives, such as establishing minimum billable hours for attorneys and paralegals, and a performance-based standard for the office manager.

If standards are not set for every activity, it is important to identify those that do require them, why the standard is required, and what the standard is. One thing is certain: If the standards set are unrealistic or not acceptable to the people involved, the result will be a frustrated and unmotivated group of employees. And, if standards are set for one group and not another, this could result, at the very least, in enormous amounts of time spent discussing this discrepancy.

Step 2: Measure actual performance. Performance appraisals are one way of measuring performance, either through direct observation or, preferably, with a written report. The primary issues here are what aspects of performance are to be measured and who is going to do it.

In some instances, quantitative measurements are possible. If the firm has a standard requiring a paralegal to bill a minimum of 1,400 hours each year, it is easy to determine whether the standard has been met. However, qualitative measurements may be just as important and more difficult to measure since they are mostly subjective on the part of the observer. For example, keeping clients happy and informed of the progress of their lawsuit is an important nonbillable paralegal function. So is contributing to the positive morale of the office by taking part in office functions, such as birthday parties and retirement lunches. In measuring the performance of a receptionist, for example, qualitative measures of performance might be more relevant than quantitative measures, or at least be worthy of an equal amount of consideration.

Typically, higher levels of management review the performance of people below them. However, coworkers evaluating each other and employees evaluating the boss are relatively new performance measuring devices gaining wider acceptance in those firms with a strong team concept.

Step 3: Compare actual performance to standards. Once the standards are established and performance measurements taken, the next step is to compare them—otherwise the control process will not be taken seriously. Your comparison measures the discrepancy between the standards and the results, or the *deviation*. It is important to agree beforehand how much deviation is acceptable. For example, if the standard is 1,400 billable hours per year and the paralegal bills only 1,300, what action will be taken?

Although statistical analysis methods can determine the exact amount of deviation and the acceptable range, your own wisdom and experience are acceptable traits to use in diagnosing the extent and severity of the deviation. Perhaps some unfortunate family circumstances prevented the paralegal from meeting the standard; or the assigned task of reorganizing the firm's law library resulted in forfeiting billable hours, yet was beneficial to the firm. On the other hand, if there is a consistent, recurring problem with this paralegal's billable hours, other action might be required.

Step 4: Take corrective action. For the control system to work, the results of the comparison between actual performance and the established standards must be quickly communicated to the appropriate parties. Doing so will allow deviations to be dealt with before performance deteriorates too far or may serve as a warning that bigger problems are in the offing. The final part of the control process, then, is to determine the course of action after evaluating the discrepancy between actual performance and the standard. There are three choices: do nothing, solve the problem, or revise the standard.

If things are, for the most part, proceeding according to plan, no corrective action may be required. Doing nothing, however, does not mean giving up responsibility. It means that no corrective action is required at the present time to reach the objectives. If, on the other hand, corrective action is necessary, do something about it immediately. Timely problem solving is the payoff from the control process.

Revising the standard is warranted when deviations are attributed to errors in planning rather than to performance problems. Perhaps the standard is just unrealistic. Typically, this occurs when planning a new task or job function. Performance quotas may be based on nothing more than estimates that prove to be impossibly difficult or too easy. If the standard is unrealistic, no employee will be able to meet it. If it is too easy, everyone will meet and exceed the quota. In either case, morale problems are likely to result.

In summary, here are the four steps in the controlling function of management:

1. Set standards.
2. Measure actual performance.
3. Compare actual performance to standards.
4. Take corrective action.

1–3 The Intangible Law Office Management Skills

The **intangible** management skills are invisible, yet they play a significant part in the law office manager's job. In his study of the managerial role, Henry Mintzberg, Professor of Management at McGill University in Montreal, Quebec, identified the different roles associated with the various management functions. His findings, as reported in his book, *The Nature of Managerial Work* (New York: Harper & Row, 1973), are grouped into the following three general categories: interpersonal roles, informational roles, and decisional roles. (See Figure 1–6.)

Interpersonal Roles

As we go about our day-to-day business our success is primarily dependent upon how well we are able to relate to, motivate, and lead others. This is particularly true for law office managers who will, depending upon the situation, assume one or more of the following interpersonal roles.

Figurehead   As the symbolic head of the law office, the office manager may be required, from time to time, to perform certain ceremonial duties such as welcoming visitors, presiding at company parties, and signing letters on behalf of the organization. In the figurehead capacity, the office manager is a reflection of the organization to those outside the firm as well as to those within.

Leader   No matter the task, the office manager sets the tone for the entire firm, serving as a guide and motivator. Strong leadership is required from the top down in order for all employees of the firm to have a sense of purpose and direction. Arguably, the law office manager may be the most visible leader for establishing the firm's internal atmosphere.

Liaison   In the role of liaison, the office manager establishes a network of external relationships with peers in professional organizations, such as the local chapters of the Association of Legal Administrators, the National Association of Legal Assistants, the Legal Assistants Management Association, or the Professional Legal Secretaries Association, as well as with peers in other law firms to

Figure 1–6 Responsibilities of the Law Office Manager

Interpersonal
Figurehead
Leader
Liaison

Informational
Monitor
Disseminator
Spokesperson

Decisional
Entrepreneur
Disturbance handler
Resource allocator
Negotiator

The law office manager wears many "hats" in carrying out his or her responsibilities.
Source: Doug Martin (t, c) and BLT Productions (b).

exchange information and provide support. The roles of figurehead and leader require a continual update of professional knowledge and skills as well as the ability to get information from sources established outside the organization. Attending luncheons, dinners, seminars, and professional association meetings are important to the firm because in the liaison role management is the link between the firm and the outside world. In other words, networking will provide you with sources of information and plug you into the always valuable communication grapevine.

Informational Roles

The second role assumed by the law office manager is to receive information, analyze and interpret it, and then decide what to do with it. Obviously, not everyone in the firm is privy to the same information—and for good reason. Do individual staff members need to concern themselves with day-to-day financial decisions? Or, does the managing partner need to know that a certain secretary is having personal problems? Given the amount of information regularly coming into and circulating around a law office, the role played by the office manager in deciding what to do with it is an important function.

Monitor   Receiving and analyzing information related to both internal operational matters and external events is a critical part of the office manager's role. This includes keeping up with trends and staying on top of developing technology as well as being aware of internal events that may have an effect upon the firm. In this capacity, caution must be exercised not to discard important information or to place too much importance on trivial matters. Maturity, common sense, and past experiences will help in making decisions about what is important and what is not.

Disseminator   As you can imagine, the person who is responsible for putting information into the communication network system is vital to the overall welfare of the firm. One example of disseminating information is attending a legal update seminar and calling a meeting to share information with others in the firm. Another is to issue a memorandum announcing the observance of a staff member's birthday. In this capacity, the office manager is once again assuming the role of liaison.

Spokesperson   The office manager is sometimes called upon to speak on behalf of the firm—most often at employee meetings. As spokesperson for the firm, the office manager must be certain that the information presented truly reflects the position of top management and does not breach any confidences. A violation of trust or confidence can cause irreparable damage both to the firm and to the individual.

Decisional Roles

To be an office manager requires the ability to make decisions, including the tough ones, and to take risks. In this role, some decisions and risks will prove to be successful while others will not turn out the way you planned. No matter the result, you will be held accountable for the consequences.

Entrepreneur   To be an entrepreneur (or more accurately, an *intrapreneur*, which means you are working for someone other than yourself) you must be willing to initiate change and take risks. Launching a feasibility study on the best way to update the firm's computer system and then making recommendations to top management is one way of being an intrapreneur. For the firm to keep up with the changing times, it is important to identify the people with intrapreneurial initiative and to support them in their decisions and efforts whether they are successful or not. Intrapreneurs must be allowed to fail, periodically, or they will not be willing to assume the risks associated with change.

Disturbance Handler   The role of peacemaker is also associated with the law office manager. Handling problems with clients or differences between co-workers is an important part of the job. This role requires better than average communication skills and the ability to listen without judging. Because emotions and feelings are involved, the way disturbances are handled is critical to both morale within the firm and the firm's outside reputation.

Resource Allocator   The office manager is often charged with determining how to allocate the firm's resources, which include time, money, equipment, information, and personnel. The decisions made in connection with the allocation of resources will determine how well the firm will be able to serve its clients and satisfy the needs of its employees.

Negotiator   The law office manager is frequently acting the role of negotiator—in bargaining with landlords, vendors, and employees, for example. Anytime you are looking for a way to resolve differences you are in negotiation. Working in a law office will provide you with ample opportunities to perfect your negotiating skills.

The role of law office manager is diverse, requiring excellent communication skills, a self-motivating attitude, the ability to lead others, and above-average strengths in time management and stress management.

1–4   The Need for Law Office Management

As with all other organizations, law firms need management in order to operate efficiently and effectively. There was a time when management in most law offices was not a planned activity. Most often, management of the law office was left to the most senior partner—or worse, to no one in particular.

The reason for this lack of attention in the past to management in law firms is rather simple. Attorneys earn money by billing clients for their time. **Billable hours,** time spent working on a client matter, are the key to the success of most law firms. Clearly, time spent on managing the firm's law practice is not billable to clients. Because management time is not billable, it produces no income for the attorneys or for the firm and, as a result, was viewed as an interference to the practice of law. For this reason, yesterday's law firms often had no formal management, no person or team specifically dedicated to overseeing the operation. But all that has changed.

Today's Law Firms

Law firms today need more effective management than ever before. Reasons ranging from advancing technology to increasing competition pose new challenges to law office managers.

Office Automation   Office automation has made the need for management critical to success. Gone are the days of typewriters and carbon paper. Most law offices are using word processing equipment and many have the most sophisticated computer systems currently available. Automation, facsimile machines, portable telephones, and the continuing phenomenon of rapidly changing technology are making information management a necessity. Software programs are also having an impact on the way law is now being practiced. Programs are currently available for calendaring, docket control, litigation support, research, accounting, and timekeeping, and more programs are on the way. Information is a resource that requires efficient management.

High Costs   The high costs associated with starting and maintaining a practice also contribute to the need for efficient management. The cost of starting up a new law practice today is staggering. A simply furnished law office for one attorney, adequately staffed and equipped to provide client services, will cost between $50,000 and $125,000, depending on location. These start-up estimates do not include a law library, salaries, or the money needed for the lawyer to live on until fees start coming in. Likewise, there are high costs involved in staying in business once the practice is established. Lawyers expect the office manager to know not only how a law firm operates financially but also how to manage it efficiently and effectively.

Competition   The number of law school graduates has steadily increased in recent years. There are more than 750,000 attorneys in the United States, making competition among lawyers rather tough and survival harder. One excellent way to cope with competition in any business is through effective management technique.

Paralegals   As a valuable resource for law firms, paralegals offer opportunities to capitalize on ways to make more money for the firm. Paralegal services can be billed to clients at a lower hourly rate than attorney time. Lawyers are delegating more tasks to paralegals and looking for new ways to make use of their skills. As with any resource, carefully planned management is essential.

Risk   The risk associated with the practice of law has greatly increased. Clients are no longer afraid to sue their lawyers when they feel there are legitimate grounds for a lawsuit. Likewise, employees are much more likely today to seek legal remedies to enforce their rights as employees of the firm.

As a result of these factors—improved technology, high costs, increased competition, the emergence of paralegals, and the risks associated with practicing law—the old-fashioned unmanaged law offices are going the way of the dinosaur.

SUMMARY

1–1

The law office manager is an important and accepted part of today's law office management team. *Management* is defined as the planned use of the firm's resources to achieve goals. Management also refers to the people who establish the firm's goals and are responsible for achieving them. Law firm management is divided into two distinct areas: practice management, which is the mix of the number and types of cases the firm will take, and operations management, which includes all nonlawyer-related, administrative functions.

1–2

The tangible law office management skills consist of planning, organizing, staffing, directing, and controlling the efforts of individuals and the firm as a whole. Planning establishes future goals and develops action plans for achieving them; organizing coordinates the firm's resources to maximize efficiency and effectiveness. Staffing involves recruiting, placing, training, evaluating, and developing the firm's human resources. Directing is the process of leading and motivating others; and controlling is a way of measuring performance and staying on target.

1–3

The intangible law office management skills fall into three general categories: interpersonal roles, informational roles, and decisional roles. While the results of these skills categories are often not clearly visible, they are nevertheless equally as important to good management as the more tangible skills.

1–4

Several factors have contributed to the need for management in today's law firms. Among them are rapidly changing office automation technology; the high costs associated with establishing and maintaining a law practice; competition among the increasing number of lawyers; the emergence of paralegals as a valuable, income-producing resource; and the risks associated with practicing law.

REVIEW

Key Terms

accountability
action plans
authority
billable hours
controlling
delegating
directing
goal
intangible
management
operations management
organizing
planning
practice management
responsibility
staffing
tangible

Questions for Review and Discussion

1. Define the terms *management, responsibility, authority*, and *accountability*.
2. Explain the difference between practice management and operations management.
3. The typical law office manager is responsible for a variety of administrative functions. What are they?
4. What are the tangible management skills and what is the purpose of each? What are the intangible management skills?
5. What are the steps involved in successful planning?
6. Explain the difference between being efficient and being effective. If you had to choose one concept over the other, which would it be and why?

7. Name the resources requiring management in the law office.
8. How can you get more control over your time?
9. When should you consider delegating work to others?
10. What steps are involved in delegating?
11. In establishing controls, what aspects require consideration and why?

Activities

1. In front of the class, or in groups of three, one student assumes the role of the law office manager who is delegating the task of gathering all billable hours for the litigation department for the end-of-the-month billing cycle. If the role play is conducted in front of the class, the class will observe, make notes, and give feedback to the delegator on the process. If the role play is conducted in triads, the third person serves as observer.
2. From the following list, check three or four items that create time management problems for you.

Meetings   _____
Drop-in visitors   _____
Telephone interruptions _____
Paperwork   _____
Red tape   _____

Lack of policies   _____
Lack of personnel   _____
Procrastination   _____
Failure to plan   _____
Too many policies   _____
Improper scheduling _____
No self-discipline   _____
Doing too much at once _____
Lack of skills   _____

Now brainstorm with your group to find at least two possible solutions for each item identified.
3. Invite the manager or administrator from a local law firm to speak on "A Day in the Life of a Law Office Manager."
4. Chances are, some of the activities or tasks you perform could be delegated to someone else. Take a few minutes to make a list of some tasks you should consider delegating.

_____

_____

_____

_____

_____

_____

_____

_____

_____

_____

CHAPTER 2   Tracking Revenue and Expenses

OUTLINE

2–1   Types of Legal Fees and Costs
     Retainer Fees
     Contingent Fees
     Fixed Fees
     Statutory Fees
     Hourly Fees
     Legal Costs and Overhead Expenses
2–2   Practice Management Concepts
     How Fees Are Determined
     Formula for Setting Hourly Fees
     The Leveraging Concept
     The Mix of Business (Practice Management)
2–3   Keeping Track of Time
     Why Timekeeping Is Important
     Timekeeping Systems
2–4   Keeping Track of Costs and Expenses
     Telephone Charges
     Facsimile Charges
     Photocopy Expenses
     Messenger and Courier Service Expenses
     Ethical Considerations
2–5   Client Billing Procedures
     Manual Billing
     Computerized Billing
     Billing Dos and Don'ts

COMMENTARY

Congratulations! You have been hired as the first Office Manager at Dunn & Sweeney. Dunn & Sweeney, you discover, is a fast-growing firm composed of 15 attorneys (5 of whom are partners), 4 paralegals, 10 secretaries, 1 full-time receptionist, and 1 part-time office services clerk. In your first meeting with the Managing Partner, Richard J. Sweeney, you are told that the firm has been experiencing some cash flow problems. The firm receives fees from several types of legal matters: contingency cases, clients who are charged by the hour, a few fixed fee situations, and some statutory cases. Traditionally, the firm has advanced all client costs and absorbed all overhead expenses. Statements for services rendered are prepared sporadically by individual secretaries when they have time. Mr. Sweeney has asked you to attend next month's meeting of the firm's Executive Committee with a report and recommendations for improving cash flow. Since cash flow is a result of money coming into the firm, and money flowing out, you decide to take a look at the firm's revenue stream and its billing system and procedures.

OBJECTIVES

In Chapter 1 you learned that law office managers, as an integral part of the management team, perform a variety of functions and assume many roles. After completing this chapter, you will be able to:

1. Define the common types of legal fees.
2. Explain how legal fees are determined.
3. Distinguish between legal cost and overhead expenses.
4. Explain the "value added" surcharge cost recovering method.
5. Compute hourly fees for attorneys and paralegals.
6. Discuss the leveraging concept.
7. Project revenue based on hourly fees.
8. Discuss and describe types of timekeeping systems.
9. Explain the reasons for and methods of tracking overhead expenses.
10. Discuss manual and computerized billing systems.

2−1   Types of Legal Fees and Costs

Lawyers sell their services for a fee. The regular collection of fees ensures that the firm will have money available to meet overhead expenses and to provide income for all members of the firm. There are a number of types of legal fees. Prior to commencing work on a legal matter, the attorney and client will agree on how fees and costs will be handled. Many states now require that all fee and cost arrangements between attorney and client be in writing.

Retainer Fees

There are several types of retainer fees, as well as several meanings for the word *retainer*. The most common usage of the word **retainer** applies to the fee paid by a client at the beginning of a specified matter and is usually nonrefundable. The **case retainer** may be the entire fee due for the case or may represent only part of the fee. Case retainers are typical in litigated divorces and criminal cases, but many firms require a retainer in all situations to bind the client to the firm before work is performed.

A **retainer for general representation** is common for businesses, school boards, public entities, or anyone requiring continuing legal services. A flat annual amount is charged for general representation with the services included and those excluded carefully spelled out in a written agreement. For example, some charges, such as for litigation matters or raising public funds, are not included in most general representation agreements. The general representation retainer provides the client with the ability to forecast annual legal expenses more accurately for budgeting purposes, and provides the law firm with a steady flow of cash.

Although relatively uncommon, the **pure retainer** binds the law firm to the client by including, among other things, the provision that the firm will not represent a competitor of the client and will keep the client advised of changes in laws or regulations that might have an impact on the client's business.

Contingent Fees

Contingent fees are conditional: they are paid only when a legal matter has been successfully resolved, whether by trial or settlement, and when the money has been received from the unsuccessful party to the lawsuit. Contingent fee arrangements are most common in plaintiff accident lawsuits, product liability matters, and collection cases. In contingent fee matters, if no money is recovered, there is usually no fee due.

The percentage amount to be paid to the law firm is agreed upon between the client and the firm prior to commencing legal action. Typically, contingent fees range from 25 percent to 50 percent of the total money awarded. Different percentage divisions may be agreed to depending on whether the case is settled or goes to trial. For example, a contingent fee agreement might state that the lawyer's fee is 25 percent if the case is settled, 33⅓ percent if the case goes to trial, or 50 percent if it is appealed.

Limits on the amount of fees an attorney can charge in contingency matters have been imposed by some states; likewise, most states prohibit contingent fee arrangements in certain types of cases, such as family law matters and criminal cases.

Fixed Fees

Fixed fees, sometimes called **flat fees,** are usually associated with the standard services performed by most law firms. These include uncontested divorces, routine adoptions, preparation of a simple will, and forming a small business corporation. In addition, some firms might have a fixed charge for performing such services as making a court appearance, attending or taking a deposition, and preparing a motion or answers to interrogatories.

Statutory Fees

Statutory fees are set by state legislatures. They vary from state to state and are most common in probate estate and real estate transactions. These percentage fees are calculated on a graduated scale based on the value of the assets being transferred.

Hourly Fees

Hourly fees are the rates charged to the client for time spent on their legal work. The hourly billing rate for attorneys and paralegals is determined after considering many factors, including education, experience, and geographic location of the firm. One formula for determining hourly billing is discussed in Section 2–2.

Legal Costs and Overhead Expenses

Some costs are involved in all legal actions. These can include the court filing fees, process server's fees, fees for witnesses, and costs for transcripts of testimony. Costs associated with taking legal action are either advanced by the client prior to commencement of the action, with additional requests for costs submitted as they are incurred until the matter is resolved, or advanced by the law firm and repaid at the conclusion of the case. In either event, costs are paid by the client to the firm and are in addition to the legal fees.

In addition to the costs associated with taking legal action, many law firms also bill clients for *overhead expenses*, such as photocopies, postage, facsimiles, messenger service, telephone charges, secretarial services, and word processing. Overhead expenses appear either as itemized entries on the client's statement or as a surcharge. A surcharge is a percentage figure, usually no more than 5 percent, that is calculated on the total bill. This "value added" percentage method for recapturing overhead expenses, while less costly to the firm than providing a record of itemized charges, can be unfair to clients if the percentage figure is too high.

2−2   Practice Management Concepts

Establishing adequate cash flow takes a long time in most law firms because, historically, lawyers have a tendency to wait until the work is completed, or nearly complete, before issuing a statement for services. Only recently have law firms begun to realize that delayed billing creates financial chaos.

Because time can be measured accurately, it has become the standard on which many legal fees are based. Additionally, time-based billing allows the office manager to prepare more precise budgets by being able to forecast cash flow with greater accuracy.

How Fees Are Determined

Contingent fee percentages are agreed to between the lawyer and the client based on an estimate of time required to resolve the matter and on how confident the attorney is of a successful outcome. Statutory fee percentages are established by state legislatures. Fixed fees are determined by estimating attorney or paralegal time required based on past experience in handling similar matters and custom within the local legal community. Retainer fees, too, are based on an estimate of time to be spent on a client's legal matters. Hourly rates can be determined in a variety of ways. One way is to use a simple expense-based formula.

Formula for Setting Hourly Fees

Basic hourly rates for partners are often established using a formula such as the one below, which considers both the overhead expenses attributable to each attorney and the compensation they expect to receive.

$$\frac{\text{Overhead expenses} + \text{Required compensation}}{\text{Number of billable hours}} = \text{Hourly rate}$$

For example, assume that a partner's share of annual overhead expenses is $55,000, personal income requirements are $225,000, and the partner typically bills a minimum of 2,000 hours each year. Based on this formula, the partner's hourly rate would be:

$$\frac{\$55,000 + \$225,000}{2,000} = \$140.00 \text{ per hour}$$

The actual billing rate, however, might be higher than this expense-based calculation suggests because, in determining hourly billing rates, factors such as reputation, years of experience, and community standards are also considered.

The Leveraging Concept

Suppose that the custom in the community is a lower hourly billing rate than that calculated by the expense-based formula described above. In this case, the law firm, or lawyer, has several options: (1) move the practice to an area that would support the hourly rate; (2) cut overhead costs; (3) lower personal income expectations; or (4) hire associate attorneys and paralegals to make up the difference through a concept known as **leveraging.** Leveraging is the process of making a profit from the services performed by others. For years, lawyers have been hiring associate attorneys not only to provide them with an on-the-job training opportunity, but also to provide the firm with a source of additional revenue. With the emergence of paralegals, law firms have found a valuable new resource that can also provide additional income for the firm.

When calculating the hourly rate for associate attorneys or paralegals, a third factor—profit—is added to the equation. Associate attorneys and paralegals are expected to produce a profit. If they do not, and are merely an additional expense, there is no reason to hire or retain them. To calculate the hourly rate for a paralegal, assume the expense of providing office space and supplies, equipment, and secretarial support for the paralegal is $12,000; salary, employer tax contributions, and benefits are $36,000; and the firm's minimum profit requirement is equal to the total expense of the paralegal, or $48,000. Also assume that the firm has established a standard for its paralegals of 1,400 billable hours each year. According to our formula, the hourly billing rate for the paralegal, then, would be about $69 per hour:

$$\frac{\$12,000 + \$36,000 + \$48,000}{1,400} = \$68.57 \text{ per hour}$$

Similarly, the hourly rate for an associate attorney might be:

$$\frac{\$30,000 + \$75,000 + \$105,000}{1,900} = \$110.53 \text{ per hour}$$

Billing rates for associate attorneys and paralegals vary widely, just as they do for partners. It is quite common to find hourly rates for legal services higher in larger law firms and in major metropolitan cities than they are in smaller firms in suburban or rural areas.

There are, of course, other methods used to determine hourly rates, but this simple formula is surprisingly accurate for determining a base to which appropriate adjustments can be made. Determining the amount of attributable overhead costs can be difficult. However, the simplest way is to assign a percentage-share-of-usage figure to overhead expense items, such as office rent, supplies, equipment, and secretarial support.

The Mix of Business (Practice Management)

At Dunn & Sweeney the hourly rates for legal services are:

Partners	$175
Associate attorneys	$110
Paralegals	$ 70

If the firm were to bill all of its work on an hourly fee basis, you could calculate the annual potential fee income as follows:

$$\frac{\text{No. of}}{\text{timekeepers}} \times \frac{\text{Hourly}}{\text{rate}} \times \frac{\text{Required}}{\text{billable hours}} = \frac{\text{Total expected}}{\text{fee income}}$$

Or,

5 partners	× $175	× 2,000	=	$1,750,000
10 associates	× $110	× 1,900	=	$2,090,000
4 paralegals	× $ 70	× 1,400	=	$ 392,000

Projected annual fee income $4,232,000

Although hourly income potential for the firm appears adequate to meet its needs if all clients were being billed at the hourly rate, three of the five partners at Dunn & Sweeney are litigators, and six associate attorneys and two paralegals also work in the litigation section. All current litigation cases at this firm are on a contingent fee basis. Since the firm has been in existence for only five years, even though the future revenue potential for the backlog of quality litigation lawsuits is great, the firm expects to receive only $150,000 in fees from litigation matters coming to a close this year.

The other two partners in the firm, who are not handling any contingent fee cases, have several hourly fee clients and also take as many fixed fee cases as they and their paralegals can handle. Together with the fees billed by the four remaining associates, the income generated by all timekeepers (excluding the litigation section) has been close to $2,000,000 for the past three years. The litigation attorneys project fees next year from cases coming up for trial to be $1,000,000 and $1,500,000, respectively, for the next two years.

As a law office manager you should be able to develop best case, worst case, and probable income projections for your firm. Best case income projections might reflect a situation where everyone is producing at maximum capacity and the firm prevails in all the contingent fee cases. Worst case projections could be that illness strikes one or two top billable hour timekeepers and the firm loses a contingency case or two in trial. Probable income projections are usually somewhere in between best case and worst case. It is of prime importance to document *how* you arrive at your projections, since this is the information you will use to develop budgets and make decisions for the firm in the coming year.

2–3   Keeping Track of Time

When considering law firm cash flow, one of the most important items for attention is how the billable timekeepers—attorneys and paralegals—keep track of their time.

Time is a paradox. Everyone wants more of it, yet we have all the time in the world. Getting the most from your daily 24-hour allotment requires good time management skills and an equal amount of self-discipline. The problem in many law offices is that while everyone is conscious of the value of time, many are rather lax in recording how their time has been spent. Perhaps in no other profession does the axiom "time is money" hold more truth. Yet, as office manager, you will find time sheets with large blocks of unaccounted time because the timekeeper is not diligent about recording time spent on client matters throughout the day. When timekeepers wait to record their time until the end of the week, their memories are rarely able to reconstruct a detailed analysis of their day-to-day activities. Law firms stand to lose hundreds of thousands of dollars each year from faulty timekeeping.

Why Timekeeping Is Important

Time records provide the information from which court documents, such as accountings in bankruptcy cases, and billing statements to clients are prepared. In addition, time records can provide the law office manager and the timekeepers with useful management information. For example, supervising attorneys can use time reports to review the work of associate attorneys and paralegals to see how long they are taking to perform certain tasks, on which projects they may be spending too much or too little time, and in which areas they may require more training, as well as to monitor their overall performance.

Time records can also be used to motivate the timekeepers. For example, in some law firms weekly or monthly summaries of time reports are circulated in an effort to stimulate competition among the timekeepers and departments.

Since most people underestimate the amount of time involved in performing tasks or litigating a case, timekeeping is an important self-management tool. Keeping track of time will point out poor work habits and tasks that could be delegated and can provide a realistic profile of how long projects actually take to complete.

From an administrative point of view, time records alone are the ultimate measure of profitability of any one case, a particular department, or any one attorney or paralegal. Based on time records, a firm might decide to revise its goals, make a change in long-range strategy, reward or terminate an employee, or hire additional staff.

Timekeeping Systems

You can see that keeping accurate time records is one key to the success of the law firm. But just how do you go about keeping track of time? Here are some typical methods.

Converting Time into Decimals   Most law firms convert time into decimals for ease and accuracy in recording based on the following conversion table:

0–6 minutes = .1 hour	31–36 minutes = .6 hour
7–12 minutes = .2 hour	37–42 minutes = .7 hour
13–15 minutes = .25 hour	43–45 minutes = .75 hour
16–18 minutes = .3 hour	46–48 minutes = .8 hour
19–24 minutes = .4 hour	49–54 minutes = .9 hour
25–30 minutes = .5 hour	55–60 minutes = 1.0 hour

With the converted decimal system, time can then be recorded using any of a variety of timekeeping systems.

The Time Planning System   The time planning system is basically a daily or weekly appointment calendar with spaces provided for writing in appointments, things to do, and the amount of time spent for billing purposes. Some time planners, such as the one shown in Figure 2–1, also have spaces for assigning priorities to each item on your list, as well as a place to enter expenses and record memos.

Figure 2–1　Time Planner

NOVEMBER 1992

S	M	T	W	T	F	S
1	2	3	4	5	6	7
8	9	10	11	12	13	14
15	16	17	18	19	20	21
22	23	24	25	26	27	28
29	30					

DECEMBER 1992

S	M	T	W	T	F	S
		1	2	3	4	5
6	7	8	9	10	11	12
13	14	15	16	17	18	19
20	21	22	23	24	25	26
27	28	29	30	31		

JANUARY 1993

S	M	T	W	T	F	S
					1	2
3	4	5	6	7	8	9
10	11	12	13	14	15	16
17	18	19	20	21	22	23
24	25	26	27	28	29	30
31						

INSTRUCTIONS: List all items to be done today, prioritize items according to importance, and number them in the order in which you will perform them.

Monday, December 28, 1992　　363RD DAY – 3 DAYS LEFT

Priority Order Code	To Be Done	Time Estimate Hrs. 1/10s	Appointments	Hours	Memos & Expenses
				8	
				9	
				10	
				11	
				12	
				1	
				2	
				3	
				4	
				5	

Tuesday, December 29, 1992　　364TH DAY – 2 DAYS LEFT

Priority Order Code	To Be Done	Time Estimate Hrs. 1/10s	Appointments	Hours	Memos & Expenses
				8	
				9	
				10	
				11	
				12	
				1	
				2	
				3	
				4	
				5	

Wednesday, December 30, 1992　　365TH DAY – 1 DAY LEFT

Priority Order Code	To Be Done	Time Estimate Hrs. 1/10s	Appointments	Hours	Memos & Expenses
				8	
				9	
				10	
				11	
				12	
				1	
				2	
				3	
				4	
				5	

Source: Law Publications, Inc., Los Angeles, CA (1980). Reprinted with permission.

The success of the time planning system is dependent on the timekeeper's entering enough information so that the person who transcribes the planner will be able to prepare the client's statement from its contents. Although this type of system requires a considerable amount of clerical support, if it helps in recording additional billable hours, it is probably worth the extra effort. One advantage of the time planning system is portability. For attorneys and paralegals who spend a great deal of their time away from the office, this type of system may be favored over other timekeeping methods.

The "One-Write" System Another type of manual timekeeping is the "one-write" system, which comes with or without carbons and is a convenient way to record billable hours and services performed. It is called a "one-write" system because you make each entry just once. Since no recopying or dictation is required, there is no chance of transposition errors. You can also record associated client expenses and costs on a "one-write" expense record form. (See Figure 2–2.)

After time and expenses are recorded, the self-adhering, perforated strips are peeled off and attached to the accompanying client/case service record form. A photocopy of the form can be submitted with the client billing, or the service record form can be transcribed and condensed for billing purposes.

The Machine System Machine systems for recording time require that all client files have an assigned number and that the file number be available when the work is being performed. The machine system has a built-in clock to record time in decimal units, a numerical keypad for encoding the file number, and a preestablished code for the work performed. Here is an abbreviated example of a work-performed code system:

Code	Work Performed
01	Telephone call to client
02	Telephone call from client
03	Prepare letter to client
04	Draft legal document
05	Attend deposition

The machine system offers the flexibility of assigning up to 99 coded work designations to fit almost any law office task. Time is recorded on a roll of paper, similar to an adding machine roll. At the end of the timekeeping period, the codes must be transcribed for billing purposes by a secretary or billing clerk. When using the machine system, care must be taken to transcribe the codes accurately and to remember to start the clock when commencing the task and turn off the clock when finished. Otherwise, you might find a six-minute entry for preparing several pages of interrogatories or a five-hour telephone call appearing on the client's statement!

Computerized Timekeeping Systems The continuing proliferation of software packages designed specifically for law offices indicates a growing interest in using computers to record time. Most law office managers are excited by these programs because they often eliminate several steps, as well as errors, by combining the timekeeping and billing processes. For example, you can purchase a software package that not only allows you to turn on and off a stopwatch that tracks time but also creates an electronic time slip for each billable activity: you simply enter the user's name, the client's name, an optional case

Figure 2–2   Time Record

DECIMAL CONVERSION

CODES FOR DESCRIPTION OF SERVICE

CLIENT TIME		NON-CLIENT TIME	
A – Court Appearance, Hearings	R – Research	E – Education and Reading	X – Bar Association, Community Activities
C – Conference	S – Study and Review		
D – Drafting	T – Telephone	M – Management and Office Administration	P – Personal
L – Letter or Dictation	V – Travel		

IN 6 or 12 MINUTE INTERVALS USE:
6 minutes = .1 hour   36 minutes = .6 hour
12 minutes = .2 hour   42 minutes = .7 hour
18 minutes = .3 hour   48 minutes = .8 hour
24 minutes = .4 hour   54 minutes = .9 hour
30 minutes = .5 hour   60 minutes = 1.0 hour

IN 15 MINUTE INTERVALS USE:
15 minutes = .25 hour
30 minutes = .5 hour
45 minutes = .75 hour
60 minutes = 1.0 hour

TIME RECORD

Date	Lawyer	Client & Case	File No.	Description of Service	Time	Hours	Decimal
					FROM / TO		
					FROM / TO		
					FROM / TO		
					FROM / TO		
					FROM / TO		
					FROM / TO		
					FROM / TO		
					FROM / TO		
					FROM / TO		
					FROM / TO		
					FROM / TO		
					FROM / TO		
					FROM / TO		
					FROM / TO		

(Left margin, each row: Bend Tab Back)

FORM TR

Figure 2–2 *continued*

| Client Matter | CLIENT SERVICE RECORD - PAGE | File No. Attorney |

INSTRUCTIONS: This form is for use with attorney Time Record supplies. Open one Client Service Record for each billable matter. Number each form behind the word "page". If more than one lawyer records time against the matter, use one of the three columns on the right of the form, and post each lawyer's time into a separate column. Monthly, or at the time of billing, multiply each lawyer's recorded hours by his billing rate, and enter the total time-dollar value of all attorneys in the "Dollar Balance" column. When a client is interim billed, subtract the amount of the bill (or the amount specified by the billing attorney) from the "Dollar Balance" column, and describe the billing beneath the last time strip pasted to the form.

PASTE TIME STRIPS HERE

Form CRS

| Attorney ↓ | | | Dollar Bal. |
| Balance F'wd. → | | | |

Source: Daniel J. Cantor & Co., Inc., Philadelphia, PA (1975). Reprinted with permission.

number or name, and the activity performed. This program even allows you to keep track of billable telephone calls without changing programs.

Future programs will interface with some PBX telephone systems, allowing for the metering of phone calls from the time the receiver is picked up to the time it is put down. With this type of software, the value of time spent is automatically calculated and inserted on the timeslip, as well as onto the several types of management reports it generates.

Both custom-designed and off-the-shelf software programs are gaining popularity among law office managers and attorneys for keeping track of billable time. The reason is clear: When computerized systems are used by attorneys and paralegals, most time records—especially those kept on activities performed in the office—do not need to go through the additional step of being transcribed by a secretary or the bill preparer, thus eliminating errors and saving time.

2–4 Keeping Track of Costs and Expenses

It is important to the financial welfare of the law firm not only to keep records of time but also to keep records of client-related costs and expense items. The costs associated with litigation, such as court filing fees, witness fees, and transcripts of depositions, are often recovered by the prevailing party in the lawsuit, thus necessitating the keeping of accurate records. Costs associated with legal matters are sometimes advanced by the firm, or they may be paid by the client.

Additionally, it is not unusual for expense items, such as long-distance telephone calls, photocopies, and messenger services, to be paid by the client. In order to charge expense items back to the client, however, the client must be aware that he or she will be billed for these. Consequently, accurate records must be kept.

Telephone Charges

Preprinted long-distance call record forms, such as those shown in Figure 2–3, can be used to track telephone calls, or you can create your own forms. This manual recordkeeping system usually recaptures only a minimal percentage of actual telephone expenses because people who place the calls forget to write down complete information. If remembering at the end of the week how time was spent is difficult, trying to recall several telephone numbers and the reasons for the calls is virtually impossible.

Another drawback to a manual system is that the office manager must compare the monthly telephone bill with all the call record forms to determine the actual amount of the call in order to bill the client. This is a time-consuming task producing only marginal results. Several companies, however, including some telephone companies, have electronic and computerized systems to track telephone expenses. One popular device uses a numeric or alphanumeric data entry terminal that records who is making the phone call and for whom. Without entering the proper input commands, the user is virtually locked out of the telephone system and cannot place outgoing calls.

Likewise, most local telephone companies, through their central switching location software system, can provide you with a monthly itemized list of telephone calls placed within their service area from each telephone in the firm. This type of call tracking system gives the manager more control over telephone expenses because it monitors each individual telephone in the office. But you

Figure 2–3 Preprinted Long-Distance Call Records

LONG DISTANCE CALL RECORD

Date _____ Time Start _____ Time Stop _____ Total Time _____

CLIENT/CASE _____ FILE NO. _____

Place Called _____ Phone No. _____

CALL   ☐ To _____ Of _____
       ☐ From

SUBJECT _____

_____

WHAT I SAID _____

_____

_____

_____

WHAT HE (SHE) SAID _____

_____

_____

_____

_____

Amount $ _____

Charge to: _____   TAX $ _____

_____   TOTAL $ _____

Signature _____

TELEPHONE CONFERENCE RECORD

Date _____ Time Start _____ Time Stop _____ Total Time _____

CLIENT/CASE _____ FILE NO. _____

CALL   ☐ To _____ Of _____
       ☐ From

SUBJECT _____

WHAT I SAID _____

_____

_____

_____

WHAT HE (SHE) SAID _____

_____

_____

_____

_____

_____

Signature _____

Telephone call records provide both a summary of the conversation for the client's file and a record of the expense item. *Source:* Law Publications, Inc., Los Angeles, CA (1976). Reprinted with permission.

will still need a way to track and recapture telephone calls made through your long-distance carrier, as well as a method for attributing telephone calls to individual client matters.

A medium-sized law firm can spend $75,000 or more each year in telephone services. Assuming that 75 percent of these costs are billable, with a good tracking system you could expect to recover about $57,000 of your annual telephone expenses.

Facsimile Charges

There are several methods to keep track of facsimile charges. One way is to keep a log next to the facsimile machine with the date, client case number, and number of pages. You can then either charge the client on a per page basis or reconcile the log to the monthly statement received from the telephone company. A data entry terminal, similar to the one mentioned above for tracking telephone calls, using a numeric or alphanumeric code, is another way to keep track of who is sending facsimiles and to whom.

Perhaps not since the microwave oven has any piece of technology gained such wide acceptance in so short a period of time and become a standard piece of equipment in the law office as the fax machine. Since even in the smaller firms the number of faxes sent each week can number in the hundreds, many now have more than one facsimile machine to keep work flowing. A typical busy, small law firm will send and receive over 1,000 facsimile pages per month. At an average per page cost of $1.50, the amount recovered can be nearly $18,000 per year.

Photocopy Expenses

The modern-day law office cannot survive without at least one photocopy machine; and, depending on the size of the office, you would be wise to have one or more backup photocopiers for emergency or deadline situations. One of the more frustrating events in a law firm is to have work come to a halt because the photocopy machine has broken down or is being serviced.

Debit card cost control systems, metered "key" access systems, and coded data entry terminals are common ways for law firms to control access to the photocopier and to record client account billing information. Of course, it is also possible to record the information manually on a preprinted form, but this method is the least efficient and least effective way to track photocopier usage.

A typical busy copier makes about 50,000 copies per month. With approximately 80 percent of these copies billable at an average of 10 cents per copy, you may be able to recover about $4,000 each month per copier.

Messenger and Courier Service Expenses

Most law firms in major metropolitan areas are addicted to messenger services. Procrastination, poor time management, too many deadlines, and unreliable postal services have contributed to the rise in use of messengers and overnight couriers.

Costs vary from company to company and are changed frequently, currently ranging from $10.00 and up for next-day air letters. All messenger and courier services provide the sender with a completed form which can be used to track a lost or delayed package. This same form can be used to reconcile the monthly statement and allocate charges to the appropriate client.

It is not uncommon for even smaller law firms to incur monthly charges of $300 to $500 for these overnight or same-day delivery services.

Ethical Considerations

Your job as office manager requires that you monitor and control expenses. The custom in many parts of the country is to charge the client for some or all of the firm's overhead expense items. However, working together with the partners, you must look at each expense category and establish a policy on which ones will be charged back to clients.

For example, if the decision is to charge for photocopying and facsimiles by the page, what is a fair and reasonable amount to charge? Should a surcharge be added to the clients' bills for telephone expenses, or will calls be billed at actual cost—or at all? Are clients to be billed for messenger services that are required because of someone else's poor planning or procrastination?

Charging clients for these and other overhead expenses is a widespread practice among lawyers. By doing some routine monitoring of these expense items, you will no doubt be able to establish policies that are fair and equitable to both the firm and the client. In any event, to guard against possible disputes, clients should be informed of all costs and expenses they will be expected to pay.

2–5   Client Billing Procedures

The firm's billing procedures are critical to cash flow. Billing should be centralized, with one person accountable for this vital law office management function. When left to individual secretaries, preparation of client statements is often relegated to the bottom of the work pile and rarely includes all the costs incurred on behalf of the client. Centralized billing, then, is most often the responsibility of the office manager, the bookkeeper, or an accounting clerk.

Manual Billing

Some smaller law firms type individual client statements from the timekeeper's handwritten records. If kept in some organized format on a daily basis, this may be the most efficient way to bill clients. When preparing client statements manually, however, the typist must take care in transcribing the timekeeper's notes and in calculating the bill accurately, remembering to add any costs and expenses incurred on the client's behalf.

Computerized Billing

Many law firms, small and large, have turned to computerized billing not necessarily to save time—because computerized billing can actually increase staff time—but to increase the firm's profitability. One major payoff from a computerized billing system is the indispensable management reports it provides, which can make the firm more profitable.

With any computerized billing system, unless each timekeeper has a computer that uses a software program to create timeslips, someone must input the information into the program in order for the computer to generate the client bills and management reports. This task is typically performed by individual secretaries, since they are most familiar with the cases as well as the timekeeper's handwriting and can correct entries as they are made.

Another way of handling this time-consuming task is to have one person enter all timeslips into the computer. This method frees up secretarial time, keeps all billing information in one location, and helps to ensure that the bills get out on a regular schedule.

In addition to providing some consistency to billing procedures, computerized billing programs can tabulate billable hours in a variety of useful ways for the office manager and the lawyers. All of the quality billing software can total billable and unbillable hours on a monthly, annual, and cumulative basis. The more sophisticated programs can correlate this information with other billing data and show an individual lawyer's write-ups, write-downs, or write-offs and their overall efficiency on a given case or in a given area of law. These reports would also show that a paralegal is more efficient when setting up a corporation, for example, than when handling a tax matter.

Other management reports can identify the profitable and unprofitable areas of the practice; how much income is attributable to clients brought into the firm by a particular partner; and which activities, such as research and document drafting, might be producing excessive unbillable hours for some timekeepers. They can also provide a list of aged accounts receivable as well as a report of unbilled work in progress for use in forecasting future income.

Billing Dos and Don'ts

No matter which procedure the firm uses, here are some suggestions for creating and maintaining a good billing relationship with the firm's clients.

Do communicate the firm's payment expectation to the client before work is begun. Communication with the client regarding billing should be done by the attorney who will be representing the client. However, some attorneys feel awkward in this situation and the office manager is given the task.

Don't assume anything when it comes to what you think the client may know. Make sure the client is aware of the attorneys' and paralegals' hourly rates or the published fee schedule for the work to be performed. Clients should also know what costs and expenses will be charged to them, when statements are prepared, and when the firm expects to be paid.

Do discuss the timing of charges to be incurred. For example, if the expected fee is $4,000, tell the client it is reasonable to expect that $2,000 will be billed in the first month, $1,000 in the second month, and $1,000 in the third month.

Don't be afraid to ask the client if he or she will be able to pay the charges as they are incurred. If payment cannot be made, this information will allow you to make alternative arrangements to be paid something each month on your terms. If you cannot offer an extended payment plan, and the client is unable to pay your statements as received, the firm cannot afford to work for that client. When offering any form of extended payment plan be sure to take a look at the Federal Truth in Lending legislation, which has been interpreted to include installment billing arrangements even when no finance charge is included.

Do get an agreement in writing. Some states—California is one—now require attorneys to "contract for services in writing if it is foreseeable that total expenses to a client, including attorney fees, will exceed $1,000, or the matter is a contingency matter. Hourly rates, other standard rates and charges, the nature of services to be performed, and the respective responsibilities of the attorney and the client are to be included in the contract." Whether or not such an agreement in writing is required by law, it is a sound business policy.

Don't send out bills sporadically. Make it a practice to send itemized bills at the same time each month. Doing so shows the firm is as serious about getting paid as the phone company and Mastercard. If, for some reason, you cannot get the bills out on time, send a letter explaining why the bill will be delayed. It is important to keep the psychology of expectation in the client's mind. However, if you do this more than twice in a year, the firm's credibility and professionalism might be questioned.

Do print a payment due date on your bill. Everyone is accustomed to seeing a specific payment due date on bills. "Payable upon receipt" has no meaning, but a specific payment due date allows clients to schedule payment to the firm along with their other bills. Payment due dates will also allow you to know when payments are overdue and to follow up immediately.

Don't use bills with aging columns. Printing the aging of receivables columns is tantamount to extending credit and will slow down your cash flow. Many clients will assume that if you print "current, 30 days, 60 days, 90 days and over" at the bottom of your statement, they can make payments whenever they want to.

Do include a self-addressed return envelope. We are all accustomed to receiving a return envelope with our bills. By including a return envelope with the client's bill you are once again establishing an expectation of being paid just as any other creditor.

SUMMARY

2–1

There are several types of legal fee arrangements. Among them are retainer agreements, contingent fees, fixed fees, statutory fees, and hourly fee rates. In addition to being charged a fee for services performed, clients are typically expected to pay all costs associated with their legal action. In many instances, clients are also charged for certain overhead expenses, such as long-distance telephone calls, photocopies, and messenger service associated with their legal action.

2–2

Legal fees are determined in several ways. Both contingent fees and statutory fees are percentage-based fees. Fixed fee and retainer fee agreements are determined by estimating the amount of time to be spent on the client's matter. One way of determining hourly fee rates is to use a cost-based formula. Experience, reputation, and community custom are factors to be considered in determining fees for professional services. The types and number of cases being handled by the firm are important to the revenue stream, or cash flow. Through a concept known as leveraging—making a profit from work performed by others—the firm is often able to increase its profit potential by hiring paralegals and associate attorneys.

2–3

Time is a valuable resource for the law firm. Fees are billed based on time spent working for a client. There are several types of timekeeping systems, most of which convert time into decimal units for ease and accuracy in recording billable time. Notes regarding services performed are recorded manually or by using a computerized timekeeping system. Client statements are then prepared from these time records.

2–4

In most cases the prevailing party is able to recapture costs advanced for litigation. Thus it is important that the law firm keep an accurate record of these costs. Many law firms also charge clients for certain overhead expense items, such as photocopies, facsimiles, telephone calls, and messenger services. Both manual systems and sophisticated cost-recovery systems are available to track and record this information. The reports generated from these systems can provide the office manager with useful information for controlling overhead expenses.

2–5

Whether client statements are typed on an individual basis or produced by a computerized billing system, good client relations require that clients be thoroughly informed of what they are expected to pay, when they are expected to pay, and that billing will be done on a regular schedule.

REVIEW

Key Terms

case retainer
contingent fees
fixed fees
flat fees
hourly fees

leveraging
pure retainer
retainer
retainer for general representation
statutory fees

Questions for Review and Discussion

1. What are the common types of legal fees?
2. How are legal fees established?
3. Explain the difference between legal costs and overhead expenses.
4. What is the "value added" surcharge method of recovering overhead expenses?
5. What is the formula for computing hourly fees for partners? For associate attorneys and paralegals?
6. Explain the concept of leveraging and how it applies to the practice of law.
7. What is the formula for projecting revenue based on hourly rates?
8. What are some timekeeping methods used in law firms?
9. Why do law firms want to keep track of overhead expenses and what are some methods used?
10. What are the advantages and disadvantages of manual and computerized billing systems?

Activities

1. Contact two or three software vendors for information on timekeeping programs. Invite them to demonstrate their programs to the class.
2. Ask those students who work in law firms to bring samples of their timekeeping methods to class for discussion.
3. Discuss ways to motivate timekeepers to be more diligent in their timekeeping habits.
4. Conduct an informal survey among local law firms regarding their practice of charging clients for photocopies, long-distance calls, and other client-related overhead expenses.
5. Based on the practice management information given for Dunn & Sweeney in Section 2–2 (see "The Mix of Business," pp. 28–29), and using the formula

$$\frac{\text{No. of}}{\text{timekeepers}} \times \frac{\text{Hourly}}{\text{rate}} \times \frac{\text{Required}}{\text{billable hours}}$$

$$= \frac{\text{Total expected}}{\text{fee income}}$$

calculate your estimate of potential income for the firm for this year. Remember that all litigation cases at Dunn & Sweeney are handled on a contingent fee basis. Therefore, you cannot include in your billable hour calculations anyone who is assigned to the litigation group.

PART TWO

THE TANGIBLE

LAW OFFICE

MANAGEMENT SKILLS

Chapter 3
Administrative Effectiveness in the Law Office

Chapter 4
Law Office Facilities Management

Chapter 5
Information Management in the Law Office

Chapter 6
Basic Finance for the Law Office Manager

Chapter 7
Personnel Management

CHAPTER 3   Administrative Effectiveness in the Law Office

OUTLINE

3-1   Making Good Impressions
    Choosing a Telephone System
    Voice Mail
    Managing the Reception Staff
3-2   Records Management
    Creating Files
    Filing Systems
    Selecting Filing Equipment
    Organizing Active Files
    Managing Inactive Files
3-3   Managing the Law Library
    Function of the Library
    Automating the Library
3-4   Managing Office Equipment and Consumables
    Purchasing Equipment
    Renting and Leasing Equipment
    Tax Considerations
    Managing Office Consumables

COMMENTARY

As the office manager at Dunn & Sweeney you are directly responsible for the efficient operation of the law firm. After only a short time with the firm you have noticed that the reception desk is so busy that calls are answered only after numerous rings and that callers are left on hold for too long; too much staff time is devoted to locating misplaced files; the firm is rapidly running out of file storage space; and some office consumables are overstocked and others are in short supply.

Since effective administration of the law firm is the office manager's responsibility, you need to take immediate steps at Dunn & Sweeney to allow the firm to function more smoothly and economically.

OBJECTIVES

In Chapter 2 you learned that law firms create revenue from several types of legal fees and through a concept known as leveraging. You also learned that in addition to fees for services rendered, law firms are generally reimbursed for costs and overhead expenses associated with legal action. After completing this chapter, you will be able to:

1. Develop criteria to evaluate or select an office telephone system.
2. List areas for consideration when hiring reception staff.
3. Define records management.
4. Explain four types of filing systems.
5. List criteria for consideration in selecting filing equipment.
6. Discuss ways of organizing active files.
7. Explain some of the different ways law firms manage inactive files.
8. Discuss how automation is used to manage the law library.
9. List the items that will affect your office equipment management decisions.
10. Discuss different types of inventory and control systems for office consumables.

3–1   Making Good Impressions

A very good case could be made for making the receptionist the highest paid staff position in the law firm. Whether on the telephone or face-to-face in the lobby, the receptionist is often the first and most frequently contacted person in the entire firm. Yet often little attention is given to how well this administrative area functions. Here are some guidelines for assessing effectiveness in this key position.

1. Are incoming calls answered by the second or third ring?
2. Are callers left on hold for more than 15 seconds?
3. Are the telephones adequately staffed?
4. Is the reception staff properly trained to answer the phones professionally, to transfer calls without interruption or take accurate messages, and to page discreetly?
5. Does the staff know how to route inquiring calls from prospective clients?
6. Does the receptionist know how to handle emotional or rude callers?
7. Is the receptionist professional at all times?

As these guidelines suggest, the reception function consists of two key elements—equipment and staff. Let's assume that at the moment your firm is not considering relocating its offices to larger quarters. But, keeping in mind that moving is an option for any law firm outgrowing its space, there are certain items to consider when evaluating your current system or future needs.

Choosing a Telephone System

Not so long ago selecting an office telephone system required little or no thought. You simply called the local telephone company, asked to be hooked up, and within a matter of days a technician came to install your black, rotary dial telephone. Without much thought or effort, you were able to communicate with clients. Not so today! Law office managers are now faced with a number of decisions before choosing a telephone system.

Telephone Instruments   Individual telephone instruments now come with a variety of features. Among them are call holding, call waiting, call forwarding/busy/no answer; conference call and call transfer capabilities; do-not-disturb buttons and distinctive rings; hands-free speakers, speed dialing, and busy indicators. The cost of business telephones now ranges from about $300 to $1,400 per station, depending on their features.

System Features The ability to route calls is just one feature available on modern telephone systems. You can also have an accounting system built in or added on to some systems which have the capability of generating billing information using client codes. Twenty-four-hour remote dictation and transcription service through a centralized location that can be accessed by attorneys when they are away from the office is also available on some systems. For the convenience of both the attorneys and clients calling into the office, consider having an 800 line installed. Not only will an 800 line save time and aggravation for members of the firm when calling from a remote location; it is also another way to build goodwill with clients.

Buy or Rent You will also need to decide whether the firm should purchase its own telephone system or rent one from the local telephone company. Believe it or not, your telephone equipment and usage fees may, over time, exceed your rent for office space. For example, if your phone bills are $3,000 a month, you are committing $360,000 for phone service over the next 10 years, and that excludes any increase in rates. That much money requires attention to detail. The cost and benefits of owning your own equipment must be carefully weighed against the cost and benefits of procuring these from your local telephone services provider.

Traffic Traffic refers to the volume of calls, in numbers and duration, that occur within the law office. Keeping traffic statistics will help you determine if you have the correct number and type of telephone lines as well as adequate reception staffing needs. Most telephone vendors have developed forms and guidelines to help you gather this vital, predecision information.

Expansion Capabilities Too often the ability to expand the telephone system is overlooked. As the firm grows, lack of system expansion capability can result in poor responsiveness to clients as well as increased expense if the entire system has to be replaced. Excess capacity can be included in the initial configuration or acquired as needed. You will want to know the approximate cost of adding to the system, either initially or later, as well as how many instruments can be added before any additional cost is likely to be incurred.

Reliability When the telephone system is not working in a law office, business is interrupted. Before choosing a vendor, you need to know the average time between system failures; the average time it takes to repair a problem once on site; the amount of time the power can be off before a computer program is lost; the amount of time required to reload and self-test the system, if required; and, in the event of a power failure, whether relays can be installed for limited calling in emergencies.

Maintenance and Installation All telephone systems require routine maintenance and repairs. Not only should you be concerned with how many local, trained maintenance personnel the vendor has, but you should also know what contingency plans are in place in the event of a personnel strike or a disaster.

How are incomplete calls or static on the lines handled? Will the vendor follow through with the telephone company until the problem is resolved, or will you be notified only that it is the operating company's (usually one of the Bell Telephone companies) problem? In the latter case, the potential for finger-pointing exists between the two vendors, which will usually require excellent assertive communication skills on your part to resolve.

How long will the vendor take to install your telephone system? Depending on the size of the system and the efficiency of the vendor, installation can take anywhere from two weeks to twenty-six weeks. When planning a move, making arrangements for telephone service is a priority.

How does the law office manager cut through all the advertising hype to determine what system is best for the firm? One way is to hire and work closely with an independent telecommunications consultant. Today's telephone systems are extremely complex and costly, allowing few opportunities for errors in judgment. Working with a consultant gives you vital technical expertise and allows you to control the bidding and evaluation process.

Whether you work with a telecommunications consultant or on your own, before you purchase a communications system you will want to request proposals from several vendors. In preparing a request for proposal (RFP), the vendor needs a brief history of the law firm, the current system you are using, the number and types of instruments you require, your best estimate of communications needs for the future, and your maintenance requirements. Vendors can then respond with detailed cost proposals from which you can make a decision.

In summary, here is a list of considerations when evaluating a telephone system:

1. Telephone instruments
2. System features
3. Buy or rent
4. Traffic
5. Expansion capabilities
6. Reliability
7. Maintenance and installation

If just selecting the telephone system seems extremely complicated, let's consider voice mail, one of the many options now available for making your telephone system work more efficiently.

Voice Mail

For many law firms a voice mail, or voice messaging, system is solving many routine communications problems. Voice messaging is not a high-tech answering machine. It is a computer-based solution for managing resources more effectively. Here is a description of how voice mail works.

When a client calls the law firm and the attorney is not able to take the call, the receptionist can route the caller to the attorney's voice "mailbox," where the client can leave a message of any length. These automated call handling systems store incoming spoken messages in voice mailboxes, which can be accessed only by code. Messages are stored on a computer disk, not on tapes such as those used on answering machines, so the recipient hears only the messages left in his or her mailbox. There is less chance for error in message-taking, and the receptionist is free to handle more calls. In addition, voice mail can perform other functions, such as automatically paging the attorney when a call comes in or letting the recipient know when there is "mail" waiting to be picked up. Why should your firm consider a voice messaging system? Here are three reasons.

1. Voice messaging helps people communicate. Voice messaging enables clients to say what they have to say with a single call. Because clients can get right to the point and leave messages of any length, a message will also reflect their emotional state and the urgency of the situation. Often, because the attorney has more information about the nature of the client's call, only one response call is necessary, thus saving time. In addition, voice mail allows the recipient to retrieve messages when convenient and without interruption to other activities.

2. Voice messaging never sleeps. Even in the late night or early morning hours when attorneys are often still toiling away, messages can be phoned in for colleagues or staff to hear the next morning. Law firms with branch offices around the country and abroad also benefit from saving on long-distance calls made in off-peak hours to other time zones.

3. Voice messaging serves the clients. Ten seconds on hold can be an eternity to a caller. Likewise, waiting for someone to answer the telephone can be just as frustrating when it takes more than three rings for a response. An optional feature, such as call attendance, will automatically route calls from clients to a predetermined backup line when the line is busy so that no caller is left waiting for his or her call to be answered.

Additionally, voice mail protects client confidentiality. When clients do not have to identify themselves and the nature of their call to a receptionist, there is less likelihood that confidences will be breached inadvertently. Since client confidentiality is a critical issue in all law offices, voice mail is another way to make clients feel secure about discussing all aspects of their case with the attorney.

Voice mail is not for all firms—not because of possible client resistance, since just about everyone is familiar with answering machines, but because buying the equipment can cost from $10,000 to about $50,000. For firms with fewer than 50 employees, voice mail service companies are a cost-effective alternative to purchasing a system. Calls to the customer's phone are forwarded to the service office, where the voice messages are recorded. The user then calls the service, punches in an identifying code, and listens to the recorded messages. Voice mail service companies charge a monthly fee for each mailbox. Although more expensive than an answering machine, the services provided by voice mail service companies cost much less than a receptionist and are available 24 hours a day. Voice messaging can be a valuable time-saving tool for increasing productivity and responsiveness to clients.

Managing the Reception Staff

The reception function is one of the most important administrative areas in the law firm. Skillful handling of calls and visitors enhances the firm's credibility and competence with clients, court personnel, government officials, and business acquaintances, as well as making the job easier for attorneys and all members of the staff. On the other hand, careless performance of the reception duties can lose prospective clients for the firm or alienate present ones.

Large law firms generally have a central reception area staffed with one or more receptionists who sit at a desk answering telephones and greeting visitors. In addition, when large firms occupy several floors in a building, a smaller reception area is likely to be found on each floor. In small law firms, secretaries may add reception duties to their list of responsibilities.

In most law firms, the receptionist is the first contact a client has with the firm. So, whether this function is being performed part-time by a secretary or other staff members or is the responsibility of one or more full-time receptionists, it is imperative that those who are likely to perform the tasks be properly trained. Here are some areas for particular attention.

Staff Selection   Although it would seem that just about anyone could answer the telephone and greet visitors, surprisingly few people do it well. Because of the high visibility of the receptionist position, the office manager should pay particular attention to the attitude and appearance of candidates for the job. Whether the person selected is a career receptionist or someone who sees the job as an interim step, his or her attitude must reflect the importance of the position.

A relaxed, friendly, yet businesslike manner reflects the firm's confidence, empathy, and professionalism. In addition, poise, graciousness, a pleasant voice, and old-fashioned manners contribute to the firm's image. Unfortunately, there has been such a noticeable decline in manners and graciousness throughout all levels of business today that some colleges, universities, and private training companies are now offering courses in what were once considered common courtesies. The law firm that pays attention to these seemingly small details can favorably enhance its public image.

The overall appearance of the receptionist is equally important to the firm's image. Small firms in rural communities may have a very informal atmosphere where casual clothes are customary. Law firms in urban areas, on the other hand, are usually more formal in appearance and business suits are common for both men and women, regardless of position. Because the receptionist helps to create an image of the firm, her or his (yes, there are male receptionists in law firms) appearance should be a reflection of the firm and its clients.

In addition to answering calls and receiving visitors, a law office receptionist might typically perform other tasks, such as keeping certain client records and posting to client expense accounts; maintaining and preparing the office calendar for weekly distribution in the firm; scheduling conference room activities; receiving, sorting, and distributing incoming mail; and sending and receiving facsimiles and messenger service items. The variety of duties and functions associated with the reception position make this a pivotal position in any law firm.

Client Confidentiality   When clients come to a lawyer, the matters to be discussed are often highly sensitive, personal, or emotional issues, such as divorce or bankruptcy. Not only must all members of the firm protect and preserve client confidences as a matter of courtesy; the American Bar Association Rules for Professional Conduct require that client matters be held in strict confidence.

For clients to feel free to discuss all aspects of their case with attorneys, paralegals, and secretaries, they must feel that confidentiality is important to everyone in the law firm, starting with the receptionist. At the reception desk, computer screens, client files, message slips, and scraps of paper must be hidden from view of anyone who might be in the reception area and then put away or disposed of properly. Clients should be greeted quietly and their arrival discreetly announced without using their names, if possible. For example, "Your 10:30 appointment is here" is preferred over "Jack Smith is here to see you about his divorce matter."

When a client is calling into the firm to speak with an attorney, paralegal, or secretary, the receptionist can also aid in protecting confidences by asking, "Will Ms. Jones know what this is regarding?" instead of, "May I tell Ms. Jones what this is regarding?" Calls should not be put through while a client is in an attorney's or paralegal's office, unless otherwise instructed.

Here are some procedures for maintaining client confidentiality in the reception area.

- Do not leave client files out where others might see them.
- Dispose of waste paper and message slips properly—filing or shredding them is best.
- Be discreet in answering the telephone and announcing callers or visitors.
- Never discuss client matters outside the office, or with others in the office, when conversations could be overheard.

Staff Security The law firm is responsible for providing a safe working environment for its employees. Unfortunately, there have been enough reported instances of unhappy clients who have forced their way into a law office, terrorized the staff, sometimes taking hostages or shooting people, that staff security is uppermost in the minds of some law office managers.

Since the receptionist is uniquely vulnerable—often sitting in an unprotected, exposed area cut off from others—this area requires particular attention. Some firms are enclosing the reception desk and immediate surrounding area with protective glass, leaving it accessible only from a locked interior corridor. This solution to a security problem has the added benefit of protecting client confidences because conversations with the receptionist cannot be overheard by people sitting in the reception area.

In addition to protecting the receptionist, making the reception area a separate room with doors to attorney and staff offices accessible only by code or buzzer systems also provides security to the entire firm—including access to client files. Security in the law office serves two purposes: it protects the members of the firm, and it protects clients.

3−2 Records Management

Do you remember when PCs (personal computers) were new and there was great excitement about the dawning era of paperless offices? That didn't happen. Instead, the use of more computers in more law firms has led to generating more paper than ever before, resulting in the need to manage, store, and retrieve all that information more efficiently and effectively.

Arguably, a law office's most valuable resource is its clients' records or files. Proper management of these records and files—from creation to destruction—will save time, money, and frustration. **Records management** is the systematic storage of records for quick retrieval upon demand. Records management can be done manually, with a computer, or by using a combination of both systems.

Whichever system your firm uses, with planning and some well-thought-out procedures for dealing with records, the firm will save money in both employee time and use of office space for file storage.

Creating Files

There are several steps involved with creating a new file, whether the file is for a new client of the firm or for a current client. The first step involves completing a routine information sheet for the firm's records with such items as the client's name, address, and telephone numbers, as well as other parties to the action and their attorneys, fee arrangements, billing arrangements, and any noteworthy comments regarding the client or the case. Some firms create their own forms for this purpose. The new case memo form shown in Figure 3–1 is illustrative of the types available from supply houses.

Checking for Conflict of Interest   Once all the pertinent information has been gathered, and before an actual file is opened, research of current and past clients must be conducted for a possible **conflict of interest.** A conflict of interest exists in a situation where regard for one duty leads to disregard of another. For example, an attorney representing both parties in a divorce action may discount the needs of one party in favor of the other; or, unknowingly, an attorney in your firm may have a financial interest in a corporation that asked one of the lawyers to represent it in a litigation matter. The potential for a conflict of interest is particularly high when there are several lawyers in the firm. In all cases, once an actual conflict of interest exists, the attorney must withdraw and new counsel must be engaged. Since substituting counsel is costly and embarrassing, care should be taken to ensure that no possible conflict of interest exists before agreeing to represent any party in a legal action.

The process of checking for conflicts of interest usually begins with a paralegal, then through a records management clerk, and finally with the lawyers themselves. Law firms that are fully automated will run a check on their client database for any of the names appearing on the new case memo. Smaller firms without a computerized client database rely on their alphabetical client file card index, as well as on the memories of their attorneys.

Once the conflict check is completed, a physical file can be opened. Most law firms use some sort of a multipart, preprinted form with carbons attached, similar to the one shown in Figure 3–2, when opening new files. With one typing, copies of all relevant information regarding the case are provided for the attorney and secretary, bookkeeping, central filing, and the file itself.

Managing the Client Database   Information pertaining to a new client is also entered into the law firm's database as soon as the file is opened. Whether the firm is automated and all client records are accessed by computer or whether the firm uses a manual index system to keep track of its clients, the integrity of any system is dependent upon the accuracy of the information in it. Accuracy, in turn, is largely a function of how often the system is updated to keep it current.

A client database serves several functions. One is to provide accurate information about clients to those who may need that information in the law firm. Most of the client database software programs include an activities file for each client, which will provide an up-to-date status report so that telephone calls can be returned or consultations held without chasing down a client's paper file. This results in a tremendous time saving for both attorneys and staff.

Another advantage of a computerized database is to be able to compile various lists of clients with common criteria. For example, you can pull up a list of clients whose last names begin with the letter *P.* Or you can compile a list of all your corporate clients, print a mailing list, and keep them informed of new legislation that might affect their businesses.

A database can also tell you whether new business is a result of referrals, networking, or holding seminars. Once the database has been created, its uses are almost unlimited. But the information on it must be kept up-to-date and managed wisely for maximum advantage.

Figure 3–1   New Case Memo Set

NEW CASE MEMO SET

CLIENT INFORMATION

CLIENT _____   FILE NO. _____

ADDRESS _____   DATE OPENED _____

_____   ☐ NEW CLIENT   ☐ PRESENT CLIENT

PHONE(S): HOME _____   BUSINESS _____

CASE INFORMATION

FILE TITLE _____

MATTER _____

_____

_____

TYPE OF CASE _____

REFERRED BY _____   OBTAINED BY _____

RESPONSIBLE ATTORNEY _____   ASSIGNED TO _____

ADVERSE PARTY _____

ADDRESS _____

PHONE(S) _____

OPPOSING ATTORNEY _____

ADDRESS _____

PHONE(S) _____

FEE ARRANGEMENTS

☐ FIXED FEE OF $ _____   ☐ HOURLY RATE AT $ _____   PER HOUR

☐ HOURLY RATE AT $ _____   PER HOUR PLUS _____ % OF AMOUNT ☐RECOVERED ☐SAVED

☐ ESTIMATED FEE IN THE RANGE OF $ _____   TO $ _____

☐ CONTINGENT FEE OF _____ % OF AMOUNT ☐RECOVERED   ☐SAVED ☐OTHER _____

☐ FEE TO BE DETERMINED ON BASIS OF ALL RELEVANT FACTORS ☐ RETAINER OF $ _____ PER ☐ MONTH ☐YEAR

   NUMBER OF HOURS OF SERVICE COVERED BY RETAINER: UP TO _____ HOURS PER ☐ MONTH ☐YEAR

   EXCESS HOURS TO BE BILLED AT $ _____ PER HOUR.

☐ OTHER _____

BILLING ARRANGEMENTS

BILL ☐ MONTHLY   ☐ QUARTERLY   ☐ ON COMPLETION   ☐ OTHER _____

☐ TOWARDS FEE & COSTS

☐ RETAINER OF $ _____   RECEIVED ON _____   ☐ $ _____ TOWARDS FEE

☐ $ _____ TOWARDS COSTS

☐ CLIENT'S DEPOSIT ACCOUNT OF $ _____ RECEIVED ON _____

   TOWARDS FEES AND COSTS AS INCURRED. ACCOUNT TO BE MAINTAINED AT $ _____ UNTIL COMPLETION.

NOTES

_____

_____

_____

_____

_____

_____

_____

_____

_____

Source: Law Publications, Inc., Los Angeles, CA (1984). Reprinted with permission.

Figure 3–2   New Case Multipart Set

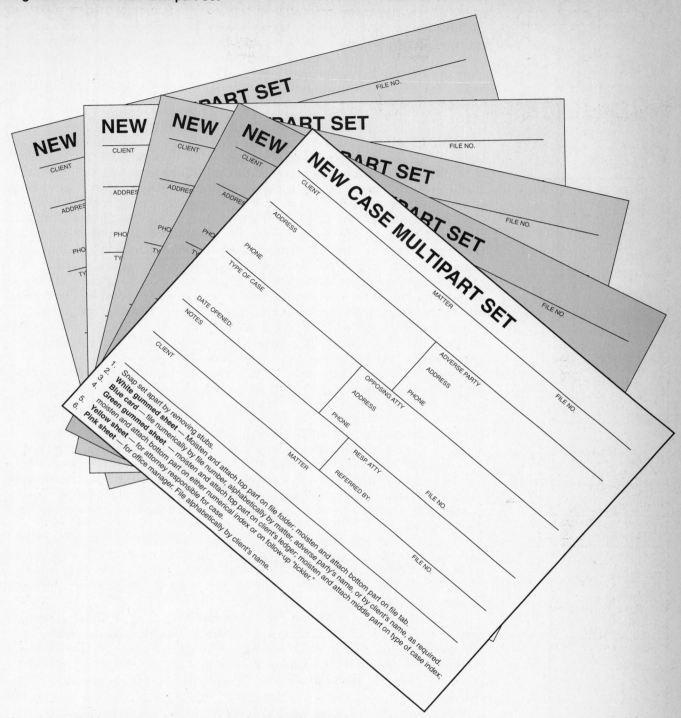

Source: Law Publications, Inc., Los Angeles, CA (1974). Reprinted with permission.

Filing Systems

In most law offices you will find one of the three basic filing systems—alphabetic, numeric, and subject files—or combinations of the three, with the newest system for records management, bar coding, beginning to find its way into law firms.

Alphabetic Files Strict alphabetic filing is the arrangement of files, or materials, by the name of the client, organization, or title (when used for creating forms files). Precise rules exist for filing alphabetically, and unless everyone is familiar with them, unlimited opportunities exist for misplacing the files. Perhaps worse than the frustration caused by misplaced files, alphabetical filing thwarts any attempt to maintain client confidentiality because anyone can locate files just by looking under the client's name, and the tabs of any files lying around can be seen and read easily.

Numeric Files Because using numbers is more accurate than using letters for filing purposes—most people can remember that 17 comes after 16, but many have difficulty remembering whether McDonald comes before or after Madison—most law firms today, especially those with a computerized billing system, use a numeric filing system. If your firm is currently computerized, or if you are contemplating it, before implementing a numeric filing system it is important to check the limitation on the number of digits your computer program will accept. Most programs will allow you to use up to a total of eight characters (including letters, decimals, and digits) in numbering your files.

Here is one example of a numeric filing system: A small firm might choose to include the year in their numbering system, as a reminder of when the file was opened, as well as the sequential number of the file. The first file opened in 1992 would then be assigned the number 92-0001, the second file would carry the number 92-0002, and so on. This system has the added advantage of letting you know exactly how many new files were opened in any year.

Another example of a numeric filing system might be to assign each area of the practice a one thousand series, then number each new file sequentially in the series. At Dunn & Sweeney, for example, the litigation department files are in the 1000 to 1999 range, so file number 1067 means that the file is the 67th litigation file opened. Wishing to track the number of cases brought into the firm annually, Dunn & Sweeney also uses the year as part of their numbering system, adding it at the end like this: 1067.92. Corporate clients with several files can be assigned their own numbers, still incorporating the basic numbering plan. For instance, all Jade Corporation files are in the 6000 series. Consequently, file number 6125.92 is the 125th file opened for Jade Corporation, and it was opened in 1992.

Some firms use a combination of digits and letters, such as 92-0001 LT. This file number tells us that the first file opened in 1992 was a litigation file. File number 92-0025 EP would indicate that the 25th file opened in 1992 was an estate planning client. A quick periodic audit can tell you where the firm is, or should be, placing its marketing emphasis.

All numeric filing systems also require some kind of alphabetic client index, or you will not be able to locate the file using only the client's name. The multipart sets described in this chapter provide copies for filing in the attorney's and the secretary's alphabetic index. In addition, one notebook should be kept in a central location with each file number recorded as it is assigned to a file so that subsequent files will have the correct number in sequence. Assign the opening of files to one person to eliminate the possibility of recording errors.

Using a numeric or an alphanumeric system provides you with almost limitless combinations. In deciding which to use, remember the two primary objectives in law office records management: The first objective is to be able to retrieve information quickly, and the second is to provide information to assist in practice management.

Subject Files Reference files, personal files, and form files may be maintained according to the subject to which they relate. In law firms, form files are the mainstay of the filing system since so much of legal work is repetitious. These "boilerplate" forms are usually filed according to categories such as family law, real estate, personal injury, and probate, with subdivisions for various forms within each subject category. Using form files saves money for the client and the firm; but one major drawback with any type of subject file is that there may be a problem in getting two people to agree on what to call the file. And, at times, even one person may have trouble deciding on a name. To be useful then, subject files and form files should have a written, cross-referenced guide indicating under what subject certain materials are to be found.

Filing systems can also be arranged according to department, division, region, and geographic location, but these systems are more likely to be found in the law department of a large corporation than in private law firms.

Bar Coding Files   In just a few years bar coding has progressed from an obscure supermarket-based device to mainstream records management in organizations that must manage numerous paper files. Still underutilized in law firms, bar coding is one way to eliminate records management drudgery, promote efficiency, save money, and keep track of files. By applying bar codes to individual files, then scanning the bar codes of the files in use at the end of the day at the desk of their last location, you can keep track of files easily. Instead of spending hours locating a file, you simply enter the file number into the computer and its last known location will appear on the screen.

Implementing a bar code system requires a personal computer, a laser printer, some software, and a reader. Bar code software cannot yet be purchased off the shelf, but it can be easily programmed by a knowledgeable computer programmer. Bar code readers tend to fall into one of five categories: light pens, stationary fixed beam scanners, hand-held lasers, stationary moving beam scanners, and imaging array readers. These electronic readers analyze patterns of thick and thin lines and spaces from objects of almost any size or shape, making only one error for every 350,000 characters read and operating at speeds equivalent to producing 300 typewritten pages per hour. Bar codes can be programmed to read the alphabet or numbers, or a combination of each, making the system ideal for almost any type of records management situation. Figure 3–3 illustrates several types of bar code configurations.

Figure 3–3   Bar Codes

Bar codes, using a combination of letters and numbers, are a way of improving a records management system.

The cost of this technology has continued to fall, making bar coding affordable for many law firms. Since the software can be used with many types of hardware, a medium-sized law firm might be able to install a bar code records management system for less than the annual cost of a file clerk.

In the future, bar coded client files might be used in conjunction with bar coded employee identification cards to record billable time. The application of bar code technology to the law firm environment is now at the point where automation was ten years ago. As law firms and programmers become more familiar with the technology, no doubt other uses for a bar code system will be found.

Selecting Filing Equipment

Filing equipment and storage space are required to contain the paper records of a law firm. This, in turn, presents the office manager with several concerns and challenges in utilizing high-priced office space effectively. Because of the ever-increasing cost of storing paper records, many law firms are questioning the need to maintain paper files, as well as which paper files to maintain.

There are some legitimate reasons for keeping paper records, however. For one thing, attorneys are used to paper. It is visible and they can touch it. Most attorneys get very nervous when suggestions are made about getting rid of their hard-copy files. Also, in some cases it is just more economical to keep records in their original paper format than to transfer them to any other record-keeping system. Here are some criteria to help you make the right filing equipment selection.

Types of Filing Equipment   Because use of office space influences equipment buying decisions, there has been a gradual shift from the lateral filing cabinets to open-shelf filing or to high-density mobile filing shelves, which are now gaining popularity.

The ubiquitous *lateral filing cabinets* have some advantages, even though they take up more space than other types of storage equipment. These cabinets can be purchased with locks and can be made fireproof. They are particularly good for storing financial records of the law firm, personnel files, and other high security documents.

Many law firms have turned to *open-shelf filing systems* to save space. These systems are also faster to use, and are more accessible than filing equipment with drawers. However, they too are stationary and require aisle space.

In file-intensive environments, such as law offices, *high-density mobile storage systems* have become very popular. High-density mobile filing systems, such as those pictured in Figure 3–4, rest on wheeled carriages that roll on tracks imbedded in the floor. They are easily moved manually with a handle, or with a chain-driven drive shaft, or by pushing a button on the end of the carriage. Mobile filing systems include floating-aisle systems, which allow you to adjust the width of the space between aisles, to rotate files, and to use vertical and horizontal file carousels.

Because of their versatility (any kind of shelves or racks can be put on carriages, even lateral files with locks) and their efficient use of space (they will hold three to four times as many paper files as filing cabinets), high-density mobile filing systems are particularly well-suited for large central file storage, for shelving the law library, and for creating open-office work spaces with files, desk space, and a nearby copier and fax machine. (See Figure 3–5.)

Figure 3–4 Mobile File System

Mobile systems are easily moved with handles. *Source:* Photo courtesy of CenterCore, Inc., Wayne, PA.

Effective Use of Space Obviously, the more files you maintain, the more you need to use space effectively. One way to maximize storage space is to expand the files vertically—all the way to the ceiling, if necessary. Another way is to review the files periodically and move inactive files out of the office for storage in an off-site facility.

Frequency of Use Some systems are so condensed that they cannot be accessed by more than one or two people at a time. Others that are expanded vertically to the ceiling require a ladder to reach them. While not all files need to have immediate accessibility, frequency of use should be a major factor in selecting your filing systems.

Security All client files should be secured and unavailable to anyone outside the firm. Within the firm, some files, such as personnel and financial records, should have restricted access. Unless you can house files in a locked room, you will have to consider purchasing some units with locking devices.

Adaptability Many law offices need to change their floor plans from time to time. Flexible and adaptable mobile filing systems permit you to vary the

Figure 3–5 High-Density Mobile File System

Not only will high-density file systems hold more files than conventional equipment; they can be moved about on tracks at the press of a button. *Source:* Photo courtesy of CenterCore, Inc., Wayne, PA.

number of aisles. Dividers and other types of filing supply accessories will allow you to make changes in an open-shelf system. Future growth requirements should be taken into consideration when selecting filing equipment.

Productivity   No matter what kind of file storage system you select, if the files you want to work on cannot be found, productivity is lost. It is important to pay attention to file retrieval methods and refiling procedures. In the past, retrieval of filed information has been completely manual. Automated filing systems are gaining popularity, however, and as more attorneys become accustomed to using computer terminals at their desks, these automated systems could replace the customary stacks of files typically found in most law offices.

In summary, use these criteria to select filing equipment:

1. Effective use of space
2. Frequency of use
3. Security
4. Adaptability
5. Productivity

Organizing Active Files

Once you have selected your file storage equipment, it is time to consider how you are going to keep your files in order. Lawyers tend to surround themselves with files. They stack them on their desks, on tables, on the floor, credenza, and sofa. Locating a file, then, can mean picking up each file and looking at its label. Selecting the right supplies to deal with the massive amounts of paper and files generated by the average law office presents the office manager with yet another challenge. Here are some ideas for organizing your files.

Use Color   There are two methods of color-coding files. One way is to use colored labels. If your filing is done alphabetically, assign each letter of the alphabet a color and then select the appropriate colored label to correspond with the name on the file. More than one label is usually placed on each file for ease of identification. Color coding speeds up the filing and retrieval of folders. It is much easier to find the blue labels than it is to search for the letter *M*.

Another way to use color-coding is to purchase colored file folders. By assigning a color to each subject, such as red for litigation, brown for real estate, and green for estate planning, you will know that when searching for a litigation file, for instance, the only ones you need look through are the red ones. Color coding the files is an excellent way to cut down on misfiling errors, and it provides the ability to scan instantly without reference to letters and numbers.

Hang Files   Hanging folders are often the backbone of many filing systems. These, too, come in colors and in both letter and legal sizes. If you need to file small items that tend to fall out of regular hanging folders, try a hanging file jacket. They resemble a hanging folder but open only on the top.

If you are dealing with the opposite problem—trying to file thick documents that stick out and hide the tab—there are box-bottom hanging folders, as well as box-bottom shelf folders, suitable for holding larger amounts of documents. The bottoms of these folders open flat, with a strip of cardboard reinforcement, and will provide an opening of from one inch to four inches.

Use Binders   Another alternative to box-bottom folders for storing large documents is the two- or three-ring binder. Binders come in a variety of colors and sizes, provide easy access to documents, store neatly on shelves, and are less fragile than traditional file folders.

You will find client record management simplified and more efficient by using a combination of filing material resources.

Managing Inactive Files

Attorneys like to keep everything—forever. While there may be a good reason to keep much of the documentation in a client's file for a period of time after the case has been resolved, the rising cost of office space and off-site warehousing facilities makes an equally good case for designing procedures for systematic file evaluation and review. Often it is best to give some, or all, of the file contents back to the client or to destroy them rather than pay for storage, in some remote location, for material never to be looked at again.

Records Retention Some documents, by law, must be retained for certain periods of time. The retention of other documents is left to the discretion of the firm. Figure 3–6 is a records retention guideline compiled by the Association of Legal Administrators. Finding suitable storage equipment and facilities for these items alone requires good planning and careful budgeting.

Micrographics Another way to store client files and documents is to use microfilm or microfiche. Just about everyone is familiar with **microfilm,** a process in which paper documents are put on a roll of film cartridge or jacket of film, and **microfiche,** a sheet of microfilm containing rows of images in a grid pattern. These are the systems commonly found in libraries for storage of newspapers, magazines, and other print media. The user inserts the film cartridge or the sheet of microfilm into a reader to access the information, or into a reader-printer if a photocopy of the information is required.

Plain-paper printing technology has now been incorporated by the major vendors in their micrographics systems, making microfilming a viable alternative in storing inactive files. It is now possible to store the information contained in one filing cabinet on a small roll of film and, if required, to produce a legible copy within minutes.

Micrographic technology is developing at a rapid pace. In the not too distant future, you can expect reader-printers linked to computers to search the microfilm automatically for the required documents, then transmit that film to remote sites via facsimile or laser technology. As this technology is developed and becomes affordable, you could also keep active files on microfilm, thus greatly reducing the amount of office space needed to store client records.

Micrographics equipment is not inexpensive. You can expect to pay upwards of $25,000 for the basic equipment and supplies. However, for medium-sized and large firms this cost may be easily justified in terms of reduced on-site space requirements and increased productivity.

Optical Disk Storage Optical disk technology is best suited for large law firms with huge databases and frequent retrieval activity. Documents are put onto a disk with the use of a scanner. Information can then be retrieved on a computer screen and printed out on a printer. Some systems have **split-screen** capability. Documents can be retrieved in original form and displayed on the left side of the screen while modifications are performed to a copy on the right side of the screen. The integrity of the original document is preserved through a locking mechanism in the software. The split-screen technology works particularly well for long forms that require occasional modification, such as real estate leases and lengthy securities documentation. Since 13 or more file drawers of information can be stored on one disk, one of these systems would significantly decrease your records storage space requirements.

Optical disk technology is relatively new and expensive, with systems ranging from $50,000 to $1,000,000. However, optical disk technology went from being the new kid on the block to a viable contender in the records management industry in just five years. It is possible that both an optical disk storage system and a micrographics system will be standard records management equipment in future law firms.

Paper Shredders Many law firms have purchased paper shredding machines for the purpose of not only disposing of inactive files that they no longer wish to retain but also protecting client confidentiality. One hard look at the amount

Figure 3–6 Records Retention Guide

Type of Records	Retention Time
Accident reports/claims (settled cases)	7 years
Accounts payable ledgers and schedules	7 years
Accounts receivable ledgers and schedules	7 years
Audit reports	Permanently
Bank reconciliations	2 years
Bank statements	3 years
Capital stock and bond records: ledgers, transfer registers, stubs showing issues, record of interest coupons, opinions, etc.	Permanently
Cash books	Permanently
Charts of accounts	Permanently
Checks (canceled—see exception below)	7 years
Checks (canceled for important payments, i.e. taxes, purchases of property, special contracts, etc. Checks should be filed with the papers pertaining to the underlying transaction)	Permanently
Contracts, mortgages, notes, and leases (expired)	7 years
Contracts, mortgages, notes, and leases (still in effect)	Permanently
Correspondence (general)	3 years
Correspondence (legal and important matters only)	Permanently
Correspondence (routine) with customers and/or vendors	2 years
Deeds, mortgages, and bills of sale	Permanently
Depreciation schedules	Permanently
Duplicate deposit slips	2 years
Employment applications	3 years
Expense analyses/expense distribution schedules	7 years
Financial statements (year-end, other optional)	Permanently
Garnishments	7 years
General/private ledgers, year-end trial balance	Permanently
Insurance policies (expired)	3 years
Insurance records, current accident reports, claims, policies, etc.	Permanently
Internal audit reports (longer retention periods may be desirable)	3 years
Internal reports (miscellaneous)	3 years
Inventories of products, materials, and supplies	7 years
Invoices (to customers, from venders)	7 years
Journals	Permanently
Magnetic tape and tab cards	1 year
Minute books of directors, stockholders, bylaws, and charter	Permanently
Notes receivable ledgers and schedules	7 years
Option records (expired)	7 years
Patents and related papers	Permanently
Payroll records and summaries	7 years
Personnel files (terminated)	7 years
Petty cash vouchers	3 years
Physical inventory tags	3 years
Plant cost ledgers	7 years
Property appraisals by outside appraisers	Permanently
Property records, including costs, depreciation reserves, year-end trial balances, depreciation schedules, blueprints, and plans	Permanently
Purchase orders (except purchasing department copy)	1 year
Purchase orders (purchasing department copy)	7 years
Receiving sheets	1 year
Retirement and pension records	Permanently
Requisitions	1 year
Sales commission reports	3 years
Sales records	7 years
Scrap and salvage records (inventories, sales, etc.)	7 years
Stenographers' notebooks	1 year
Stock and bond certificates (canceled)	7 years
Stockroom withdrawal forms	1 year
Subsidiary ledgers	7 years
Tax returns and worksheets, revenue agents' reports, and other documents relating to determination of income tax liability	Permanently
Time books/cards	7 years
Trademark registrations and copyrights	Permanently
Training manuals	Permanently
Union agreements	Permanently
Voucher register and schedules	7 years
Vouchers for payments to vendors, employees, etc. (includes allowances and reimbursement of employees, officers, etc., for travel and entertainment expenses)	7 years
Withholding tax statements	7 years

Source: Association of Legal Administrators, Vernon Hills, IL (1987). Reprinted with permission.

of paper filling the firm's trash cans everyday is usually reason enough to give serious thought to managing this waste more effectively.

If you do not want to purchase your own equipment, mobile shredding trucks can be found in just about every urban area. However, the cost of purchasing a unit is low enough, ranging from about $1,900 to $20,000, that many firms are buying their own. Paper shredders come in sizes ranging from heavy-duty with built-in compactors, for firms that shred more than a ton of paper each week, to small personal shredders. Mid-range units and larger units, which are designed for frequent, heavy use, are more appropriate for most law firms, since even the smallest law firms produce unbelievable amounts of paper. (See Figure 3–7.)

Here are some factors to consider when buying a paper shredder.

1. Security. If a high degree of security is required, then consider the cross-cut shredders, which cut paper both vertically and horizontally into confetti-like particles. Straight- or strip-cut models, which cut paper into spaghetti-like strips, are better suited for handling computer printout sheets and large volumes because of their higher cutting capacity and greater speed. Cross-cut shredding is virtually impossible to reconstruct, but it costs about 20 percent more than straight-cut models. The sensitivity of the work performed by the firm will dictate which level of security is sufficient.

2. Volume. To ensure trouble-free operation, do not underestimate the amount of paper to be shredded. Some shredders come with automatic on/off switches that respond when a piece of paper is inserted and shut off when the process is finished. An automatic reverse process is designed to prevent paper jams, and some shredders will even deliver a power surge to handle a job that might otherwise overload the machine. Often, in an attempt to save money, the wrong size machine is selected. It is best to select something in the midrange, at the very least, because the firm will grow into it almost immediately.

3. Material. What kinds of material are you going to run through your shredder? If you are going to be shredding computer printout sheets, you will need a shredder with a throat large enough to accept this size paper without folding it over. In all likelihood, however, you will also be shredding materials such as paper clips, staples, cardboard, ribbons, and diskettes. Make sure the machine you choose has cutting heads that can handle these items.

Paper shredders have become common equipment items in law offices because of the confidential nature of the work performed. Whether shredding is centralized and the responsibility of one individual or decentralized throughout the office, buying the right equipment is essential to getting the job done with the least amount of trouble.

In summary, consider these items when buying a paper shredder:

1. Security
2. Volume
3. Material

3–3 Managing the Law Library

The practice of law revolves around the use of reference materials. The law library is to the attorney as a laboratory is to the scientist. More than just a collection of books, the law library is a system for organizing and disseminating information.

Small firms often pay little attention to the operation of the library, being satisfied when new loose-leaf inserts for the books are kept up to date. Large

Figure 3–7 Sample Shredding Cuts

Strip/ribbon cut

Top security crosscut

Crosscut/particle cut

Shredding protects client confidentiality. *Source:* Photo courtesy of Cummins-Allison Corp., Mt. Prospect, IL.

firms often use the services of outside library consultants to keep their libraries functioning at optimum efficiency, or they employ a professional librarian.

Computer applications are not only appropriate for managing today's law library; they can allow small law firms and even solo practitioners to gain more control over this integral part of the firm with relative ease.

Function of the Library

Before making any decisions about hardware or software, first consider what functions your library performs. Is it simply to warehouse state statutes and reports? If so, then automation is not necessary. You can get by with a simple manual file system for checking in materials as they are received.

However, if the library is to offer not only statutes and reports but also treatises, form books, on-line databases, form files accessible by subject, and various kinds of indexing capabilities, then you must consider how automation will help you accommodate these resources as well. In addition to gaining more information services from your library, automation can also give you more control over the collection of materials and the library budget. (See Figure 3–8.)

Automating the Library

Automating your library might include cataloging information, gaining access to reference materials, creating files, and establishing an inventory system.

Figure 3–8 Law Office Library

A functional law office library integrates privacy and working space with easy access to research books. *Source:* Photo courtesy of CenterCore, Inc., Wayne, PA.

Cataloging Using a database management system to create an index, you can list by author, title, and subject all research materials in the firm. Cataloging allows you to gain control over all the books, photocopied articles, law reviews and journals, continuing education seminar books, and pamphlets that are otherwise likely to be sitting on shelves and tables all over the office. Cataloging books and materials requires using call numbers, such as are used in other library systems, to tell you where materials are located.

Reference Materials By now, most attorneys and paralegals are familiar with LEXIS and WESTLAW, the two best known, computer-assisted legal research systems. Both are easily accessed through a personal computer and both systems are easy to learn. The installation of WESTLAW or LEXIS can eliminate the need to purchase many of the books previously owned by law firms. Since installing a basic law library runs about $100,000, plus another $20,000 in annual update maintenance fees, the relatively low monthly fee charged by these computer-assisted legal research databases can look very attractive.

Legal research, however, is not only concerned with finding precedence in case law, or specific state or federal regulations and statutes; it also includes locating information in many subject areas. Given today's overly litigious environment, where some very bizarre situations may become the subjects of lawsuits, virtually any kind of information may be required by researchers. For example, in addition to case law, these are some typical subject areas that a paralegal might research:

- Product warranty and guarantee information by product and industry
- Typical procedures used by physicians
- Patents, trademarks, trade name usage, and copyright
- Information on specific products
- Information about a specific industry
- Information about specific businesses
- Identification and location of expert witnesses
- Case-related pending state and federal legislation
- Congressional and regulatory information

Table 3–1 shows some of the leading on-line database information companies. Most of the systems in Table 3–1 are designed for infrequent users—they use simple commands and you pay only for the time on the system. Check with your local law library to see what database systems it has available and with your local bar association for any discounts to members who sign on to any of these or other database services.

Table 3–1 Leading On-Line Database Information Companies

Company	Product
LEXIS, NEXIS, MEDIS	Abstracts and full text of articles on financial, medical, legal, and general interest topics.
Dialog Information Service	340 databases with abstracts and full-text articles on technology, medicine, business, and the sciences.
COMPUSERVE Information Service Co.	Text of general and business articles, on-line shopping, historical stock quotes, dozens of user bulletin boards, and abstracts.
Dow Jones News/Retrieval	Corporate information, business articles, and stock quotes.

Form Files To avoid duplication of effort and needless expense to clients, you can put forms, legal briefs, and memoranda into your automated library system and catalog them by subject for easy retrieval. The creation of an on-line form file that can be accessed by everyone is one of the most cost-effective ways to use your automated database.

Inventory You can set up a system for checking in the library materials you receive in the firm on a daily, weekly, monthly, or annual basis so you will know when you last received the *ABA Journal*, for instance. You can also set up a checkout system, by category, that will enable you to monitor usage of publications. This system allows you to consider cancelling certain publications that may no longer be needed by members of the firm.

   In summary, here are some areas to consider when automating your law library:

1. Catalog (for access to materials by author, title, and subject)
2. Reference materials (both law-related and nonlaw-related)
3. Form file (for frequently used forms, briefs, memos)
4. Inventory (of available materials and usage frequency)

3–4 Managing Office Equipment and Consumables

When it comes to paying the bills for office equipment, including furniture, photocopiers, and telephone and computer systems, you have a choice. You can purchase the equipment, lease it, or rent it.

Purchasing Equipment

When purchasing outright, you pay a set price and own the equipment, or you can finance the purchase with a loan, repay it in installments, and take title to the equipment once the loan is repaid. Although some people like to own everything, each acquisition should be considered independently, keeping in mind the following factors.

Cash Flow Paying sizable sums up front for office equipment will have a different impact on cash flow than making installment payments over several months. In addition to the impact on cash flow, there are tax ramifications and overall profit consequences to consider on both rental and outright purchase transactions. If the firm has an abundance of cash and an outright purchase is possible, get the advice of a tax expert before concluding the transaction.

Obsolescence For law firms that like to take advantage of changes in technology, leasing or renting can offer greater flexibility. However, if the equipment can be used over a long period of time, then ownership could be more profitable. For example, the outright purchase of a postage meter and scale in most cases is probably a better choice than leasing or renting this equipment, and the same is likely to be true with report binding equipment and typewriters for occasional use. On the other hand, future technology will no doubt make obsolete any computer system or photocopy machine on the market today.

Maintenance and Insurance   If you decide to purchase equipment you will be solely responsible for insuring it against damage or loss, and for maintaining and servicing it after the warranty period has expired. You can sometimes obtain maintenance contracts with outside service vendors, and you can, of course, add the equipment to your office insurance policy. One very important item to consider in your maintenance contract is whether the vendor will provide replacement equipment while yours is being serviced and at what price.

Renting and Leasing Equipment

In most cases renting is ideal only for short-term needs, such as replacing a malfunctioning copier or providing a temporary secretary with a computer, because the cost of renting office equipment for the long term is much higher than purchasing it or leasing. However, if you are really concerned with keeping abreast of state-of-the art technology, renting equipment gives you the greatest amount of flexibility.

When you lease equipment, you make monthly payments over a stated period of time, but you do not own the equipment unless your lease agreement allows you to buy the equipment at a reduced cost at the end of the lease period. Either of these arrangements—lease or lease-and-buy—is more costly than an outright purchase. If you finance the purchase, however, the total overall cost can be at least as much as a leasing arrangement.

Because many firms lease office equipment and upgrade their systems before the leases have expired, you should be familiar with different types of equipment leases. Although there are many variations, most leases for office equipment fall into one of three categories: operating, financial, or flexible leases.

Operating Leases   An **operating lease** requires monthly payments over a fixed period of time. At the end of the term, the lessor takes the equipment back. In most cases, there is a penalty for terminating the lease early.

Financial Leases   A **financial lease** offers the option of purchasing the equipment at the end of the lease period for a predetermined fixed dollar amount (normally about 10 percent of the purchase price) or at a price based on the fair market value for the equipment when the lease expires.

Flexible Leases   A **flexible lease** allows you to change equipment during the lease period. However, in some instances, the lessor will allow this option only when the old equipment can be quickly leased to someone else, and some lessors will only provide replacement equipment at an additional price. Read the fine print of a flexible lease to make sure you can upgrade to new equipment at no additional cost.

Many leasing companies, as well as some banks and financial institutions, offer additional leasing options such as a **cancellable lease,** which allows you to get out of a contract before expiration without paying a penalty, or affords you the opportunity to upgrade or add to the equipment you originally acquired.

Despite the fact that leasing office equipment may offer many advantages, there are some drawbacks. One disadvantage is that there are usually two separate agreements—one for the equipment and one for the financing. You have to be careful that what you negotiated so hard for in equipment is accurately stated in the overall financing contract. In many cases, the third-party lessor, who provides the financing, has no contractual obligation to live up to the vendor's promises. So, if the equipment goes down and you cannot use it, you may still have to make the monthly payments on it.

Tax Considerations

You should consider the tax consequences of each option before you decide to buy, lease, or rent office equipment. Under current Internal Revenue Service rules, when you buy equipment you cannot always deduct the cost of the equipment as an operating expense or claim an investment tax credit. However, you can usually depreciate the equipment over a number of years and lower taxes that way.

Leasing equipment offers the advantage of being able to claim the monthly payments as a tax-deductible business expense. However, the IRS is now considering many types of financial leases to be the same as a conditional sales contract, which means they are considered more purchase than lease and thus cannot be expensed. Agreements that state the exact dollar amount for buy-out at the end of the lease are particularly susceptible to this interpretation by the IRS. Because of these interpretations, tax-oriented reasons for leasing office equipment are gradually disappearing.

In summary, here are some areas for consideration when deciding how to manage your office equipment budget:

1. Cash flow
2. Obsolescence
3. Maintenance and insurance
4. Type of leasing agreement
5. Tax ramifications

The decision to buy, lease, or rent office equipment requires research and the consideration of several factors. In the end, however, the firm's cash flow will probably be the deciding factor.

Managing Office Consumables

Few law firms can afford to look the other way when it comes to managing consumable office supplies. Court forms, letterhead, envelopes, paper, postage, ballpoint pens, paper clips, staples, felt-tipped markers, and three-ring binders may individually be low price items, but collectively they add up to a major expenditure for most firms.

In addition to the outlay of cash to purchase a consumables inventory, other associated cost factors include:

- Quality of goods (cheapest may well be most costly).
- Poor or inconsistent service from vendors.
- Stockroom/mailroom operational costs.
- Paperwork, purchasing, and communication with vendors.
- Storage space for inventory.
- Inefficient use of time as a result of too little or no inventory.
- Supplies that become obsolete before they are used.
- Employee waste and pilferage.

To be a good manager of office consumables requires the skills of a detective—you need to actively look for ways to reduce costs by continually seeking out new sources of supplies; you will also need to monitor internal usage of supplies without being miserly. There are three primary areas, then, of consumables management: inventory control, suppliers, and employee pilferage.

Inventory Control   Whether your inventory management is computerized or performed manually, it is a good idea to have one person directly responsible for office supplies. When one person is in charge, there is better control and a more efficient distribution system. In some firms, this task is the responsibility of the office manager. In others, it belongs to the receptionist, a senior secretary, or a purchasing manager.

In a typical law firm inventory system, standard items used by most personnel are maintained in either a stockroom or the mailroom. When something needs to be replenished, or requires a special purchase, the appropriate person is notified and an order is placed. However, rather than wait for the person in charge to be notified when stock is getting low, many firms use an inventory system commonly referred to as a **mini-max inventory system.** With this type of manual inventory system, a physical inventory of office supplies is taken once a week. When any supply falls to a preestablished minimum level, an order is placed to bring that supply up to a maximum level, also preestablished. Minimum and maximum supply levels are established by performing a past purchase analysis. Unless there is a special project requiring an unusual purchase, this weekly inventory control system will allow most firms to maintain adequate reserves without overcrowding or overspending.

Computerized inventory systems are more commonly found in larger firms with centralized purchasing. With computers, branch offices and individual departments can be more closely monitored, resulting in more efficient management of supplies. For example, consumable products waste is more likely to be brought under control with the use of a computerized inventory system.

The law firm's financial investment in supplies inventory may also be reduced with a computerized system by lowering the inventory levels. With routine inventory reporting and tracking, orders can be placed to be delivered **just-in-time** (also known as the JIT inventory system) as a supply is about to run out. With JIT, firms do not have to store large quantities of supplies, nor do they have to risk running out of frequently used items, such as photocopy paper, except in unforeseen instances of late or inefficient delivery.

Hiring an outside professional inventory management service is another way to gain control of your office consumables. Typically, these firms keep track of your firm's inventory on computer, order from their own network of suppliers, warehouse supplies until required, deliver them to your office as needed, and bill you once a month. Not only does using an outside service reduce internal paperwork and staff time; it can also reduce inventory storage space, and it often costs no more than doing all this yourself.

Suppliers   Every manager involved with purchasing is no doubt familiar with the unknown supplier who tries to peddle office supplies by phone. Using a disreputable supplier can create many problems. One way to choose a supplier is to study the marketplace for price and service, and then establish a working relationship with only those reputable suppliers who offer quality goods and consistent service at competitive prices. Getting a partnership going with your supplier is no mean feat and should be approached with a couple of points in mind.

The first point, which is obvious but important, is that the cheapest component is not always the better one in the long run. Once you factor in poor quality, down time, reworking, and aggravation, the cheapest may well turn out to be the most expensive. Effectively managing suppliers means to aim for the lowest cost when all is said and done, not the lowest initial price per unit. Because poor quality is so expensive, use much care in selecting both suppliers and products.

The second point has to do with the number of suppliers. Old thinking was that by dealing with two or more suppliers or distributors you could get a better deal by creating competition for your business. New thinking in this area advocates building a relationship with one reputable, consistent, carefully selected supplier who will, in effect, become your partner. As such, your supplier will know your firm's office supplies needs, will be able to deliver products on time and at competitive prices, on occasion allowing you to take advantage of special offcers, and will provide you with an off-site inventory storage warehouse.

It is important to shop around, but when you have found a supplier who is reliable and committed to good service, stick with that distributor. Because there are so many products on the market, and they are always changing, a close supplier relationship allows you to take advantage of the distributor's product expertise and broad product line.

Employee Pilferage   Pilferage of office supplies by employees is a cost factor that many law firms either choose to overlook or do not consider significant enough to receive attention. But perhaps you have heard of some companies where you have to turn in your old pen when it runs out of ink in order to get a new one. Inventory control of this magnitude is bound to create hostile feelings among employees. On the other hand, the absence of controls can be very costly.

According to Office Supply Order Systems, an international firm headquartered in Livingston, New Jersey, at least 20 percent of all office supplies go home with employees as fringe benefits. Late August and early September are particularly prime periods for employee pilferage. As students go back to school, paper, binders, report covers, tape, pens, glue, staplers, and scissors start disappearing from the office. This cyclical increase in the disappearance of office supplies is in addition to the regular taking home of pens, paper, staplers, and paper clips by employees—sometimes carelessly, often intentionally.

Many employees consider the following items to be fringe benefits: office supplies for home use; photocopies for personal use made on the firm's equipment using the firm's paper; personal long-distance telephone calls; use of the fax machine for personal business; and using the firm's postage to mail out their monthly bills and personal correspondence.

There are several ways to better control these items. A limited access stockroom/mailroom controlled by one person provides the most control, while an honor-system sign-out sheet will provide some, but not much, control over supplies. Use of a coded access system for photocopiers and telephones, or a manual record log, will discourage personal use of this equipment, but short of using gestapo tactics, you should expect any control system only to reduce, not eliminate, employee pilfering.

SUMMARY

3–1

Often the first impression a client receives of a law firm is the result of how they are treated on the telephone. If the telephone system is inadequate, or the reception staff is improperly trained, the result can be a loss of clients. Care should be taken in selecting a reliable telephone system to ensure that calls are answered promptly, that messages are accurately taken and received, and that client confidentiality is maintained. Likewise, care should be taken in selecting and training the reception staff. The importance of the reception function is all too often overlooked.

3–2

Records management is the systematic storage and retrieval of paper records and can be accomplished in a variety of ways. It includes creating and organizing active files, as well as deciding how and where to store both the active and inactive files of the firm. Advances in computers and other electronic equipment technology, as well as the development of new types of storage systems, have greatly increased the options in records management.

3–3

Lawyers and paralegals, law clerks, and secretaries regularly use the law library.

If the library is to be more than a warehouse of state statutes and reports, then automation should be considered. There are many computer-assisted research databases now available which are easy to use and competitive in cost when compared to the purchase and maintenance of a physical library. Since the library is the backbone of any law practice, active management of the facility is a necessity.

3–4

Cash flow and obsolescence are two key elements in the decision whether to buy, rent, or lease office equipment. If leasing the equipment is desired over purchasing, then the type of lease being offered must be investigated and negotiated. There are tax ramifications to be considered as well as maintenance of the equipment and insurance on it. One of the greatest problems in managing consumable office supplies is employee pilferage, which usually hits its apex when school starts in the fall. Developing an effective office supplies inventory control system without giving the impression you are the gestapo is truly a management skill. Whether you use a manual system, a computerized system, or rely on a JIT system, the goal is to avoid overstocking or understocking the supply room.

REVIEW

Key Terms

cancellable lease
conflict of interest
financial lease
flexible lease
just-in-time

microfiche
microfilm
mini-max inventory system
operating lease
records management
split screen

Questions for Review and Discussion

1. What criteria would you use to evaluate a telephone system?
2. Reception is an important function in a law office. What items relating to this function deserve attention?
3. What does the term *records management* mean?
4. What are four types of filing systems discussed in this chapter?
5. When selecting filing equipment, what are some considerations?
6. What are some ways to help organize active files?
7. How can a firm effectively manage inactive files?
8. How can automation improve library management?
9. When deciding whether to buy or lease office equipment, what factors are likely to influence your decision?
10. How can you effectively inventory and control office consumables?

Activities

1. After creating a specification sheet of telephone equipment requirements for Dunn & Sweeney, contact three telephone equipment vendors, including the local Bell company, and ask them for estimates for purchasing and leasing the equipment, for installation (including how long it will take), and for maintenance and insurance. Present your findings to the class.
2. Contact a records storage facility and get information about their services and the costs involved with storing records off-site. Also contact a micrographics vendor and an optical disk vendor and get information about their technology, including costs. Then develop an argument for and against each type of record storage. Which would you recommend? Why? Present your findings to the class.
3. Contact a local law firm, preferably a medium-sized or large firm, and ask for a guest speaker to talk to the class on records management and/or library management.

CHAPTER 4   Law Office Facilities Management

OUTLINE

4–1   When to Consider a Move
        Expansion
        Consolidation
        Image Enhancement
4–2   How to Assess an Office Building
        Area and Accessibility
        The Building Itself
        Standard Workletter
        The Lease
        Lease Checklist
        Services of a Commercial Real Estate Broker
4–3   Getting the Most Usage from Your Office Space
        Conducting a Needs Assessment
        The Space Plan
        Fighting the Space War
4–4   Moving the Law Office
        Select a Moving Company
        Get Estimates of Moving Costs
        Take Care of Details
4–5   Planning for a Law Office Disaster
        How to Prepare for a Disaster

COMMENTARY

It is obvious that Dunn & Sweeney is rapidly outgrowing its present office facilities. Secretaries are crowded together with little room to keep regularly used files at their desks. Paralegals are sharing cramped quarters with no privacy. Some associate attorneys have larger offices than the partners, and a couple of the partners spend so little time in their offices that they are willing to occupy smaller offices to free up space. In addition, a groundswell of complaints has developed about the lack of space for client files, the noise coming from the photocopy and fax room, the small employee lunchroom, and the increasing problems with finding adequate parking places for both employees and clients. A reading of your current office lease indicates that it will expire in about twelve months. You have been asked by the partners for an opinion as to whether Dunn & Sweeney should move their offices or stay put.

OBJECTIVES

In Chapter 3 you learned that administrative effectiveness is largely a function of managing important information and data to serve the needs of clients, to assist in making decisions and plans, and to reduce costs and improve productivity. After completing this chapter, you will be able to:

1. Discuss the reasons or circumstances that might suggest a move.
2. List the important considerations in assessing a relocation area.
3. Itemize the factors in selecting an office building.
4. Explain the difference between usable area and rentable area and calculate rent based on each.
5. Define *workletter* and its purpose.
6. Explain the differences in the most common types of leases.
7. Develop a list of commonly negotiable items.
8. Explain how increases in operating expenses are passed on to tenants.
9. Develop a needs assessment to determine amount of space required.
10. Discuss the factors involved with the actual relocation.
11. List the steps involved in planning for an office disaster.

4–1 When to Consider a Move

The decision to move your law office is almost always the result of compelling reasons and is reached only after conducting considerable research and analysis in order to justify this step. Regardless of the firm's size, the time, money, and effort expended will not allow the luxury of relocating on a whim.

What factors, then, suggest moving? Any one, or all, of the following factors might suggest that your firm consider relocating: growth and expansion of the firm, consolidation, or building an image.

Expansion

Along with growth comes the need to provide adequate working spaces for all personnel—attorneys, management, paralegals, and secretaries—for the simple fact that overcrowding leads to inefficiency. Law firms do actually outgrow their quarters. In fact, expanding in one area alone, such as becoming fully computerized, may necessitate a move.

A merger with another law firm, the creation of a new division to handle specialized litigation cases, or extensive purchases of equipment or library resource materials will, in many cases, require larger office quarters.

Consolidation

When law firms merge, some lawyers may decide to regroup and establish their own firm instead of being acquired in the merger. Or several lawyers may decide to leave a firm and open their own offices. And occasionally lawyers do retire. In these situations, consolidation rather than growth might suggest the need to relocate to smaller quarters.

Likewise, in large firms, decentralization may result in the establishment of branch offices, expanding the firm geographically while decreasing the need for headquarters space.

Image Enhancement

A law firm's desire to improve its image and status is also a valid reason to consider relocating. This motivation is anything but an ego trip because a firm's image, including its physical location, can have a direct impact on its ability to attract and retain clients as well as competent employees.

The concept of image may be vague and difficult to define, but there is no doubt about the positive impact on employee morale, on efficiency, and on productivity that results from working in a location designed to enhance the firm's image.

The reality of the competitive legal marketplace alone can, in some instances, justify a move. Some law firms will open a small office in a city that is expected to grow in order to establish name recognition and a presence in the community with the expectation that as the city expands, so will the firm.

4–2 How to Assess an Office Building

Let's assume you have decided that moving the office is a viable option. How do you choose an area? What do you look for in a building? Here are some guidelines to help you select a location and a building.

Area and Accessibility

Ready access to major highways, to an airport, to other means of public transportation and to the courthouse are specific aspects of an area that are considered important by many people in selecting office location. Attorneys who travel frequently, or who entertain out-of-town clients and visitors, are likely to consider proximity to good hotels and an airport extremely important. Having a variety of retail establishments and restaurants nearby usually rates high with employees, as might reasonable proximity to recreational, cultural, and academic facilities.

Do not overlook the distance from home that employees—attorneys and staff members—will have to travel to get to work. Also worth noting is how accessible the area is to current and future clients. Some buildings are situated close to a major highway or freeway, but the placement of on- and off-ramps makes them difficult to reach.

You will no doubt want to select a community whose general reputation is good, that is clean and attractive, and whose city government favors business growth and development. Whether you live there or not, the area you select is going to be home for the members of your firm for many hours each week.

The Building Itself

There are several factors to consider in selecting a building once the geographic area is determined. Some of these factors are obvious, while others demand close scrutiny and careful consideration. Each is important, however, because the comfort, convenience, safety, and satisfaction of both employees and clients can be affected.

Usable Area Versus Rentable Area The **usable area** is the square footage in which you can put personnel, furniture, and equipment for actual use. This should be of prime interest to you in evaluating the space offered. On a multitenant floor, for example, the usable area can vary over the life of the building as corridors expand or contract and as floors are remodeled.

The **rentable area** of a floor refers to the entire floor, including restrooms, corridors, stairwells, and elevator shafts, measured to the finished surface of the permanent outer building walls and including all interior columns and projections necessary to the building's structure. Obviously, the rentable area is fixed for the life of the building and not affected by changes in corridor size or remodeling. This measurement is used when the landlord figures the total income-producing potential of the building and when the tenant's pro rata share of a building is computed for purposes of assessing additional rent, real estate tax, utility, and service costs. Ask the landlord to provide you with the **load factor** (also known as the loss factor or the add-on factor). The load factor, stated in a percentage, is your pro rata share for use of restrooms, corridors, elevators, and building services. The load factor varies from building to building and is added to the usable area figure to determine the amount of rent charged per square foot.

Here are a couple of examples of how the load factor will affect your rent. Let's assume you need to have 1,000 square feet of *usable area*. In building 1 your pro rata share of the building's load factor is 10 percent. Therefore, you are going to be paying rent for 1,100 square feet even though you can only use 1,000 square feet. Rent in building 1 is $1.50 per square foot per month, or $1,650 monthly. In building 2, on the other hand, your pro rata load factor is 20 percent, but rent is only $1.45 per square foot per month. Is this a better deal? No. You are paying rent on 1,200 square feet but can use only 1,000 square feet, and at $1.45 per square foot, you will pay $1,740 per month, or $90 more, for the same amount of usable area as in the first building.

Each tenant's pro rata share of the load factor, then, refers to the tenant's rentable area in relationship to the building's entire rentable area. Therefore, the sum of all pro rata shares for a building should equal 1.00, or 100 percent. These are the formulas you can use to compute rentable area and usable area:

$$\text{Usable area} + \text{Load factor (\%)} = \text{Rentable area}$$

Stated another way:

$$\text{Rentable area} - \text{Load factor (\%)} = \text{Usable area}$$

Here are a couple of tips to help you evaluate more accurately any space under consideration.

1. Find out what dimensions were used to calculate the usable area measurement of a particular floor or suite. Not all building owners measure usable and rentable areas on the same basis.

2. Recalculate all per-square-foot rental quotes to reflect rent per usable square foot once you have obtained uniform quotes for all buildings under consideration and have made adjustments for usable space only. When obtaining rental quotes be sure to clarify whether the quote is on a monthly or an annual basis. Typically, on the West Coast rental is quoted on a monthly basis whereas on the East Coast quotes are more often based on annual calculations.

The two most important factors in renting space are (1) how much space can be used and (2) how much rent is being charged for that space.

Elevator Service   Before moving into a multistory office building, take a look at the elevator service. When office space is located above the first floor, elevator service is as essential as lighting, plumbing, or air conditioning because both employees of the firm and clients will regularly use the service.

Poor quality elevator service is more than an annoyance—over the course of a year it can result in the loss of hundreds of billable hours for a sizable law firm. For this reason, in areas where there is an ample supply of office building space, developers and building owners feel the pressure to provide a level of elevator service that meets the demands of tenants. This competitive pressure is so acute that you can often negotiate a reduction in rent for buildings that have slower elevator service. What should you look for?

- Elevators should be able to handle peak traffic—start of the day, noontime, and closing—without long waits or too many intermediate stops. Acceptable waiting periods during this time range from 20 to 30 seconds.
- Elevators should have adequate lighting and ventilation and should provide a smooth ride.
- Control buttons in cars and at landings should be low enough to reach from a wheelchair. And elevator doors need to be wide enough to allow wheelchair access and be roomy enough to turn a wheelchair 180 degrees.
- If escalators are being used in the building, they should be supplemented by one or two elevators.

Keep in mind that if your offices are located above the first floor, vertical transportation is an important consideration for employees and clients.

Building Management and Maintenance In a properly managed building the building manager is responsible for much more than obvious maintenance and the collection of rents. For example, the building manager is responsible for the safety, comfort, and well-being of the tenants. Because many building operating expenses incurred after the first year are passed through to tenants, the ideal building manager is knowledgeable as a mechanical and electrical engineer; familiar with building operations management; well-versed in purchasing, bill collecting, accounting, sanitation engineering, contract administration, and personnel administration; and adept at public relations. A knowledgeable and proficient building manager will be able to maximize revenue and minimize the building's operational expenses, thus saving you, the tenant, money in the long run.

Building management, then, should receive your same careful scrutiny as the physical structure of your new office home. Obviously, on-site management will reduce response time to your needs, and when building managers work there too, they usually give more attention to routine maintenance. For a quick evaluation of building management, make several random checks of the restroom facilities.

Cleaning Service Whether cleaning service is included in your lease or privately contracted, its quality and frequency are important to morale and image. Keep in mind that even when the landlord is providing the cleaning service, there is still room to negotiate. By comparing your cleaning needs to those provided, you can often upgrade these services at a reasonable cost. Figure 4–1 provides you with a checklist of typical cleaning service specifications.

Safety Life safety features, devised to guard against fire and earthquake, are an entire category of building improvements increasingly important to tenants.

Figure 4-1   Office Cleaning Specifications

Office Areas

Nightly Services (Monday through Friday)
- Gather all waste paper and place for disposal on loading dock or other designated area; tag as required.
- Empty and damp wipe all ashtrays.
- Sweep and/or dust mop all tile floors.
- Spot clean or damp mop all stains on tile floors as required.
- Vacuum clean traffic lanes on all carpeted areas.
- Spot minor stains on carpets, as required.
- Dust desks, chairs, tables, file cabinets, counter tops, telephones, and other flat surfaces within reach.
- Dust all ledges and other flat surfaces within reach.
- Remove fingerprints from doors and partition glass.
- Spot clean coffee stains, etc. from desk tops.
- Wash all drinking fountains.
- Close all drapes as directed.
- Turn off all lights, leaving only designated lights on.
- Secure all doors as directed.
- Keep janitor closet clean and orderly.
- Dust picture frames daily.
- Properly arrange chairs in offices and conference rooms.

Weekly Services
- Remove fingerprints from woodwork, walls, partitions.
- Vacuum clean all carpeted areas.

Monthly Services
- Polish or clean door kickplates and thresholds.
- Dust all door jambs.
- Dust all high partitions, ledges and wall mounted objects.
- Clean and refinish all resilient floors with a slip retardant floor finish, as required.

Quarterly Service
- Vacuum all fabric furniture.

Three Times Per Year
- Dust or vacuum all return air vents.
- Vacuum walls covered with fabric.

Semi-Annually (Twice per year)
- Lift and clean under all plastic floor pads.
- Vacuum all draperies.
- Wash all metal partitions.

Annually (Once per year)
- Wash and clean all chair pads.

Restrooms

Nightly Services (Monday through Friday)
- Clean and sanitize all urinals, commodes and wash basins to include all chrome fittings and all bright work.
- Clean mirrors and frames.
- Wet mop floors.
- Dust ledges and partitions.
- Spot clean walls, doors and partitions.
- Fill all dispensers from stock.
- Empty and remove all trash from containers, clean exteriors of containers.
- Empty and damp wipe all ashtrays.
- Report any fixtures not working properly.
- Report any light fixture burnt out.

Weekly Services
- Empty, remove and sanitize all feminine napkin disposal units.
- Spot wax traffic paths in lounges.

Monthly Services
- Clean and/or polish all door kickplates and thresholds.
- Dust all door jambs.

Bi-Monthly
- Thoroughly scrub and refinish all resilient floors with a slip retardant floor finish (lounges only).

Quarterly
- Thoroughly machine scrub all floors.

This is a list of typical services performed by cleaning professionals in an office building.
Source: Black's Office Leasing Guide: Greater Los Angeles Five County Area (New York: McGraw-Hill Information Systems, 1987). Reprinted with permission.

Some of the more common life safety features found in modern office buildings are the following.

Automatic sprinkler systems. If the temperature reaches a certain critical heat in any given area, the sprinklers will turn on and water is pumped into the system. The water flow may cause a fire alarm to sound in some installations.

Manual fire alarms and smoke detection systems. When activated, these alarms and systems alert a central control station as well as the occupants of the floor.

Smoke evacuation systems. Either manual or automatic exhaust equipment removes smoke from occupied areas.

Automatic door-release systems. These systems automatically close certain doors to isolate fire and smoke.

Elevator recall service. These are special smoke detectors that can cause elevators to close their doors and descend automatically to the first floor when smoke is detected.

Emergency stair towers. These are specially constructed stairwells designed to resist fire for a certain period of time, usually two to four hours, which is long enough to completely evacuate the largest building.

Remote stairway unlocking. Stairways are often locked from the outside for security reasons. These systems automatically unlock the doors in case of fire.

Emergency power. An emergency generator provides continued operation of the lighting system, as well as all the systems listed here, in case of a general power failure.

Central control console. Located on the ground floor and equipped for emergency use, the central control console includes multiple telephones and telephone lines, elevator location indicators, a loudspeaker paging system, and a panel that receives messages from all fire alarms and smoke detectors in the building.

Security   Law firms frequently need access to the office for both employees and clients beyond the normal office hours. Typically this has been handled by providing employees with keys and by putting a night bell outside the office door, or by putting an extension telephone at the main reception floor desk.

Some of the newer buildings have an electronic system that uses either a card reader or a keypad for password entry. Card systems are usually tied to the building's security system and will provide a printed access record—or record of attempted access, in the case of unauthorized users. Use of surveillance cameras in corridors has also become commonplace in some office buildings.

Any law firm has a sizable investment in equipment and personnel that needs to be protected. Building security should be of primary concern to the office manager.

Parking   More than a convenience, adequate parking is a necessity for your firm's employees and clients. Parking is often the reason why office space in building A rents for more than space in building B when the sites and physical features are equal.

With the recent emphasis on compact cars, more parking spaces are being devoted to them. However, not everyone drives a compact car, and those who do not will be extremely upset by nicks and dings on their car doors caused by parking spaces being too small to accommodate their automobiles. A standard size parking space is 8'6" wide by 17'6" long whereas compact car parking spaces are 8' wide by 15'6" long. You will want to choose a building that provides enough of each to meet the needs of your law firm and its clients.

Most office buildings offer either deck parking or parking under the building. There are advantages and disadvantages to each. Some of the features you want to look for in either type of parking structure are:

- Availability of covered parking in inclement weather.
- Number and location of spaces for handicapped people.
- Lighting and security during daytime and at night.
- Length of time required to get from parking lot to office.
- Location and maintenance of elevators, escalators, and stairwells.
- Supervision, control, and maintenance of facility.

Most landlords will provide a certain number of parking spaces to tenants free of charge during a specified period of the lease. Consider the welfare and morale of your *entire* staff, as well as the needs of clients, when negotiating this portion of your lease. There is usually room here to gain extra concessions or privileges from a landlord who wants your firm as a tenant.

Standard Workletter

The **workletter** is that part of the lease which itemizes and assigns a dollar value to the standard tenant improvements provided by the landlord in terms of quantity and construction quality. Tenants may upgrade standard improvements for an additional cost. Figure 4–2 is a sample of a typical workletter. Since the dollar value of the workletter is a major factor in determining the favorability of the lease, you should pay careful attention to the following areas.

Flooring   Depending on the type of equipment and the size of the installation, computer rooms may require a raised floor. A raised floor is essentially a platform set on steel posts providing up to 18 inches of space for cabling. Removable portions of the floor provide access when required.

Floor-load capacity for a law firm is a critical yet often overlooked factor. A law library or file room may require a floor-load capacity in excess of the average tenant. Normally, the floor-load capacity of an office building varies from 75 to 100 pounds per square foot. A capacity of 100 pounds per square foot will support most law libraries and file rooms. Since floor-load capacities vary greatly depending on whether the building is a high-rise, low-rise, or garden-type facility, it is important to check this feature.

Electrified Floors   Buildings with this feature are becoming quite common and are particularly appealing to people-intensive businesses, such as law firms. Because wires are encased in metal boxes, usually at six-foot intervals, concrete can be poured over and around telephone and power lines which are run through the floor to many points throughout the office, thus eliminating unsightly and unsafe wires lying about. Electrified floors provide greater flexibility in interior office design.

Ceiling Height   Most buildings have eight-foot ceilings. However, there are buildings with nine-foot ceilings, and occupying one may increase the amount of your rent as well as any tenant improvements but, at the same time, provide you with extra shelf and storage space if you take shelving all the way to the ceiling. If presented with this option, you will need to weigh the advantages and disadvantages before signing the lease.

Figure 4–2 Sample Workletter

A typical workletter for the City of Los Angeles		New Building (cost per sq. ft.)
Flooring:	Allowance of $1.50/S.F. is provided. Carpet over pad @ 80% floor area. Remaining 20% VCT.	$ 1.50
Ceilings:	Acoustical tile. (12"×12" concealed spline)	$ 2.30
Partitions:	1 lineal foot ceiling height partition with vinyl base and building standard paint. (Excludes devising partition) Allowance: 1 L.F. per 12 S.F. of office space.	$ 2.30
Doors/Bucks/ Hardware:	Entrance and interior building standard doors 3′ × 8′-6″ plain sliced white oak with oil finish. One entrance door per 3000 S.F. of office space. One interior door allowance per 30 L.F. building standard partition.	$.20 (entrance) $1.36 (interior)
Window Treatments:	Horizontal mini-blinds	$ .42
Sprinklers:	Semi-recessed head per 200 S.F. of office space.	$ .55
Electrical:	A) Lighting: (1) 2 × 4 parabolic fixture per 80 S.F. of office space $1.93 B) Switches: Single-pole @ each room $ .45 C) Duplex receptacles: 1 per 200 S.F. of office space $ .40 D) Telephone outlets: 1 per 200 S.F. of office space (home run to nearest telephone closet) $ .50	$ 3.28
HVAC:	Branch distribution, VAV's thermostat and balance (excludes exhaust fans) Allowance—1 zone per 1000 S.F. of office space	$ 3.80
SUBTOTAL		$15.71
General Conditions		$ 1.26
SUBTOTAL		$16.97
GENERAL CONTRACTOR'S OVERHEAD AND PROFIT		$ .85
TOTAL		$17.82

To establish the value of the lease proposal, you need a reasonably accurate idea of the value of the landlord's standard workletter. *Source: Black's Office Leasing Guide: Greater Los Angeles Five County Area* (New York: McGraw-Hill Information Systems, 1987). Reprinted with permission.

Partitions Since confidentiality is a primary concern in law offices, the need exists for **aural privacy.** At its most basic level, aural privacy is unintelligible— that is, while you can hear the sound of voices, you cannot understand what is being said. To provide confidentiality, partitions should completely block normal voice tones and make raised voices unintelligible. On a still higher level, partitions are capable of providing silence and completely masking any volume, such as that produced by photocopy machines or raised voices.

Several different types of partitions can be used in law offices depending on the degree of privacy required. *Demising partitions*, used to separate tenants in multitenant buildings and between tenants and public corridors, and *interior partitions* are the only types most commonly offered by the landlord. Therefore, you must determine the degree of sound acceptable for each area in your office and make any special partition requirements a part of the workletter. There is nothing more disconcerting to a client than to be sitting in a lawyer's office and being able to hear the conversation taking place in the office next door when the lawyer is using a speaker phone. Do not forget to include the employee lounge area, equipment rooms, and computer rooms when making your sound control recommendations.

Lighting Fluorescent lighting fixtures are standard in most modern office buildings, with the current most common fixture being two feet by four feet with a parabolic lens. Also known as an "eggcrate" because of its looks, the parabolic lens distributes light better than the formerly common white acrylic sheet lens which tended to create glare and reflections on computer screens. While not perfect, the parabolic lens does have a low surface brightness and is not affected by accumulating dust, thus making it a better choice for areas where computers are used.

It is sometimes difficult to negotiate a change with the building management in the standard lighting fixture for an individual tenant. However, the importance of visual comfort to all members of the firm should not be overlooked. Lawyers spend a considerable amount of time in concentrated research and study of documents. Paralegals, word processors, and legal secretaries are expected to produce legal documentation with exceptional accuracy, often against deadlines. And more people in law firms are using a personal computer than ever before. Properly designed lighting can reduce fatigue along with associated mental and physical health problems.

Heating, Ventilating, and Air Conditioning (HVAC) A building's heating, ventilating, and air conditioning system is usually referred to as HVAC. Older buildings, whether 2 stories or 40 stories, may have only a single HVAC unit located on the roof. A 40-story modern building may have four or more separate HVAC units, each controlling the temperatures of different floors, or each individual floor in a high-rise building might have its own system. Individual floor systems allow tenants to inexpensively control their own needs day or night. And if the HVAC system fails on one floor, the rest of the building is not affected.

Contemporary law offices have special HVAC needs. Computer rooms may require additional air conditioning to absorb heat produced as well as humidity controls and special fire protection equipment. Computer-controlled telephone systems often require around-the-clock, daily temperature control, and large copier systems generate a great deal of heat requiring additional air conditioning.

In addition, the practice of law is not conducted from nine to five. Client meetings and staff conferences often begin early in the morning, and work often continues late into the night. Some law firms operate on a 24-hour weekday schedule and often hold meetings on weekends. The building must be able to provide air conditioning outside of normal business hours, and usually there will be a cost for this service. It is bad enough to spend a warm, sunny day working but worse to be required to do it in a hot, stuffy office.

The Lease

Supply and demand affects the commercial real estate market more than most other commodities, and because of this, *all leases are negotiable*. A prestigious law firm, for example, can often command significant concessions based on reputation alone. But you must ask for them.

Common Negotiable Items   You should assume that everything contained in a lease is ultimately negotiable. But here are some of the most common negotiable items.

Length of the lease. Long-term leases offer financial security and may therefore be attractive to both the landlord and the tenant. Short-term leases of five years or less are renegotiable at expiration and can be advantageous to either party. If the area vacancy rate is low, the landlord has the advantage. However, if the vacancy in the marketplace is over 15 percent, the tenant usually has the advantage.

Space layout. The space plan demarcates potential reception areas, storage areas, private offices, and the overall configuration of the law firm. Sometimes the tenant pays for the floor plan; other times the development company pays. The cost usually runs about 85 cents per square foot to have a floor plan designed.

Parking space. The general feeling regarding parking spaces is that the landlord should not give more than is necessary and the tenant should not accept less than is needed. The usual computation of need is based on the average building occupancy of one person per 250 square feet, or four persons per 1,000 square feet. Assuming that each person in the firm drives a car to work, four spaces per 1,000 square feet of office space may or may not be enough for your firm.

In addition to the number of parking spaces included in your rent, you will also want to negotiate the cost of additional parking spaces for use by employees and clients. Some facilities charge for guest parking by minutes, half hour, full hour, or the day. Tenants can purchase parking stickers at negotiated discounts to validate clients' parking tickets.

Base rent. The rental rate quoted to you is the asking price, not the price the landlord is willing to accept. In most situations, particularly when the marketplace has a large vacancy factor, you can negotiate either a lower base rent or a period of reduced or free rent.

Tenant improvements. For law firms, this is a major negotiating point. Typically, the landlord will offer only standard building items and materials. The firm will want many upgrades, such as built-in cabinets, kitchen areas, interior glass and wood paneling, wallcoverings, marble flooring, better lighting and carpeting, and double entry doors. Under these circumstances, negotiate for a **turnkey clause** in the lease. Also known as a **build-to-suit-tenant clause,** *turnkey* means that all improvements have been completed and everything is in place when you walk in the door.

Other negotiable items. Other items open for negotiation include renewal options for when the lease expires; cancellation penalties in the event you wish to cancel the lease; sublet privileges to be able rent space to other attorneys who are not members of your firm; right of first refusal on adjoining office space as it becomes available in order to expand the firm as it grows without being forced to relocate; the firm's name displayed on the building, known as **signage privileges;** and the method by which operating expenses are passed through to the tenant.

Types of Leases Obviously, tenants and landlords have conflicting needs and desires. The purpose of an office lease is to document a relationship that satisfactorily resolves these conflicts. There are three basic types of leases—net, percentage, and gross—and the difference between them is the manner in which rents are computed and paid.

1. *Net lease.* Under the terms of a **net lease,** the tenant pays some or all of the real estate taxes in addition to the base rent. In a **net-net lease,** the tenant pays a base rent, some or all of the real estate taxes, plus any insurance premiums agreed to. Under the terms of a net-net-net lease (often called a **triple net lease**), the tenant pays a base rent, some or all of the real estate taxes, any insurance premiums agreed to, plus agreed upon repair and maintenance costs. While the triple net lease is unusual in office buildings, you will see it occasionally when one tenant occupies an entire building and often on the ground floor space.

Net leases can differ greatly depending upon how many extra expenses the tenant is required to pay. In some net-net leases, for example, the tenant pays rent and property taxes and is required to arrange and pay for all services, including janitorial and cleaning supplies, insurance, utilities, maintenance and repair of building (including roofs and sidewalks), and contract services such as landscaping. Do not be fooled by bargain-basement rents in net leases. Do have each item for which you are paying written into your lease.

2. *Percentage lease.* More commonly found in retail operations than in office buildings, a **percentage lease** requires the tenant to pay a percentage of the tenant's gross income in excess of a predetermined minimum, in addition to a base rent.

3. *Gross lease.* Under a **gross lease** the tenant pays only the rent and the owner pays all other expenses involved in the building's operation. Under the terms of a **modified gross lease** the tenant usually pays for janitorial service and electricity and the landlord pays for all other operating expenses.

Many office buildings operate under a **full service gross lease,** wherein the amount you pay the landlord includes all services. Table 4–1 is a composite gross rental breakdown for office buildings in a metropolitan city and a suburban area. All amounts are annual per square foot estimates.

All of the items in Table 4–1, excluding land and building, are generally referred to in a gross lease as the *base allocation* or *expense stop.* If there is an increase in any of these items above the base allocation or expense stop amount, these additional expenses will be passed through to the tenant.

Table 4–1 Breakdown of Office Building Rental Costs

	Metropolitan	Suburban
Land and building	$26.00	$20.00
Real estate taxes	⌈2.65⌉	⌈1.25⌉
Janitorial and cleaning	.75	.60
Insurance	.15	.15
Utilities	2.20	1.80
Maintenance	1.25	.60
Landscaping		.10
Management and administration	⌊1.00⌋	⌊1.00⌋
Total (Annual)	$34.00	$25.50
(Monthly)	$ 2.83	$ 2.13

Note: Bracketed portion represents operating expenses. *Source: Black's Office Leasing Guide: Greater Los Angeles Five County Area* (New York: McGraw-Hill Information Systems, 1987). Reprinted with permission.

Increases in a Lease All leases usually include two types of annual increases. One type provides for an increase in base rent. It can be a fixed annual percentage amount, such as a 5 percent increase each year, or a fixed annual dollar amount, such as $.50 per square foot, or be based on the Consumer Price Index (CPI) percentages compiled for your geographic region. Since the CPI fluctuates, the method by which the increase is calculated is negotiable. For example, you could establish the CPI increase as of the anniversary month of your lease, or it could be an average of the percentage figures over the six months preceding the anniversary date. Because CPI figures can fluctuate widely, particularly in times of rampant inflation, you will want to be sure there is a cap, or limit, on the amount of the annual increase.

The second type of increase covers the operating expenses of the building. It is calculated either by using a **base year** or an **expense stop** on operating expenses. For example, using the base year method, assume that the base year in Table 4–1 is 1992. The landlord will cover all operating expenses incurred during that year, which are estimated to be $8 per square foot for the metropolitan area building. Near the 1993 anniversary date of your lease, you will be presented with an accounting and an invoice for your pro rata share of any increases in operating expenses over the amount set down in the base year, and your rent for the next year will be increased accordingly.

If the increase is calculated by using the expense stop method, you agree to accept the landlord's projections that the building can be operated within a certain budget. If the landlord's projections are inaccurate, any expenses incurred over the expense stop amount will be passed through to you, even in the first year of the lease. In a new building, if you agree to the expense stop method of calculating passed-through operating expenses, you could be presented with a very large bill at the end of the first year and subsequent years because the landlord lacks historical data on which to make projections.

The base year increase is usually best for the tenant because it limits your upward exposure on increases by establishing a base allocation and requires an accounting. Obviously, the higher the expense stop or base year allocation for any given rental rate, the more advantageous the deal is for the tenant.

Lease Checklist

Prior to drawing the lease, both the landlord and the tenant should agree to and have a thorough understanding of the following:

- Location and size of space
- Options for expansion
- Length of initial lease and any options to extend, expand, cancel, or sublet
- Exact rent per square foot and list of specific services provided
- Method of measurement (rentable or usable square feet) and tenant's load factor
- Quantity and quality of interior work to be performed by landlord
- Normal operating hours of the building and cost of extra use
- Base year and increase provisions in the lease
- Parking spaces defined by number, location, and cost
- Local zoning ordinances pertaining to use of space
- Recital of actual space usage (i.e., to practice law)
- Date of possession and date rent starts

Services of a Commercial Real Estate Broker

Locating suitable offices for your firm and negotiating the lease take a considerable amount of time and expertise. A professional commercial real estate broker who represents tenants exclusively will not only educate you about the marketplace but will provide much needed information and support during the entire process.

Interview several brokers, then choose one with whom you feel comfortable and work exclusively with that individual. Working with more than one broker eliminates competition and the possibility of getting a better deal; in fact, you might inadvertently drive up the price in a building you want because of a falsely perceived increase in demand for space in that building on the part of the owner. Professional brokers know the market and the landlord so they know better than anyone how to negotiate for the best terms. Brokers are paid a commission by the landlord, and using one will not affect the price you pay since commissions to brokers are a standard budget item for any building owner.

The amount of time required to search out, get documentation for, and negotiate your new office facility necessitates that both you and the attorneys give serious thought to working with a professional broker.

In summary, when you decide to relocate your firm, here are ten key areas for consideration:

1. Area and accessibility
2. Usable area versus rentable area
3. Elevator service
4. Building management and maintenance
5. Cleaning service
6. Life safety features
7. Parking
8. Standard workletter installations
9. Type of lease
10. Services of a professional broker

4–3 Getting the Most Usage from Your Office Space

Most people who work in a law office will agree that a comfortable, well-designed office not only contributes to productivity but also enhances the firm's image in the eyes of clients and employees.

If you were to make a list of all the items that make you and others in the firm more productive, no doubt your list would include personal computers, telephones, copiers, facsimile machines, typewriters, and other electronic devices. But if you did not include the setting in which all of these tools are used, you overlooked a major item.

A well-designed office environment encourages coworkers to communicate better and produce more, and by so doing becomes as much a business tool as any administrative procedure or electronic device. *Today's Office* magazine (August 1989) considers the office environment to be a bargain when compared to other business expenses. According to the magazine's calculations, the people who work in the office account for 70 to 90 percent of office overhead costs while the physical office structure represents only 2 to 3 percent of total expenses. Office furnishings, equipment, maintenance, and related costs make up the rest.

When it comes to creating a comfortable, productive office environment, you do not want to be penny-wise and pound-foolish. For example, if you buy inexpensive secretarial chairs in order to save a few dollars, you may have to pay back the savings many times over with lowered productivity caused by fatigue and back strain, as well as by lowered feelings of self-esteem and morale.

The office environment is made up of several interdependent systems: people, floor plans, furniture, equipment, lighting, air quality, and acoustics. These interdependent systems are constantly changing, and for that reason your office should be designed with the ability to adapt to changing needs.

Because of the complexity of knowledge required to create a proper office environment for your law firm, you might consider retaining the services of a space planner or facilities management expert. Like the commercial real estate broker, these professionals can help you get the most productive use of your office space. Their services are often provided by the building owner or can be negotiated as part of your lease.

Conducting a Needs Assessment

To get a more accurate determination of space required, you would be wise to conduct a needs assessment by interviewing everyone in the firm. You will want to create your own checklist of points to cover in your assessment. Here are some ideas to get you started.

1. Is the space you currently occupy too large, too small, or adequate?
2. What do you particularly like about your current space?
3. What would you like to see improved?
4. What are you unwilling to part with under any circumstances?
5. What items would you like to see incorporated into a new office facility? (Include both individual office space and facilities for the entire firm.)

Remember to include future growth in your space needs assessment, and keep the number of questions to 10 or less. Fewer questions that are well thought out are more likely to get a higher response than a two-page questionnaire. Most people do not need to take long to think about their answers, so try 15-minute one-on-one interviews to gather the information instead of circulating a memorandum and waiting for a response.

The Space Plan

Whether you use the services of a professional space planner or decide to plan the office environment yourself, with or without the help of the off-the-shelf computer software, here are some space planning guidelines.

In general, you should allow about 200 usable square feet per person to determine your overall usable square footage needs. How the space is allocated will vary depending upon the firm's desired image, the individual desires of partners, the kinds and amount of office machines and equipment, filing and storage requirements, the size of the law library, conference rooms, audiovisual facilities, and personnel amenities, such as lunchrooms and quiet rooms.

The following list will help you figure space requirements for the typical law firm. Your requirements may vary somewhat depending on the results of your needs assessment.

- Typical partner's office: 250 to 400 sq. ft. (4 to 5 windows in length).
- Typical associate's or manager's office: 150 to 250 sq. ft. (3 to 4 windows in length).
- Typical paralegal's office: 100 to 150 sq. ft. (2 windows in length).
- Secretary or clerk—partitioned open space: 50 to 100 sq. ft.
- Conference rooms: Theatre-style or classroom seating requires 15 sq. ft. per person; conventional conference seating requires 25 to 30 sq. ft. per person.

- Reception room: Receptionist and seating for 2 to 4 people requires 125 to 200 sq. ft.; for receptionist and seating for 6 to 8 people figure 200 to 300 sq. ft.
- Mail room: About 8' to 9' in width, includes 30" counters against each wall with a 4' aisle between. The length of the room depends upon the number of people working in the room and the amount of mail activity.
- File room: Allow about 7 sq. ft. per file cabinet. Aisle width varies from 3' to 4' with a minimum aisle width of 2'6".
- Library: Allow 12" for book shelves against walls, 24" for back-to-back shelves. Minimum aisle space of 2'6". With seating for 4 to 6 people, and room for a small copier, a small library will require 175 to 450 sq. ft.
- Employee lunchroom: Allow 15 sq. ft. per person, not including kitchen. Kitchen and serving area should be a minimum of 1/3 to 1/2 of the dining area.
- Clerical pool area or word processing room: Allow 80 to 100 sq. ft. of usable area per person.
- Corridors and circulation: Figure 15 to 20 percent of the total usable area for all of the above-listed areas. Public corridors should be about 6' wide, principal office corridors about 5' wide, and secondary interior corridors range from 3'6" to 4'6" in width. Clearance between desks should be at least 3'. If secretaries are located in corridors, then allow 10' for width. This allows for the standard 5' long secretarial desk and 5' passageway, which is comfortable passage for two people. Minimum for this type of corridor is 8' in width.
- Coat closets: Allow 1 lineal foot for 4 coats, or 3" per person. In many offices, particularly those located in the Sun Belt, coat closets are overlooked, and only thought of on the first rainy day.
- Standard door sizes: The standard office door is 3' × 7'; double entrance doors are either 5' wide (two 2'6" doors) or 6' wide (two 3' doors).

Other space planning considerations should include:

- Drinking water: A water purification system will cost less than bottled water.
- Coffee stations: Depending on the size of the firm, locate several of these throughout the office. A coffee station requires, at the minimum, cold water lines for automatic coffee makers, a small refrigerator for milk, and a supply storage cabinet.
- An employee lunch area should include a full-size refrigerator with ice maker, double sink with garbage disposal, microwave oven, dishwasher, trash compactor, an instant hot water dispenser on the drinking water system, and a specially ducted exhaust system to prevent cooking odors from spreading throughout the office.
- One or more showers and change rooms for employees who like to exercise during lunch hour, or who work unusual hours.

Fighting the Space War

Ever since people have occupied offices, the space within them has been contested. Employees want a comfortable and spacious working environment. Management, always conscious of real estate costs, wants usable and productive space. Computers, printers, and the growing use of other electronic equipment, along with their cables and wires, seem to intensify, rather than lessen, the space war.

Although there are several different approaches to the use of space, two of them—open plan areas and private offices—seem to be effective for law firms.

The main attraction of open plan areas is flexibility. As the office environment changes, through expansion or consolidation, desks, screens, files, and other furnishings can be shifted about quickly and inexpensively to satisfy your changing needs. Several office furniture manufacturers discovered during the 1980s that circular workstations, or pods, as they are commonly called, can reduce the amount of space required by as much as 40 percent. (See Figure 4–3.)

Soundproofing and privacy are achieved with padded separation panels. Glass panels will provide a sound barrier but allow you to see out. In addition, these movable wall systems are available with power panels containing dedicated circuits allowing you to plug in computers and other equipment almost anywhere. Movable wall systems with power panels work especially well when your office has an electrified floor.

Several types of workstation configurations are illustrated in Figure 4–4, but you are actually limited only by your own creativity and imagination.

Attorneys and paralegals will always require privacy. But due to the cost of office space, the trend is now toward smaller and less luxurious offices, especially for associate attorneys. (See Figure 4–5). Instead, more emphasis and money are being put on a well-furnished conference room or two where clients are met.

In addition to being able to assist you in getting the most use from your office space, professional space planners usually have several reliable sources for

Figure 4–3 Office Pods

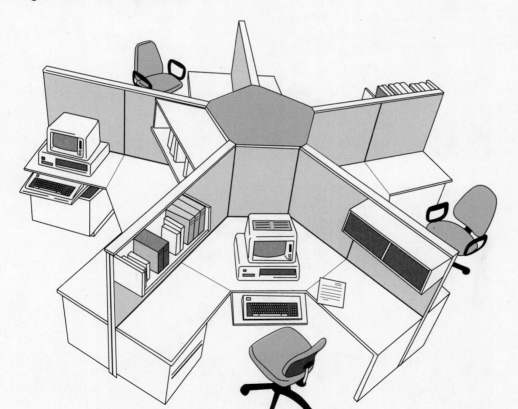

The "Pentapod" has five workstations that can be individually fitted to provide functional and aesthetic requirements. This design represents an efficient use of space and people. *Source:* Courtesy of CenterCore, Inc., Wayne, PA.

Figure 4–4   Workstations

Workstations can be designed to be functional and private. *Source:* Photos courtesy of
Steelcase, Inc., Grand Rapids, MI.

Figure 4–5   A Contemporary Law Office

This law office places a high premium on open space as well as on comfort. *Source:* Photo courtesy of Steelcase, Inc., Grand Rapids, MI.

furniture, wall coverings, and carpeting. Whether you use the services of a professional or do it yourself, the furniture you choose should be comfortable and attractive as well as functional and practical.

4–4   Moving the Law Office

Moving your law firm's office furnishings requires as much consideration and planning as selecting a site and space planning. To ensure that the actual move goes smoothly, follow these suggestions.

Select a Moving Company

At least three months prior to your move-in date, begin your search for a reliable moving company. Since the final costs are unlikely to vary significantly when you work with established companies, you will want to find a company that has had experience in moving law firms—particularly in moving law libraries.

Because only a few books can be packed in each box, and because hired packers typically pay little attention to keeping the books in order, it is almost impossible to keep books in their proper sequence when packed in boxes. If your moving company says they will pack your library books in boxes, find another company that uses rolling carts. Rolling carts can hold entire shelves of books. By numbering the carts as they are filled, there is less chance you will find the volumes out of sequence in your new library.

Two staff members will be needed on moving day to help supervise the library move. One will be needed in the old location to answer questions and to keep the books in sequential order and one in the new office to ensure that books are removed and then shelved sequentially.

The moving company should be familiar with your current and new locations, traffic patterns, parking restrictions, and access to freight elevators and stairs. You should visit the movers' facilities to look at the equipment they use and to judge their professionalism. Watch a job in progress, if possible.

A good moving company can help you in ways other than just transferring your furniture and equipment from one office to another. Often they will accept advance shipments of new items from the manufacturer, warehouse them, and then deliver and assemble the items on moving day. Likewise, they often will handle the removal and transportation of old furniture you are donating or selling. A good mover should be as much a professional advisor as the real estate broker and space planner.

Get Estimates of Moving Costs

Once you have selected two or three professional moving companies, you will request a proposal from each one. Assume that each member of the firm will pack his or her own personal belongings and the contents of their offices. The mover will take care of the library, supplies, and bulk items.

Marking, tagging, and planning will take place during business hours, but the actual move will be done at night or on the weekend. The efficiency gained by over-the-weekend moves more than offsets the cost of overtime. The move should begin at the close of business on a Friday night and be completed, with furniture and equipment in place, plugged in and ready to use at the new location by Monday morning. When possible, schedule the move over a holiday weekend to give yourself extra time to get everything set up. If your firm is really big, consider closing the office down the last week of the year to facilitate the move.

Moving costs will vary depending on the size of the law library, the amount of filing cabinets to be moved, the number and size of elevators at both locations, and how close the moving van can get to the buildings. Moving costs also vary by geographic region and according to labor rates. Because of the expense involved with the actual move, you might be tempted to get the employees more involved in packing, tagging, and marking boxes, furniture, and equipment. Resist this temptation—unless you have several idle employees. There is very little to be saved by using valuable employee time to perform manual labor. Instead, get several estimates and work with only the most professional moving company.

Take Care of Details

Relocating any size law firm is a major expense which requires that you use all of your management skills. The more planning and organization that goes into the process, the less likely little things—such as getting the new phone and fax numbers months in advance so directory listings will be up-to-date and getting stationery, business cards, and announcements to clients printed and mailed to coincide with the move date—will be overlooked.

You will need to take charge of directing and controlling the events leading up to the move and the actual move itself. Communication with attorneys, staff, and the moving company is critical. Taking control to guide and monitor the move itself is also the office manager's responsibility. In fact, the fewer people who get involved in the moving process from beginning to end, the better. Your management skills will allow you to perform with grace even under this kind of pressure.

4–5 Planning for a Law Office Disaster

The potential for disasters has always existed. But perhaps because we have become more dependent on technology, or because in the last few years disasters have shook, pummeled, and burned our cities, heartland, and shores, office managers have become increasingly aware of lurking dangers that could wipe out a law firm overnight—if the firm is not prepared to cope with emergencies.

In addition to natural disasters, such as earthquakes, floods, hurricanes, landslides, and tornadoes, emergency planning needs to include preparation for technological disasters, such as fires or electrical brownouts or blackouts; water main, gas main, or sewer breaks; pipeline or industrial explosions; transportation disruption; or nuclear power plant or other hazardous materials accidents.

Social disasters, such as bomb threats or violent intruders; health disasters, such as epidemics, pollution, and stress; and personal problems that might result in a long-term illness or disability, or disbarment or death of a lawyer—all deserve an equal amount of attention when you prepare your firm's emergency or disaster plan.

How to Prepare for a Disaster

The American Bar Association, the American Red Cross, and utility companies have numerous publications to help guide you in structuring an emergency preparedness plan. In addition, your local fire department can tell you about scheduled safety seminars or provide on-site instruction, including CPR training. Your building management can provide you with guidelines and instructions on how to evacuate the building, the location of fire extinguishers, and other lifesaving measures.

It is not enough to just gather information from these and other resources—you need to actually put together a written plan which will vary in detail based on the size and location of your law firm. Here is a checklist of points to include in your plan to get you started.

Appoint a Safety Coordinator The safety coordinator is responsible for: (1) getting emergency planning information from the various agencies; (2) meeting with the building management to ascertain what planning has been done; (3) appointing and coordinating the activity of safety monitors for each floor if your firm occupies more than one floor in the building; (4) posting vital information and conducting evacuation drills; (5) educating office personnel; (6) acquiring and storing food, water, and first aid supplies; and (7) developing a plan to communicate with employees at home in the event the office is inaccessible for a period of time.

The goal of your disaster plan should be to make sure that every employee of the firm knows what to do, who to call, and where to go in case of an emergency.

Safeguard Records and Data Duplicates of all vital records should be stored off-site so that the firm will be able to continue to serve its clients and substantiate any claims. Vital records would include (1) the firm's current court calendar; (2) business records, such as billable time and receivables information, leases, partnership agreements, inventory of physical assets, and insurance records; (3) current client lists, client files lists, and other important business contacts; (4) backup disks for the computers; and (5) any client records, files, exhibits, or transcripts which, if lost, would seriously injure the outcome of the client's legal transaction.

Ensure the Continuity of the Practice Make arrangements in advance for a location from which the firm can operate temporarily. Often, another law firm would be able to provide you with temporary quarters. Or perhaps a business client would be able to come to your rescue. Access to some telephones, compatible computers, and a desk or two for a few days will allow you to keep in contact with clients, court personnel, other counsel, and employees until you can get the firm back together.

Check Business Insurance Policies Get in touch with your firm's business insurance professional and discuss the options in your policy. Note whether reimbursement is allowed for the replacement cost of the damaged or destroyed property, or whether reimbursement is limited to the depreciated actual cash value of the property. Then compare the cost of the two different types of coverage. Since the cost of equipment usually goes up from year to year, if coverage is limited to the depreciated actual cash value of the property, replacing all the electronic equipment in your office could create a substantial financial burden for the firm.

Other options and riders to consider include (1) **business interruption insurance,** which provides for the loss of income caused by the interruption of an ongoing business due to a disaster; (2) **extra expense insurance,** which protects against increased costs in finding and maintaining an alternate place for doing business while your office is being repaired, or in locating and setting up new quarters; (3) **valuable papers coverage,** which provides replacement for loss, damage, or destruction of client files and office records; (4) **accounts receivable coverage,** which provides protection for loss due to the inability to collect accounts receivable when the records have been lost, destroyed, or damaged; and (5) **electronic data processing equipment coverage,** which protects all electronic data processing equipment, including computers, against physical loss.

Plan for the Unavailability of a Lawyer Steps should be taken by each lawyer, particularly the sole practitioner, for the continuity, or wrap-up, of the practice in the event the attorney becomes incapacitated or disabled, is disbarred, or dies. Advance arrangement should be made with one or more lawyers, either inside or outside of the firm, to represent clients of the unavailable attorney. Advance authority from clients to associate with other counsel in case of an emergency should be a routine file-opening procedure.

In addition to concern for the clients, consideration should be given to how the firm will make up the lost revenue caused by the unavailable attorney. The unavailability of a lawyer who annually generates substantial fee revenues could create serious short-term financial problems for the firm. Insurance coverage is one way to protect against this occurrence.

Disasters come in all sizes. Some are headline making and others are not. So what else could go wrong? A power failure; broken water pipes; falling ceiling tiles; shelves, file cabinets, and plants tipping over; closed airports, highways, and bridges. Good disaster planning encompasses many, if not all, contingencies.

Facilities management includes a wide range of duties and requires an equally wide range of knowledge and expertise. Fortunately, there are many professionals who can act as advisors and help you make informed choices. As always, people and planning are the keys to successful management and to quickly getting back to the practice of law.

SUMMARY

4-1

Growth and expansion of the law firm or consolidation due to retirement, decentralization, or loss of attorney personnel are reasons why a firm might decide to move. To establish a presence in a growing community or to embark on building an image are also reasons to relocate. Whatever the reason, relocation is much too costly to be done without extensive planning.

4-2

An area's good reputation and easy accessibility are usually the two major factors that will determine geographic location. Selecting the office building entails many considerations, including how the rent is being calculated; the quality of elevator service if the office is in a multistory building; the building management, maintenance, and cleaning service; safety and security features; parking; the provisions of the standard workletter; and the type of lease being offered.

4-3

A floor plan that optimizes the use of space is the best defense in the office space wars. Modular furniture systems and movable panels can provide comfort and privacy in less space than traditional furniture. It is not advisable to conserve spending when designing and furnishing a law office. An inefficient floor plan or poorly designed and furnished work stations can result in lowered productivity and health problems for employees.

4-4

The secret to a smooth relocation is selecting a professional moving company with experience in moving law firms. Particular attention must be given to moving the law library and to taking care of small details. A written timeline will help to ensure that the move occurs without a major incident.

4-5

Modern-day business disasters are the result of nature, technological occurrences, social or health-related disturbances, or personal problems. Preparing an emergency plan is now a routine part of the office manager's job and requires first the gathering of information and then the appointment of a safety coordinator. Particular attention should be given to the safeguarding of records and data, ensuring the continuity of the practice, checking business insurance coverage, and planning for the unavailability of a lawyer with the firm.

REVIEW

Key Terms

accounts receivable coverage
aural privacy
base year
build-to-suit-tenant clause
business interruption insurance
electrified floors
electronic data processing equipment
    coverage
expense stop
extra expense insurance
full service gross lease
gross lease

load factor
modified gross lease
net lease
net-net lease
percentage lease
rentable area
signage privileges
triple net lease
turnkey clause
usable area
valuable papers coverage
workletter

Questions for Review and Discussion

1. What are some circumstances which might suggest that your firm should consider relocating?
2. What are some of the important factors to consider in choosing a location?
3. In selecting an office building, what are some of the items you will consider?
4. What is the difference between usable area and rentable area, and how does it affect your rental rate?
5. What is the purpose of the builder's workletter?
6. Explain the differences among the most common types of leases.
7. What items are commonly negotiable in office leases?
8. Operating expenses are often passed through to the tenants in one of three ways. Explain the ways in which this happens.
9. What steps would you take to determine space requirements for your firm?
10. What are the most important factors involved with the actual move to new quarters?
11. What kinds of disasters should you plan for, and how would you go about preparing a disaster plan?

Activities

1. A tenant wants to rent 10,000 square feet of usable space. One building is offered at $20 per square foot and has a load factor of 9 percent. Another building rents for $19.50 per square foot, with a load factor of 14 percent. Which building offers the tenant the best deal, and what will be the rent in each case?
2. Establish criteria for new office space for Dunn & Sweeney. Select one or two areas that are suitable. Contact two or three office buildings within the acceptable areas and obtain rental information from each. After adjusting each quote based on usable area versus rentable area, compare rental rates and building amenities. Always ask for the owner's definition of the terms *usable* and *rentable*. Sometimes the answers might surprise you. The terms can mean different things to different people. Which building would you recommend and why?
3. Contact the American Red Cross, the fire department, and the telephone company for recommendations on creating an emergency plan for a law firm. Arrange for a guest speaker to come to class to talk about emergency preparedness.

CHAPTER 5 Information Management in the Law Office

OUTLINE

5–1 Inside the Microcomputer
   The Microchip
   The Central Processing Unit
   Memory
   Storage Capacity
   Auxiliary Storage
   Peripherals
   The Operating System
   Power Protection Devices
5–2 Five Steps to Cost-Effective Information Management
   Step One: Determine Need
   Step Two: Choose Software
   Step Three: Choose Hardware
   Step Four: Select Vendors
   Step Five: Networking and Other Options
5–3 Law Office Management Support Software
   Document Management Software
   Litigation Management Software
   Calendar Software
5–4 Preventing Computer-Related Management Problems
   Computer Viruses and Bugs
   Legal and Ethical Considerations of Software Usage
   The Impact of Computers on Management of Support Staff
   Coping with the Industrial Injury of the Information Age
   Eight Problems a Computer Cannot Solve

COMMENTARY

The information management systems at Dunn & Sweeney are sluggish on good days and completely dysfunctional on other days. The Atari-generation attorneys are demanding to have computer terminals in their offices, although they are not clear on how the computer will be used to help them practice law. Other attorneys will not go near a keyboard, but they do understand that efficiency in today's law firm means entering the 21st century of automation. You have been asked to research the concept of information management for law firms and to present to the Managing Partner your suggestions to fully automate Dunn & Sweeney.

OBJECTIVES

In Chapter 4 you learned that an effective facilities manager is able to assess the law firm's current and future space requirements, select a location and an office building based on certain criteria, negotiate with the landlord for additional amenities, and provide a comfortable and safe working environment for all members of the firm. After studying this chapter, you will be able to:

1. List the main components of a computer system.
2. Describe the functions of ROM and RAM.
3. Define the terms *kilobyte, megabyte,* and *gigabyte.*
4. Discuss the two categories of printers.
5. Describe the functions of the operating system.
6. List five steps to cost-effective information management.
7. Describe the purpose of a local area network and three common topologies.
8. Discuss ways in which a scanner and SBET can augment an automated office system.
9. List three basic types of management support software and their uses in the law office.
10. Explain the difference between a computer virus and a bug and how to guard against infection.
11. Explain when you can legally and ethically copy software.
12. Discuss ways to prevent CTD and carpal tunnel syndrome.

5-1 Inside the Microcomputer

Most people do not run out and buy the first house they see. Instead, a prudent homebuyer will take time to research the housing market, assess the family's current and future needs, and seek professional advice before committing to the investment of many thousands of dollars.

Yet many otherwise prudent buyers will spend enormous amounts of money on an information management system that neither meets their immediate needs nor will accommodate a growing law practice because they failed to conduct a needs assessment, to research the market, or to seek unbiased professional advice.

In order to make sound information management decisions you need to have a basic understanding of computer-related language. Here are the nuts and bolts of computerese.

The Microchip

Microchip technology began with the invention of the hand-held calculator, and the rest, as the saying goes, is history. A **microchip** is a wafer of silicon, measuring about one-fourth inch square and less than four thousandths of an inch thick, that contains imprinted circuits through which electronic impulses travel. Through the development of microchip technology, it is now possible to capture massive amounts of data on a chip no larger than the fingernail on your little finger.

The microcomputer, commonly called a desktop computer, a personal computer, or a PC, is found in almost every law office today. Most often used by one person, the microcomputer has become, for many, the first choice in office automation equipment for law offices.

While smaller firms may rely on the microcomputer exclusively, larger firms will also use large mainframe computers to process payroll, accounts receivable, accounts payable, client billings, and any other projects requiring enormous amounts of storage. The same work can be done on a minicomputer in the medium-sized firm.

The Central Processing Unit

Commonly called the **CPU,** the **central processing unit** is the brains of the microcomputer. The CPU is usually found on a single microcomputer chip and executes the program instructions to process data. Typically the most costly component of the microcomputer, the CPU is divided into the *control unit*, which directs the computer to perform the necessary processes, such as word processing, keeping the calendar, or tracking litigation, and the *arithmetic/logic unit (ALU)*, which performs mathematical computations and allows the computer to make decisions pertaining to them. The ALU functions are performed in places on the chips called *registers*, which are very small and therefore have difficulty storing vast amounts of information. Additional chips, called *memory*, are thus used for storage purposes.

Memory

Memory, or *main storage*, is an area for storing programs and data while you are working on a program. For example, while you are creating a new document using the word processing software stored in memory, the new data you are entering is also being stored on the CPU's memory chip.

There are two major types of internal memory. **ROM,** or read only memory, is one type of internal memory. ROM means that the data is fixed—you cannot change it, or destroy it, by turning off the microcomputer. ROM integrated circuits are manufactured to store operating instructions permanently. When you turn on your PC and information appears on the screen, you know that ROM has done its job, and the micro is ready to go to work. **RAM,** or random access memory, is the second type of internal memory. Since new information can be stored and removed from RAM, the information in RAM is said to be *volatile*. In other words, any information in RAM can be lost when the power is turned off unless you have taken the steps required to save it before closing down the system.

Storage Capacity

Microcomputer storage capacity is expressed by the number of memory cells on each chip. When the microcomputer is operating, the CPU reads electronic signals that represent the binary number system, which is composed entirely of zeroes and ones. A **bit** refers to these individual binary digits which will be either a zero or a one. Eight bits are required to make one **byte,** or character. For example, 01101001 might be read by the CPU as the letter *b*.

In the metric system, **K** is the symbol for 1,000. However, a **kilobyte,** or K in computerese, actually represents 1,024 bytes or characters of information in the memory of a microcomputer. Therefore, when you hear that a computer has a 256K or 512K memory, that means the computer has 256 × 1,024, or 512 × 1,024, locations for storage. A **megabyte** equals 1,024K, or about a million-character storage capacity, and a **gigabyte** is 1,024MB (megabytes) or about a billion characters.

Because the cost of memory storage capacity has decreased over the past few years as technology has allowed manufacturers to develop better and more economical chips, even a small law firm should consider a system capable of storing gigabytes. The ability to increase a computer's memory capacity, by plugging additional expansion boards into the motherboard, is one of the most important considerations when purchasing a microcomputer system for long-term use.

Auxiliary Storage

The most popular forms of auxiliary storage for microcomputers are the diskette and the hard disk. **Diskettes,** also called *floppy disks,* are made of a thin, pliable, magnetically coated plastic on which data is stored. Floppy disks come in three standard sizes, 8 inch, 5¼ inch, and 3½ inch, and each can store about 180 pages of data on one side of the disk. Double-density diskettes can store about twice as much information as the single-density ones.

A **hard disk,** made from nonbending, rigid aluminum, can store about 5,000 pages of data and rotates within the CPU at a much higher rate of speed than floppy disks, thus providing faster retrieval and storage capabilities. Most hard disks are built into the microcomputer in an airtight, sealed unit and are not subjected to the wear and tear of floppy disks. However, should the hard disk be damaged by a bounce on the desk or in being moved from one location to another, all data stored on the hard disk could be lost. For this reason, all data on a hard disk should be **backed up,** or copied onto another disk, regularly.

In a law firm daily backup of the system is normal, often taking place automatically in the early morning hours when no one is likely to be using the system. Some of the more sophisticated systems will automatically perform backup functions several times throughout the day without interfering with work flow. While there is no need to become paranoid about backing up your system, keep in mind that if the system "crashes" for any reason, you are likely to lose all of the information that is not currently backed up. For a law firm, the possibility of losing all data created in just one morning is a grim thought.

Peripherals

The input and output devices connected to the microcomputer are called **peripherals.** The most popular input device is the standard keyboard, known as *Qwerty,* which was developed in the late 1800s by Christopher Sholes. While other keyboards have been created, and attempts have been made from time to time to recruit converts, the Qwerty keyboard has continued to be the standard and is certainly the one most familiar to typists.

Another input device is called the **mouse.** The mouse is a small desktop pointing device which, as it is moved across the desk, also moves the **cursor,** a blinking arrow, dash, or other symbol on the screen that tells the typist that the system is ready for input or where typed characters will appear on the screen.

Output peripheral devices include the printer and the video monitor. Printers are classified according to the way printing is accomplished. Similar to old model typewriters, *impact printers* have a mechanism that strikes a ribbon, transferring the characters onto paper. Types of impact printers include dot matrix, daisy wheel, thimble, and line printers. Some people refer to these types of printers as *letter quality printers* because even though they are slow and noisy, their quality is suitable for most office correspondence.

Nonimpact printers include ink jet printers, which deposit droplets of ink onto the paper, thermal printers, which use heat to produce characters on paper, and laser printers, which use a small laser beam to keep images on the paper. Laser printers are fast and quiet (although more expensive than the other types) and are favored by high-volume, paper-producing organizations, such as law firms.

The CRT (cathode ray tube), or *video monitor*, is another common output device. These high-resolution television screens, or monitors, are either monochrome—typically green, amber, or white—or color, displaying a range of colors that are especially good for graphics but often confusing and distracting for word processing.

The **modem** is another peripheral device that converts microcomputer-generated electrical digital signals into audio signals and transmits them via telephone lines over long distances. Actually, a modem is both an input and output device that allows a microcomputer to communicate with another micro, a minicomputer, a mainframe, or other compatible office automation equipment using telephone lines. Since messages can be transmitted across town or around the world, a modem is standard equipment for law offices that subscribe to research or informational databases. (Figure 5–1 illustrates some of the various computer components.)

The Operating System

The **operating system,** simply defined, is a software program that manages the operation of the microcomputer. It loads specific programs, oversees the storage of data, and controls all the peripheral devices. The *DOS*, or disk operating system, goes to work loading a portion of the operating system into memory as soon as the computer is turned on. Several types of operating systems have been developed by different manufacturers. Some of the more familiar ones are MS-DOS, PC-DOS, Apple-DOS, and UNIX.

Typical functions of a disk operating system might include library commands, which are single-word commands, such as Clear (the screen) or Delete; a utility

Figure 5–1 Computer Components

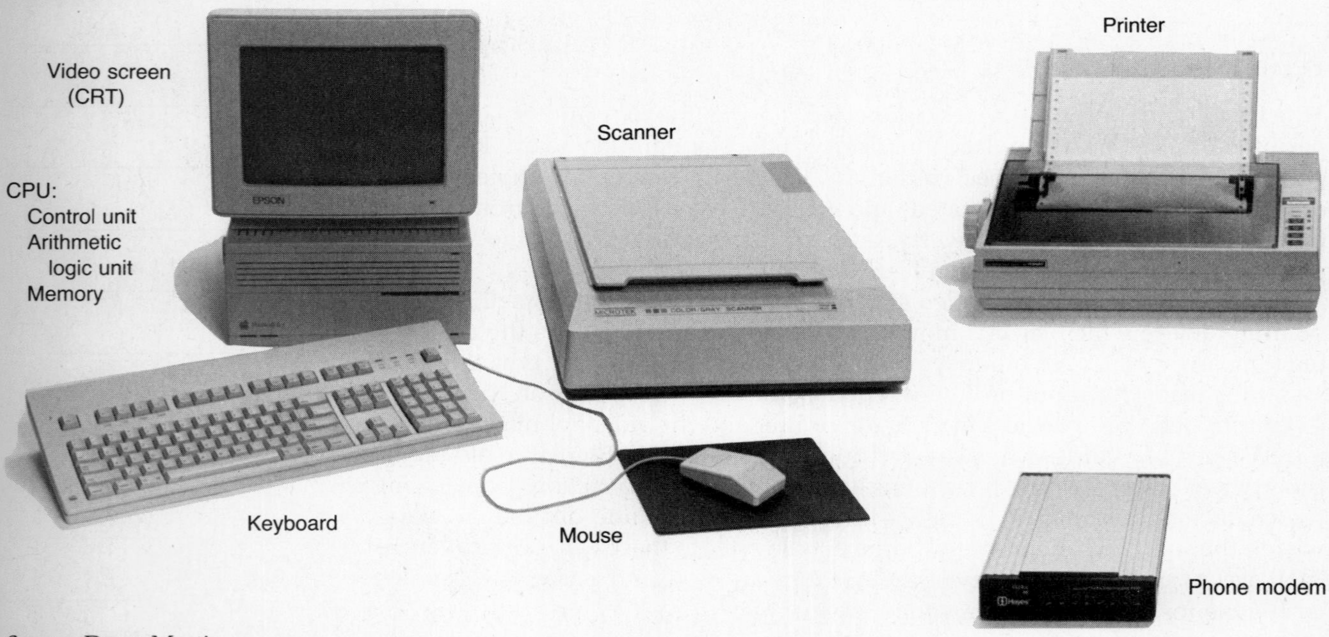

Video screen (CRT)

CPU:
  Control unit
  Arithmetic
    logic unit
  Memory

Keyboard

Scanner

Mouse

Printer

Phone modem

Source: Doug Martin.

program to accomplish routine tasks, such as backing up disks or *formatting* disks (preparing disks to store data); and the system operating routines that tell the microcomputer what to do.

Power Protection Devices

Since electrical power disturbances can cause a loss of data, or the creation of incorrect output data, power protection is of concern to all microcomputer users. Power disturbances can be caused by air conditioners and copiers being turned on and off, by lightning, or by a complete loss of power due to downed wires. Isolation transformers, surge suppressors, and transient suppressors are external devices that will block or reduce potential power disturbances. Alternative sources of power such as generators or batteries can provide emergency electrical current when commercial power is unavailable. As law firms become more dependent upon microcomputers, good power protection devices and alternative sources of emergency power will become increasingly critical.

5–2   Five Steps to Cost-Effective Information Management

Ask 20 people which microcomputer is best and you will probably get 20 different answers. Who is right? Everyone is! Whether you are going to install a new information management system, or are looking to expand or upgrade your current one, you can considerably ease the decision burden by approaching it logically. One rule of thumb is to buy neither more than you need nor less than is required to do the current job *and* allow for expansion.

Step One: Determine Need

First you will want to conduct an *end-user* needs survey. An end user is anyone who will input information or use output from the computer system. Using the following checklist, or one you develop, the end-user survey should answer two vital questions: Who is going to use the system, and What do they want it to do? You will want to cover these items in your survey.

Potential Computer Users   Lawyers, paralegals, law office managers, secretaries, and word processors will no doubt want to use the system. Library and personnel managers, as well as accounting and administrative staff, are also likely users. Some users might want a computer for home use, or a portable one to take to court or the law library.

Integrated Data and Word Processing   An integrated system usually means that from any desktop unit you can work with words or data, or both. However, many secretaries and word processors have no need to work with data. Their work is primarily in the area of document creation with little or no need to compute figures. (See Figure 5–2.) On the other hand, some attorneys, and most certainly accounting personnel, will require data computation capability in addition to word processing. Needs vary according to tasks.

Figure 5-2 DocuLiner Software

DocuLiner software lets you revise the original document without destroying it. *Source:*
Photo courtesy of CompuLaw, Ltd., Culver City, CA (1991). All rights reserved.

Litigation Support   An automated litigation support system can save time by searching thousands of pages of court transcripts for all information pertaining to a subject upon which contradictory evidence was presented, for example. Tasks of this type are typically performed by a paralegal or attorney and take many hours to complete. A litigation support system can save time and free up personnel for other tasks.

Client and Case Management Information   How much client and case information is needed and how will the information be used? Conflict of interest checks, current case status reports, and the ability to generate client mailing lists are only a few of the several options available from this type of database.

Calendaring Automated calendaring can keep track of everyone's schedules and provide daily reports with case reminders, appointments, client names, and other pertinent information such as the status of a client's account.

Forms Standard forms can be organized and stored so that they can be retrieved, modified, and printed, saving secretarial and paralegal time that would otherwise be required to input boilerplate language.

Billing Automated billing systems can greatly reduce billing time as well as generate information about each client's account. In addition, some systems are able to generate one bill at a time, or bills for the clients of a particular lawyer, or bills for clients whose balances exceed a certain amount. (See Figure 5–3.)

Time Posting Automatic time posting and the breakdown of accounts receivable into billed fees, unbilled fees, billed costs, and unbilled costs allow the firm to be more financially efficient. An example is shown in Figure 5–4.

Telephone and Copier Charges Telephone and copier charges can be automatically posted directly to client accounts at specified intervals.

Banking Some systems will generate checks, receipts, and bank deposit slips and post entries to clients' accounts automatically, as well as prepare daily transaction reports on all the firm's accounts.

Management Reports What kind of management reports would be helpful, how often are they required, and who will see them? For most firms, management reports would include aged accounts receivable reports, aged work-in-progress reports, on-demand trust account reports, profitability reports by area of specialization, and timekeeper reports. (See Figure 5–5.)

Telecommunications Requirements How much time is spent away from the office performing research, and how much time is spent searching for information in the library? Legal research and general information databases might save the firm both time and money.

Desktop Publishing and Typesetting Desktop systems allow you to professionally prepare any written material and are particularly useful for preparing newletters to clients, prospectuses for corporate clients, or any reports requiring tables, diagrams, charts, or other graphics.

Laser Printing Outside printing costs can be virtually eliminated with laser printing. Some systems can print your letterhead and court forms, as well as document text, with the same look as forms prepared at a print shop.

Budget To what extent does your firm wish to automate, how much money will be earmarked for this purpose, and over what period of time?

Figure 5–3   Time and Billing Software

These are just some of the tasks that can be automated in your law firm. As you conduct your survey, you will find questions being raised about other tasks. The next step, then, in conducting your needs assessment is to determine which areas are immediate, which are on the horizon, and which are future dreams.

Step Two: Choose Software

No doubt selecting software will be a complex task since the members of your firm will have varying needs. You can safely assume that word processing

Figure 5–4   Client Ledger Card

Client billing information is displayed on individual ledger cards. *Source:* Photo courtesy of CompuLaw, Ltd., Culver City, CA (1991). All rights reserved.

software will be high on almost everyone's list and that several people will also want data computing capability.

High among the several factors to consider in choosing software is the popularity of the software you select. This is not to suggest that you buy what everyone else is buying, but that you take into consideration how easy it will be to find employees, either part-time or full-time, who are familiar with the programs. For several years now, WordPerfect, a word processing software program, has been very popular with law firms. No doubt this is due, in part, to its capabilities and reliabilities when used on networks, but also to the manufacturer's responsiveness to the legal market. Much of the same can be said about Lotus 1-2-3, a popular data processing program.

While you might be tempted to purchase custom-designed software, or a less well-known, off-the-shelf program, keep in mind that if you have to spend

Figure 5–5 Legal Ledger Software

Management reports can be generated by Legal Ledger software. *Source:* Photo courtesy of CompuLaw, Ltd., Culver City, CA (1991). All rights reserved.

hours training each person who will use it, you have gained very little by going against the trend.

Once your firm's needs have been assessed, add these following items to your list of software considerations:

- How easy is the program to learn, what kind of training is available, and how responsive is the manufacturer's helpline?

- What type of security is provided? You will want unique passwords for users as well as controlled staff access to different parts of the system, such as accounting and personnel information.
- The ability to enter data without memorizing special codes will accelerate the training process and be less frustrating to users. Likewise, a system that requires the memorization of special commands takes more time to learn and is more frustrating to most users.
- Look for the ability to interrupt what you are doing, move to another function, and return to your current task easily.
- Also look for the ability to input data in one part of the system and have it automatically integrated systemwide without rekeying.
- Easy error correction, including recovery of lost or deleted data, is also helpful.
- Automatic data backup will provide insurance against oversight.

Step Three: Choose Hardware

After your software has been determined, it is time to review your equipment options. Most software is machine-specific—that is, it is designed to run on certain types of equipment which are listed on each software package. Because software is machine-specific, you will always want to select software before buying hardware.

As discussed earlier, when putting together your microcomputer system, questions will arise about printers, modems, monitors, keyboards, and external storage. Remember that peripherals must also be compatible with the hardware you choose. In addition to compatibility, you must also consider whether:

- The computer equipment will be able to be upgraded as technology advances without throwing out the current system.
- Other peripheral equipment, such as printers and scanners, can be added.
- Workstations can be easily added or removed as the size of the firm changes.
- Workstations can talk to each other sharing programs and data simultaneously.

Step Four: Select Vendors

The amount of service you receive from a vendor will vary. However, unless your firm has an in-house MIS (management of information systems) specialist, you should be looking for a **turnkey system,** a system that is completely installed with all hardware, software, and your firm's database in place when you sit down to use it. When selecting a vendor, you will also want to consider these factors:

- Reputation for reliability, quality repairs, and maintenance
- Length of time in the marketplace
- Availability of 24-hour telephone support
- Ability to provide on-site service in four hours or less
- Ongoing training support
- System updates
- Types of financing offered
- References from current users

In most cases vendor selection should be based on the quality of service provided, not on price.

Step Five: Networking and Other Options

Is a local area network (LAN) suitable for your firm? Take this short quiz and find out.

1. Are two or more people using computers in your firm?
2. Do you need to purchase individual software programs for each computer user?
3. Do you find yourself often transferring data from one computer to another on a floppy disk?
4. Do you have to wait to use equipment, such as a printer, that is attached to someone else's computer?

If you answered yes to any or all of the above questions, networking might be a useful addition to your office automation plan.

Local Area Networks A local area network (LAN) can be likened to a superhighway. It allows information to travel, via cables, from a minicomputer—a classification of computer introduced in 1965 by Digital Equipment Corporation (DEC) that has a much larger storage capacity than a microcomputer—or a mainframe—the largest and most powerful type of computer—to an unlimited number of individual workstations.

The way a networked system is interconnected is called its **topology.** The three most common topologies are the bus, ring, and star. The *bus topology* is similar to a freeway with many on and off ramps. Data travels along a common path (the bus) to individual workstations connected to it. (See Figure 5–6.)

Ring topologies are similar to the bus except that the ends are tied together so that data travels in a circle unless diverted to one of the workstations on the LAN. The *star topology* resembles a spider with the wires, or legs, connecting the workstations to the body. (See Figure 5–7.) For instance, the telephone company's central office concept is an example of a star configuration. A LAN can be interconnected by a specific topology, or it can be a hybrid of topologies combining, for example, the ring and star configurations. (See Figure 5–8.)

The following are the most popular networks.

Ethernet. This bus system, developed jointly by Xerox, Intel, and DEC, works with fiber-optic cables (fast, clear, expensive), coaxial cables (sturdy, insulated copper wire with limited signal range), and twisted-pair cables (commonly used for phone installations and subject to signal disruptions from nearby electrical emanations). The transmission speed for this system is 10 megabits per second (mbps).

Token Ring. IBM developed this star-and-ring topology, which uses a twisted-pair cable and operates at either 4 mbps or 16 mbps, depending on the version.

StarLAN. AT&T developed this star topology, which operates at 1 mbps and 10 mbps.

LAN Capabilities A LAN should be able to extend your firm's computer operations both immediately and in the future in the following ways:

- By letting those connected share disk storage, laser printers, and other peripheral resources.
- By allowing LAN users to transfer and share data, files, text, and documents.
- By giving you the ability to write, send, and receive electronic mail, as well as build and query group calendars.

Figure 5-6   Bus Topology

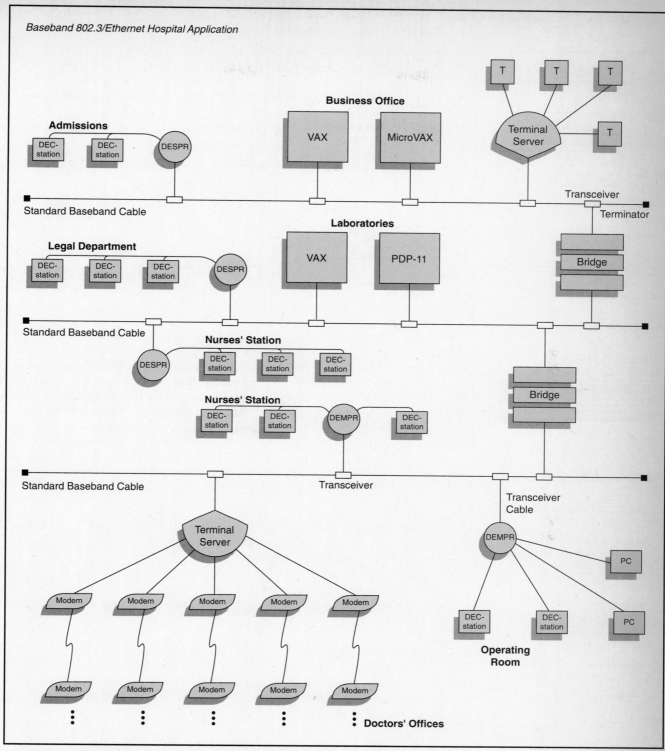

Source: Digital Equipment Corporation, Merrimack, NJ. Reprinted with permission.

Figure 5–7 Star Topology

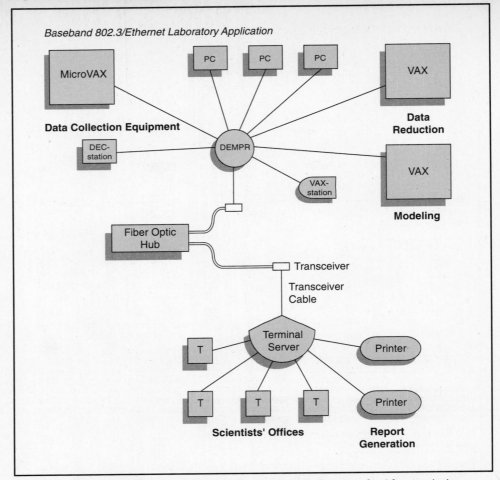

Baseband 802.3/Ethernet Laboratory Application

Source: Digital Equipment Corporation, Merrimack, NJ. Reprinted with permission.

- By permitting you to share software programs and to work as a team on a task involving use of common software such as word processing, a database, or desktop publishing.
- By allowing you to extend all of the above capabilities to other types of PCs or computers on a local level (i.e., you might want to link an IBM, or a clone, with an Apple Macintosh, or tie PCs or Macs into a minicomputer).

Choosing a LAN Now that you understand the basics of networking, here are some recommendations for selecting a LAN for your office. As with any other piece of office equipment, selecting the right network system for your firm will depend on what equipment you already have, what you want the system to do, how long you want it to operate, and your budget.

For example, if yours is a small law firm with only three to ten PCs, and you need only limited **file-server** (a computer that allows information to be used by more than one person simultaneously) and printer-sharing resources, consider the low-cost, twisted-pair wiring LANs that operate without network adapters. These include The Software Link's LANLink, Server Technology's EasyLAN, and IDEAssociate's IDEAshare.

On the other hand, if your firm needs more networking power, flexibility, and expandability, look into AT&T's StarLAN, Novell's NetWare, or Proteon's

Figure 5–8   Office LAN Incorporating Bus and Star Topologies

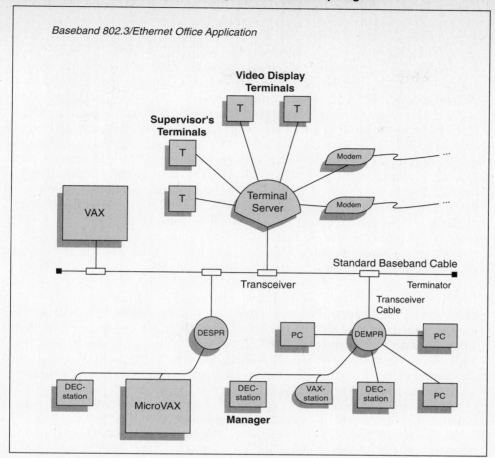

Source: Digital Equipment Corporation, Merrimack, NJ. Reprinted with permission.

ProNet. For large firms requiring corporatewide networking, IBM, DEC, and Wang Laboratories are just a few of the systems you will want to consider.

Whether you choose one of the blue-chip companies or work with a lesser-known vendor that might provide a better price-performance solution to your networking needs, your LAN will probably end up being a mix of products, vendors, cable installers, and consultants.

Scanners   Scanners, which have the ability to read pages of text or digitize photos into computer files through a process called *optical character recognition* (OCR), are becoming commonplace in many law offices. Some firms generate first-draft hard copy on an electronic typewriter and use the OCR to input the copy into the word processing system for editing, thus eliminating the need to have a word processor on every desk. Also, using word processing exclusively for text editing prevents the system from being slowed down with simple keyboarding procedures.

Office managers estimate that as much as 80 percent of a word processor's time is spent inputting information, and only 20 percent is spent editing and printing. Scanners can reduce the input time and free the word processor for other assignments, or, in some instances, scanners can reduce word processing personnel.

The three basic types of scanners are hand-held, sheetfed, and flatbed. *Hand-held* scanners are the least expensive and are designed for limited, specialized scanning needs such as adding artwork to desktop publishing documents.

Sheetfed scanners, which are currently priced from about $500 to $2,000, feature automatic document feeders similar to the ones on copiers. The types of material you can scan, however, are limited. For example, you cannot scan a page in a book with a sheetfed scanner.

Flatbed scanners range in price from about $1,000 to $10,000, and they let you scan anything—including books and magazines. Some models offer an optional automatic document feeder. All models offer high resolution and photographic quality output, the degree of which varies according to price and manufacturer.

Color scanning is still an infant in this market but is gaining in popularity as the technology continues to improve. One major drawback to color scanning is the enormous amount of memory it requires. In the future, experts believe this problem will be solved as more users switch to optical disk drives on the PCs, which have immense storage capacity.

With all they have to offer, scanners have earned their place in the efficient management of information in the law office.

Electronic Typewriters   Before you place an order for more PCs, take another look at your firm's information processing applications. You may find that a *screen-based electronic typewriter* (SBET) is more suitable to your needs. SBETs are high-end electronic typewriters (ETs) designed specifically for typing and word processing (WP). They are ideal for people who switch back and forth between word processing and typing tasks.

SBETs come in four types: personal word processors (PWPs), midsize systems, full-size typewriters, and combination ET/WP/PCs.

PWPs cannot handle lengthy documents and heavy workloads and are therefore geared toward students or home office use. Midsize SBETs are aimed at professional users and offices with low-to-medium work volume.

Full-size SBETs can handle heavy word processing, including documents of more than 50 pages; and the ET/WP/PC combination can handle that volume plus computing applications.

Ranging in price from about $400 to $3,000, all SBETs now incorporate screen-based WP software similar to mid-range PC programs. Most also have floppy disk drives. With the recent addition of spreadsheet and database software, stepped-up printers, and expansion boards, SBETs have become *the* answer to almost all secretarial applications and have eliminated the need to purchase more PCs in some offices.

How do you determine if an SBET is right for your needs? Ask yourself these questions:

- How many documents are worked on daily and how long is each?
- What proportion of the work is typing, word processing, or computing?
- Do you use a variety of paper, forms, and envelopes?
- Are graphics involved?
- What print speed do you need?
- What proportion of documents need to be saved and reused?
- Will your SBET have to interface to a laser printer or a network?
- Is your firm already standardized on WP software?

Your answers to these questions will help you make the right SBET choice. Here are some general guidelines to help you.

PWPs and midsize units are appropriate for lighter workloads, shorter documents, and limited WP need. Full-size SBETs are required for higher volumes of work and more extensive WP applications. But if you plan to network your unit or you are heavily involved in PC applications, the combination ET/WP/PC is best.

There is still a need for a typewriter or two in even the most sophisticated information management environments. SBETs are filling that need and taking their place as another shared office resource.

5–3 Law Office Management Support Software

In addition to software programs that can record billable hours, aid in legal research, or let you tap into a wealth of useful information, several other software programs are considered by some information managers to be the workhorses of today's law office.

Document Management Software

Document management software was created to manage the production, storage, retrieval, security, and backup of documents generated on a PC. When word processing was in its infancy, keeping track of documents was relatively simple. Many law firms used dedicated word processors such as Vydec and Lexitron, where documents were stored on diskettes. If someone wanted a copy of a document, they made a copy of the file and off they went. Because word processing was the exclusive domain of trained operators, document control was seldom an issue in those days.

But now, with a personal computer on every secretary's desk, it has become increasingly difficult, if not impossible, to know who worked on a document last and what changes may have been made. Lawyers who draft, revise, and edit their own work on a PC also contribute to this control problem.

Document management software offers several features to manage information more effectively, beginning with the use of header information that includes the name of the author of the document, the date, client information, and the type of document. Disciplined users of document management software find the advantages of taking the time to update the header far outweigh the few minutes required to enter the information. For example, here are some of the document management tools the software provides.

Tracking Versions When several people in the firm are making changes to the same large document, it is important that each person be working on the most recent version. Document management software allows you to keep track of various versions.

Managing Revisions With document management software you can keep useful documents intact instead of erasing each earlier version, thus allowing anyone to retrieve language from an earlier version or recreate the process of a heavily negotiated portion of a contract. (See Figure 5–2, p. 104.)

Backing Up Files created on a PC are automatically backed up to the central system with this software because it has the ability to store a second copy simultaneously.

Locking Documents When one person is working on a document, this software locks others out, thus eliminating the risk of loss of control. The latecomer is advised who is working on the document, however, so that normal work can continue.

Locating Documents Proliferating PCs have generated many documents and, occasionally, the need to find one of them. With header information such as author, date, subject, and client, document management software helps track down documents.

Archiving Automatically This software sets up a small database of information on each file. Therefore, it is possible to search that database for all memoranda and letters, or any other documents, more than a year old and have them automatically transferred to the archive files. Doing so frees up disk storage space on your computer.

Document management software allows anyone using the computer to know the whereabouts of documents as well as their provenance and pedigree.

Litigation Management Software

Litigation support software is a powerful tool for litigators and paralegals. It is a significant asset in pretrial case management as well as during the trial itself. The database can manage memos, letters, depositions, witnesses, exhibits, and other related material by providing rapid access to any data pertaining to the legal matter.

When integrated with a scanner, documents can be retrieved instantly and viewed in their entirety. For example, if you wanted to search your litigation database for all letters and memos written by Ronald Reagan, after May 1, 1985, addressed to John Poindexter, that contain in the text the phrase "arms deal" or "Iran Contra," in just a few seconds you could browse through images of the original letters including any notations penciled in the margins.

In addition, litigation support software can track a plaintiff's inventory of damages, including original cost and replacement cost; match invoices and documents to inventory items; and index and store exhibits.

One of the most common uses for litigation support software is to summarize depositions and provide for instant retrieval of pertinent information by date, subject, name, or occurrence. Complex litigation cases now require efficient management support software.

Calendar Software

Calendar software programs are designed to keep everyone in the firm up to date on the whereabouts of attorneys and paralegals, and the cases on which they are spending time. Calendar software also notes **statute of limitations** dates, the time fixed by law within which parties must take judicial action to enforce their rights. In addition, it also serves as a **tickler,** or reminder, of important dates, meetings, and deadlines. (See Figure 5–9.)

For example, tickler systems are routinely used in corporate work by attorneys and paralegals to note expiration dates of UCC filings, name reservations, and trademarks, as well as to note items to be included on the

Figure 5-9   Docket Calendar Software

Docket Calendar software lets you keep track of everyone's schedule. *Source:* Photo courtesy of CompuLaw, Ltd., Culver City, CA (1991). All rights reserved.

agenda of directors' and shareholders' meetings. Estate paralegals use the tickler to remind them of tax deadlines, trust distributions, and annual account filings.

One person, usually a paralegal, is responsible for maintaining the firm's diary and for seeing that it is distributed weekly throughout the firm. Computerized calendar systems are long-term and, in effect, provide the firm with a dual diary and reminder system that makes forgetting a deadline or appointment next to impossible.

The practice of law is just moving into the 21st century where the application of computer technology is concerned, and all indications are that clocks will not be turned back to a bygone era. Instead, as more people in the law office learn how computers and other electronic equipment can help them manage the practice more efficiently, no doubt there will be requests for more equipment, more software, and more applications.

5–4 Preventing Computer-Related Management Problems

As you might expect, along with the benefits of computers there are also some computer-related management problems. Awareness of some of these will help you prepare for handling them in the event they occur in your office.

Computer Viruses and Bugs

A computer **virus** is a program that replicates itself within the computer system. In the process, it uses up available memory and destroys existing data and programs. Although internal sabotage by a disgruntled employee is one way a virus can be introduced into a system, most viruses are introduced from outside the firm. One of the most publicized virus attacks occurred in 1987 when IBM was invaded by a virus that wished "Season's Greetings" to users. The virus attached itself to the distribution lists of every user who received it and half a million copies of the virus program quickly spread throughout IBM's worldwide electronic mail network, causing operations to come to a halt.

A **bug,** on the other hand, is a basic flaw in the initial design of the software program. And, as software programs become more complex, particularly those for the personal computer, the chances are dramatically increased that the thousands of strings of binary codes required to make up a program will end up with a bug in it. Software bugs come in several forms, such as simple errors committed at the time the program was written—the equivalent of forgetting to dot an *i* or cross a *t*. Or a bug can be the result of a more complicated interaction between two or more parts of a program that do not quite mesh. In 1989 Ashton-Tate, the publishers of dBASE IV, reported a $19.8 million quarterly loss attributed largely to bugs in the program.

There is one major difference between a virus and a bug. Viruses are intentionally caused and bugs are programming mistakes. There is not much you can do about a bug, except return the software to the manufacturer. But there are some precautions you can take to prevent a virus from infecting your computer system. Here are some of them.

- Draft and implement a comprehensive security policy that emphasizes safe computing methods and covers all computer operations. Include in this policy procedures for issuing and periodically changing access codes or passwords, and procedures for terminating or discharging employees who have access to the computer system. Make sure that networks are protected against unauthorized dial-ins from outside vendors or other personnel.
- Before using any off-the-shelf software, check to make sure the shrink-wrap packaging is intact. If the packaging has been removed, someone may have tampered with the program.
- Thoroughly test any new software on an isolated system before distributing it throughout your firm or installing it on a network.
- Check the directory information regularly, especially the file length and date of creation of your files. If you do not know why a file's date has been changed or why its length has changed, pull it out of use until you find out.

- Make backup copies of all new programs immediately after opening them and securely store the originals. In the event a virus appears on your backup copy, you still have the virus-free original.
- Limit the sharing of files and software programs, and be particularly wary of shareware programs downloaded from electronic bulletin boards. If you are hooked into any network, particularly an external network, your system is vulnerable to infection.

Legal and Ethical Considerations of Software Usage

The *Copyright Act of 1980* states that software programs are eligible for the same copyright protection as other forms of original creativity and expression. Furthermore, the act prescribes damages of $10,000 for each illegally duplicated copy of the software, and an additional $40,000 per copy if the copyright holder can prove that the copies were made intentionally.

Many firms have written policies that ban **piracy,** or the unauthorized copying of software, in an attempt to protect themselves in court, should the need arise, and to remind users of the substantial penalties involved with the intentional duplication of software. Other firms have negotiated a **site licensing agreement** with vendors, which allows them to duplicate a specified number of copies of the program for use in the law firm. A site license also eliminates the ethical issue of whether a duplicate copy can be made legally, and, since a site license usually is about 25 to 50 percent less expensive than buying the same number of individual copies, it offers a more cost-effective way of providing all workstations with copies of the software.

The Copyright Act of 1980 does permit the duplication of one backup copy of each off-the-shelf program. The problem, however, is that this backup copy can then become the source of many more copies. When Lotus Development Corporation sued Rixon Incorporated for $10 million over this issue, more people became aware of the serious ramifications involved with using pirated copies of computer software. The suit alleged that Rixon had made unauthorized copies of its Lotus 1-2-3 software and distributed them throughout the company. Without admitting any wrongdoing, Rixon paid an undisclosed amount to Lotus to settle the matter. Subsequently, other software companies began actively pursuing those firms that violate licensing agreements.

Everyone in your law office should be informed of the legal and ethical considerations of software use and the possible consequences should the Copyright Act be violated.

The Impact of Computers on Management of Support Staff

Automation technology has been gradually changing the way people work in law firms. But in just the past few years many firms have made significant changes in organizational structure, particularly in the administrative and paralegal areas. These changes are no doubt the result of improved programs and the introduction of the new generation of computers.

The emerging result of a computer-on-every-desk philosophy is a higher degree of specialization and often an accompanying need for more managerial roles. For example, word processing at secretarial desks has facilitated document production to such a degree that firms have been able to reduce secretarial staff through attorney sharing programs. Meanwhile, other tasks normally associated with the secretarial role, such as filing, photocopying, sending facsimiles, and preparing client bills, are being assigned to others. As a result, new administrative areas are developing, including Central Filing, Billing, and Office Services.

Many offices have formed their own in-house Training Department to ensure that employees are properly trained on computer equipment as well as in routine office procedures. In addition, the use of firm-specific software programs has required many firms to recruit and train their own pool of temporary workers and floaters. In these firms the manager of secretarial services works closely with the manager of the training department to coordinate and monitor the firm's daily support staff requirements.

Powerful and sophisticated computer programs require on-site management of information systems. MIS managers are often responsible for developing the firm's long-range technology plans as well as for supervising all computer operations and associated personnel, while the systems administrator is responsible for the day-to-day systems operations and maintenance. Larger firms might also employ in-house software and hardware specialists who work with users to develop databases for a specific attorney, for one area of specialization, or for purposes of practice management.

The impact of technology, however, is probably most evident at the paralegal level, with the advances in litigation support and computer-aided research being the most obvious. Computers now make it possible for paralegals to do much of the work previously done by lawyers. As a result, more than one litigation department has had to restructure its paralegal program to include positions for document clerk, paralegal trainee, paralegal, senior paralegal, and paralegal supervisor.

The transformations taking place at the support staff level are not always understood by the attorneys, even though they are aware that their dependency on a secretary to perform many functions has diminished. But all of these people, when properly supervised, can improve the profitability of the firm as well as practice management.

Coping with the Industrial Injury of the Information Age

While high technology has made many jobs in the law office easier, it has also afflicted countless numbers of workers with the industrial injury of the information age—**cumulative trauma disorder (CTD).** Cumulative trauma disorder is not a new phenomenon. However, until recently it was usually found only in manufacturing environments where hand and arm motions are repeated continuously. As automation has continued to reduce jobs to simpler tasks, and the pressure to increase productivity has cut into, or eliminated, rest periods, CTD is affecting more and more office workers.

Here is the problem. When you work on a computer, shoulder muscles are tight to support the arms and eye muscles remain rigidly focused on the screen. Each time you punch a key, the muscle running from the elbow through the forearm contracts. The muscle is attached to tendons that slide back in lubricated sheaths through the wrist to lift the fingers. The muscle relaxes, the tendons slide forward, and the finger pushes down.

In the days before computers, when a secretary used a typewriter, she (they were usually women) would periodically pause to roll out a finished page or insert a new one. There were many more hand and wrist motions involved with the typing process then. With computers, typists can move paragraphs and pages around without lifting a finger from the keyboard, and the result is a dramatic increase in the number of workers complaining of CTD. One company has estimated it will cost them over $500,000 in worker's compensation funds just to treat existing cases.

CTD problems range from swollen tendons and muscle spasms to severe nerve damage, or a combination of symptoms. CTD at its worst can result in carpal tunnel syndrome, a potentially crippling injury that often requires surgery. Here are some suggestions for preventing CTD problems in your office.

- Review workstations. Poorly designed furniture leads to bad posture, which can affect the back, the neck, and the spine, as well as arms, wrists, and hands. Chairs and keyboards that are too high or too low may force users to work with their hands bent in peculiar positions. Stiff keyboards may require too much effort to push the keys. Screens that are too high, too low, or too far away require the users to crane their necks for hours on end.
- Arm tendons should be stretched before and after long typing jobs, just as a runner stretches leg tendons before and after exercising.
- Build upper-body strength with weights. The ability of the neck, shoulders, and wrists to hold still for long periods is related to their strength.
- Take regular breaks. While there is no consensus among experts as to how often and how long work breaks should be, there is agreement that breaks are necessary, no matter how well-designed the workstation is. Some doctors recommend a 15-minute break every two hours, while others suggest five minutes every hour and a minute or two on the half hour. Some states have laws mandating work breaks.
- When taking a break, allow focusing eye muscles to get a rest by looking at distant objects. Stand up and move around. Return phone calls or perform other tasks.
- Upon returning from vacation, or a leave of absence, you will probably be deconditioned and will need time to get back into typing gradually, just as a runner who has not been exercising needs to start with short distances and work up to longer ones.

Eight Problems a Computer Cannot Solve

Because computer technology has greatly enlarged the scope of work performed by both support staff and attorneys in today's law offices, a better understanding is required on everyone's part as to what they can and cannot do.

Now that you have a better understanding of how to manage information effectively in your law office by using computers, consider eight problems that computers cannot solve.

1. *A computer will not solve vague, poorly defined problems.* You have to understand exactly what the problem is that you want the computer to solve. This requires thinking about and planning what you want the computer to do.

2. *A computer will not save you money by eliminating staff.* Instead, a computer will create new ways of doing things and new jobs.

3. *A computer will not correct errors in your manual procedures.* Since automation begins with the direct transfer of data from a manual system to the computerized system, if you put garbage in, you will get garbage out—commonly called GIGO by computer people.

4. *A computer will not be able to perform sophisticated functions such as forecasting or trend analysis until quite a few years after the system is up and running.* Before you can even think about getting your computer to perform sophisticated functions, you must spend an enormous amount of time keying information into the system. It is best to tackle only one area at a time to get the most from your investment. Like people, the computer must walk before it can run.

5. *A computer will not solve problems that call for a subjective evaluation.* Computers cannot think—but eventually they might. At the present time, though, any

decision that requires qualitative input is not appropriate for computerization. For example, the final decision to hire one person over another is arrived at by considering a broad range of personnel factors and issues that are difficult to quantify.

6. A computer will not solve all of your scheduling problems. Even with automated calendaring, litigation support systems, and gargantuan databases, there will still be scheduling problems. Automation can assist you in executing well-developed plans, but plans change frequently in the dynamic law office environment.

7. A computer's software will not take kindly to changes made by amateurs. Don't even try it. If you do not end up completely trashing the program, remember that manufacturers refuse to service programs that have been tampered with.

8. A computer will not always be right. While you might think your computer is infallible, systems can and do make errors. Faulty circuitry, a program with bugs, or a disk going bad can produce mistakes that often go undetected—for a time. Most systems function so flawlessly you tend to stop checking up on them. Do not allow yourself to fall into the trap of complacency and dependency.

Now, and into the future, one of the major challenges facing law office managers will be how to integrate new technology into the workplace in order to increase productivity while simultaneously improving employee morale and job satisfaction in a diverse work force. Law office managers will need to make a real effort to keep up with advances in computer technology and to be prepared to manage employees who may know far more about the technology than the boss.

SUMMARY

5–1

Microchip technology, first introduced in the hand-held calculator, made possible the proliferation of microcomputers, or PCs. The three main components of PC hardware are the CPU, or the brains of the computer, where information is stored in memory (expressed as bytes) on disks; the input devices of a keyboard, modem, and mouse; and the output devices, a video monitor and printer. The disk operating system is the software program that manages the operation of the PC through a library of preprogrammed commands. Information stored in memory can be lost in the event of an electrical power disturbance, but power protection devices can be used to block or reduce these potential problems.

5–2

Managers can take steps to keep their information management budgets from getting out of line. The first step is to determine who is going to use the system. The second step is to find out what the users want the system to do and to choose the appropriate software. After software is selected, step three involves the selection of hardware. Step four is to select vendors who will be responsive to the firm's needs by providing support and training throughout installation and afterwards. Step five involves exploring all the options available to expand and enhance your basic system, including a local area network, OCR scanners, and screen-based electronic typewriters.

5–3

Information management systems do not operate on hardware alone. Different types of software programs, such as document management software, allow law firms to obtain maximum efficiency by providing tools for tracking and managing document revisions, as well as by locating and locking documents in use. Litigation support software allows litigators and paralegals to locate and retrieve documents, exhibits, and other materials related to a legal matter, as well as to track and inventory plaintiff's damages. Calendar software provides the entire firm with a daily and long-term reminder of important dates and events. These and other software programs help to manage the information flowing through today's law firms.

5–4

The proliferation of computers brings new management problems to the law firm. Computer viruses—intentionally caused programs that replicate themselves within the computer, taking up available memory and destroying existing data and programs in the process—are usually an external problem occurring on networked systems. A bug, on the other hand, is a software programming mistake, which may go undetected for a period of time. Neither of these occurrences is frequent, but both can wreak havoc with your system. Other management problems can occur when software is illegally copied and passed around for use within the firm. Software is protected by copyright laws, and in the absence of a licensing agreement with the manufacturer, it is illegal to make copies of programs. Cumulative trauma disorder and carpal tunnel syndrome are health problems related to computer usage. Managers should encourage users to take regular breaks and check regularly for signs of these industrial injuries of the information age. Computers should not be expected to solve all of the information management problems in the law office. They will, however, increase productivity and improve employee morale and job satisfaction when properly integrated into the workplace.

REVIEW

Key Terms

backup
bit
bug
byte
central processing unit (CPU)
cumulative trauma disorder (CTD)
cursor
diskette
file-server
gigabyte
hard disk
K
kilobyte
megabyte
memory
microchip
modem
mouse
operating system
peripherals
piracy
RAM
ROM
site licensing agreement
statute of limitations
tickler
topology
turnkey system
virus

Questions for Review and Discussion

1. What are the main components of a computer system?
2. Define ROM and RAM.
3. How much memory can be stored on a megabyte? On a gigabyte?
4. Printers are categorized into two groups. What are they? Give examples of each.
5. What is the function of the disk operating system?
6. What are five steps in cost-effective information management?
7. Describe the three common LAN topologies.
8. A scanner and SBET can augment an automated office system. How?
9. There are three basic types of management support software for attorneys and paralegals. Describe them and their functions.
10. What is the difference between a computer virus and a bug?
11. When might you legally copy software?
12. What can you do to prevent CTD and carpal tunnel syndrome?

Activities

1. Contact two or three software companies that design programs specifically for the legal profession. Ask them for brochures and product information to share with the class; or ask them to come and present a demonstration of their products.
2. Ask a computer consultant to discuss with the class the advantages and disadvantages of networking a computer system.
3. Invite to class an attorney who specializes in copyright law to discuss the Copyright Act of 1980 and its implications in software management.
4. Organize a field trip to a local computer hardware vendor for the purpose of viewing types of input and output devices, scanners, printers and screen-based electronic typewriters.

CHAPTER 6 Basic Finance for the Law Office Manager

OUTLINE

6–1 Basic Accounting Principles
    Principle One: Entity
    Principle Two: Profit
    Principle Three: Time
    Principle Four: Profits, Property, Owners' Interest, and Debt (PPOD)
    Principle Five: Income
    Principle Six: Expense
    The Accounting Cycle
6–2 How to Read Financial Statements
    What Kind of Information Should You Track?
    How Do You Organize the Information?
    How to Interpret the Basic Financial Statements
6–3 How to Develop Budgets
    Partner Compensation
    Partner Capital
    Billing Rates
    Steps in Preparing Budgets
6–4 Cash Flow Management
    Recognizing Cash Flow Problems
    Typical Responses to Cash Flow Problems
    Components of Cash Flow Management

COMMENTARY

By now you know that much of your position as Dunn & Sweeney's law office manager involves money—keeping track of money coming into the firm from fees and money going out of the firm to pay salaries, overhead, and expenses. However, you still do not feel too confident in your response when a partner asks, "How are we doing?" Also, you are concerned that while the firm is showing a profit on its financial statements, there is no excess balance in the checking account. How is it possible to show a profit and not have enough money to pay the bills?

OBJECTIVES

In Chapter 5 you learned that managing information in the law office requires, in addition to a basic knowledge of how computers work, the ability to assess and select appropriate software and hardware and an awareness of typical computer-related management problems and solutions. After studying this chapter, you will be able to:

1. Discuss the basic principles of accounting.
2. Define PPOD and ALPIE.
3. Explain the difference between the balance sheet and the income statement.
4. Define the terms *income* and *expense* for accounting purposes.
5. Explain the purpose of a trust account.
6. List the steps in the accounting cycle.
7. Explain the difference between gross profit and net profit.
8. Compute the liquidity ratios, the average collection period, and a profitability ratio.
9. Develop an income budget, the annual billing and collection budget, a monthly budget, a net income budget, and a cash flow budget.
10. Discuss the components of cash flow management.

6–1 Basic Accounting Principles

You do not need to be a certified public accountant (CPA) to understand basic accounting principles. To say that these basic principles are inherent is a gross overgeneralization, but it is safe to assume that you have achieved a certain level of understanding of accounting fundamentals by this time, even if your formal education has not included accounting.

Before we get into the principles of accounting, and to test your existing understanding of the basic accounting concepts, review the following information about Dunn's and Sweeney's first month together as partners and be prepared to answer these accounting questions:

1. How much **profit** (excess of money earned over total expenses) did the firm make during the month?
2. How much **property** (anything of value owned by the firm—cash, equipment, buildings, or anything with a market value) did the firm have at the end of January?
3. What was the value of the **owners' interest** (expressed in dollars) at the end of January? Owners' interest means the owners' original capital contribution to start the firm *plus* profit. Owners' interest is also called owners' equity or capital.
4. How much **debt** did the firm owe at the end of the period? Debts are the claims of creditors, such as banks, against property of the firm.

Alfred A. Dunn and Richard J. Sweeney had been practicing law for a few years when they decided to form a partnership beginning on January 2. They each took $7,500 from their personal bank accounts and opened a business bank account. Then they went to look for office space to rent. No strangers to good luck, they immediately found office space in a great location and paid three months' rent in advance, or $3,000, from their partnership account. Next they went to the phone company and paid $1,200 to lease telephones and connect the service. Their next stop was for office supplies, stationery, and business cards, which came to $800.

The next day their loan for $20,000 was approved by First City Bank and they signed a note payable in one year to the bank. The money was deposited into the business account. That afternoon they leased office equipment and furniture for $5,000 and paid for it with a check drawn on the business account. Their wives volunteered to be secretaries until they could afford to hire others.

By January 5 Dunn and Sweeney had settled into their offices and received their first clients. Their good luck prevailed, and by the end of the month they had generated $10,000 in fees from clients.

Figure 6–1   PPOD Worksheet

DUNN & SWEENEY
Profit Calculation for January

Fee income was: $_____

Rent was: $_____

Telephone and office supplies were: $_____

Office equipment and furniture were: $_____

Total expenses were: $_____

Profit for January was: $_____

DUNN & SWEENEY
Operating Results as of January 31

Fee income was: $_____

Profit was: $_____

Owners' interest was: $_____

Debt was: $_____

DUNN & SWEENEY
Property and Claims Against Property

Property		Claims Against Property	
Cash in bank	$_____	Debt owned bank	$_____
		D&S profit for Jan.	$_____
		D&S investment	$_____
Total property	$_____	Total claims against property	$_____

The acronym PPOD—profits, property, owners' interest, and debt—represents the four accounting variables that hold your answer to Dunn & Sweeney's operating results in January. You can use any method you like to calculate the amounts necessary to answer the PPOD questions. Record your answers on the worksheet provided in Figure 6–1.

The purpose of using the worksheet in Figure 6–1 is to illustrate that the basic principles of accounting are common knowledge. To help you further understand accounting concepts, the following basic principles provide definitions, methods, and practices based on accounting fundamentals. It is important to understand each principle as it is presented, since later concepts will not make sense if you do not understand the earlier ones.

Principle One: Entity

In accounting each **entity,** or business, has its own set of financial transactions and records. Law firms are business entities and may be organized as a **sole proprietorship,** owned by one person, a **partnership,** owned by two or more persons, or a **professional corporation,** owned by one or more attorneys with special statutory protection for the owners against debt and some types of liabilities. A law firm, for example, could be composed of one or more partnerships and one or more professional corporations with a separate set of accounting records kept for each entity. The major differences between a partnership and a corporation are how profits and losses are treated from an accounting perspective and the extent of personal liability for the partners or owners.

Principle Two: Profit

All organizations strive to make a profit, except some nonprofit organizations such as charities. **Gross profit** is the difference between fee income and the costs of producing that income, such as salaries for attorneys, paralegals, secretaries, and other overhead expenses. **Net profit** is the difference between gross profit and any other expenses such as taxes. The term **bottom line** is often used to refer to net profit because it reflects any money remaining after taxes and all other expenses have been paid and because the amount appears at the bottom of the income statement.

Principle Three: Time

Because the financial activity of a business entity is more easily evaluated if it is divided into time periods, businesses operate on a **fiscal year,** a 12-month period usually running from January 1 to December 31. Some entities, however, use other 12-month periods. For example, July 1 to June 30 or October 1 to September 30 are noncalendar fiscal years.

Fiscal years are usually further divided into quarters to help management make better decisions. For instance, if the period just passed had a loss or lower than expected profits, immediate steps can be taken to make corrections. Also, by grouping financial information into periods, you can compare time periods against each other to see how the business is doing.

At the end of the accounting period, the books are **closed**—no more transactions will occur in that period. The information is then summarized and accounting statements are prepared. The purpose of closing the books is to answer the PPOD questions. The PPOD answers are given in two main statements like those illustrated in Figure 6–1.

The Balance Sheet   One of the statements, the **balance sheet,** shows property, debts, owners' interest (sometimes called owners' equity), and profits. Profits always belong to the owners. Part of the summary you prepared for Dunn & Sweeney under the heading "Property and Claims Against Property" (Figure 6–1) is a balance sheet. Both the owners' investment and profit for January are shown.

Why is this statement called a balance sheet? It is called a balance sheet because property held is *always* equal to claims against the property. Since all property is claimed either by the owners or by creditors, the statement is in balance.

The Income Statement   The other accounting statement in which you will be particularly interested is the **income statement.** It shows the firm's income minus all expenses for the period, as well as the profit or loss for the period. The portion of the worksheet in Figure 6-1 called "Profit Calculation for January" is an income statement.

Profits of the business belong to the owners and are therefore a part of the owners' claims (interests) on the balance sheet. In most situations owners have two types of claims or interests in the business. One is a claim for their initial capital contribution (the monies Dunn and Sweeney took from their personal accounts to start the business account) and the second claim is for any profits the business has earned but have not been paid to the owners.

Principle Four: Profits, Property, Owners' Interest, and Debt (PPOD)

Owners, managers, lenders, and tax agencies want the PPOD answers. Accounting is the only way to provide any of them with the information they want. Let's review PPOD.

Profit   Profit is the excess of income after expenses over a given period of time. $I - E = P$ is the equation to express profit. If expenses exceed income, the result is a loss.

Property   Anything of value owned by the firm is considered property. Included in this category would be cash, accounts receivable, office equipment that the firm purchased, and the office building it owns. Property is referred to as **assets** in accounting.

Cash is the only asset Dunn & Sweeney have at the moment. Their clients all paid them immediately upon presentation of a statement (they really are two lucky attorneys) and they leased furniture, equipment, and office space. But what would happen if they decided to buy the office building for $250,000 and while they own it, its value increases to $500,000? Would the increased value be reflected on the balance sheet? No.

In accounting, *historical cost* or *original cost method* is used for reporting the value of almost all assets, which means that the balance sheet is often inaccurate in terms of current market values. By ignoring increases in the market value of assets, the historical cost method also reflects the *principle of conservatism* which is, simply stated, to "never anticipate profits but always show losses as soon as they are reasonably certain." Although this can be misleading to anyone who has no background in accounting, it is necessary to have a standard method of reporting cost, and the historical cost method is the one adopted by accounting professionals.

Property, or assets, is usually divided on the balance sheet into current assets and fixed assets. **Current assets** include cash or property expected to be changed into cash or used up within a year. **Accounts receivable,** a charge account owed by clients that the firm can collect, and small amounts of office supplies such as paper and envelopes would be included in current assets but typically are not in law firms. (A discussion follows later in this chapter on cash accounting and the treatment of accounts receivable in service businesses.) **Fixed assets** are those intended to be used for more than one year. These would include buildings, equipment, and the law library.

Owners' Interest   Owners' interest, as you will recall, is also called capital, proprietorship, owners' claims against assets, or owners' equity. All the terms mean the same thing. You will also recall that all business property is claimed by two classes of claimants—creditors and owners. By law, creditors' claims are considered to be more important than owners' claims. That means that creditors are to be paid before the owners are paid. Why? Creditors *lend* money or sell goods on credit to law firms, and the firm has a duty to its creditors to pay back the value loaned.

Equity is another accounting term with more than one meaning. When you have equity in your home, for example, you are referring to the present market value of the house less any outstanding mortgage debt. Owners' equity, in business accounting terms, is the difference between historical cost and present debt. Market increases are ignored until the asset is sold.

Debt   Business debts are also called **liabilities.** Some common forms of liabilities are loans to banks and **accounts payable,** monies owned by the firm to suppliers of goods and services. Debts are divided for balance sheet purposes into short term debt, or **current liabilities,** which are to be paid in less than one year, and long term debt, or **fixed liabilities,** which are to be paid in more than one year.

PPOD   What do the attorneys really want to know when they ask, "How are we doing?" They usually want an answer to only one of the Ps and the D—property (cash) and debt—because these are the two main factors influencing cash flow. The other balance sheet items are not as important in the day-to-day operation of the firm but are more critical on a quarterly or annual basis.

Accounting and the law are very similar in at least one respect—they are both confusing. Many of the terms used refer to the same thing, and some terms have multiple meanings. A review of the material presented to this point is suggested before you continue with the next principle.

Principle Five: Income

In accounting **income** means something of value that has been received by the firm in return for services provided to clients. The valuable thing received is always an asset, usually cash or an account receivable. However, law firms have been given the title to real property, recreational vehicles, automobiles, and boats in return for services rendered. It is important to note that in accounting income is neither cash nor other property. It is merely an entry in the books, or an accounting recognition, showing that fees have been earned by providing services to clients. It is easy to confuse income with property. To clarify, remember that to be recognized as income the new asset, usually cash, must be *earned* by the firm.

The terms *sales* and *revenues* are frequently used to imply the receipt of earned assets. Referring again to Figure 6–1 and the attendant information, the partnership received assets that were not earned. These were in the form of Dunn and Sweeney's capital contributions from their own savings accounts and cash received from the bank loan. Since these two receipts of assets were not earned in exchange for services provided to clients of the partnership, they were not reflected as income. Some people use the word *earnings* to mean profits, but to an accounting professional, earnings include only earned revenues, and profit is net income.

To illustrate further, suppose a Mr. Jack T. Ripper hears that Mr. Dunn has an outstanding reputation among lawyers in the community. In anticipation of future legal problems Mr. Ripper retains Dunn & Sweeney to represent him. The firm has a policy of requiring a retainer fee in the sum of $10,000 for any new clients who are not personally known by any of the partners. Mr. Ripper brings in a cashier's check for $10,000 made payable to Dunn & Sweeney. How should Mr. Ripper's deposit for future services be handled on Dunn & Sweeney's books?

To answer this question, it is helpful to know about another accounting principle called the *principle of truth and balance (TAB)*. This accounting premise defines truth as an accurate reflection of the events of the transaction, and balance means that at least two accounts in the books must be changed in the same amount with each transaction. An example of balance is demonstrated in Figure 6–1, where the statement of property and claims against property (the balance sheet) were equal.

Truth, in accounting terms, requires full disclosure. The legal requirements for truth in reporting financial information are high because accounting statements are relied upon by lenders, creditors, investors, and tax authorities. So high are the legal requirements for truth in accounting that misstatements may result in actionable fraud, be considered a criminal offense, or constitute the basis for a civil lawsuit.

What should Dunn & Sweeney do with monies received but not earned? They should deposit them into the clients' **trust account,** an account set up for the purpose of depositing monies being held by one party for the benefit of another. Sums are then transferred to the firm's **operating account,** the one used for day-to-day transactions, when they have been earned. Law firms always have at least one trust account into which sums belonging to the clients are deposited for safekeeping. Monies held in trust actually belong to the client. Any sums remaining after the close of the client's legal matter must be returned to the client. State and local bar associations usually have guidelines for establishing and maintaining client trust accounts. Check with both your state and local bar associations to make sure you are in compliance with their guidelines.

All organizations that are purely service oriented (including law firms) use the *cash accounting method* to report income. This means that the firm does not recognize revenues until the cash is received and deposited into its own bank account. In other words, accounts receivable are not counted as an asset of the firm even though the fees have been earned.

Cash accounting allows you to use net operating cash flow to measure performance, which is important for law firms. It keeps the firm from overextending itself based upon the expectation of future income from accounts receivable. Many law firms have a high number of uncollectable accounts.

In addition to allowing you to measure performance based on net cash flow, another reason for using cash accounting is that it saves the firm money in taxes. With the cash method, taxes are paid only on income received. The other most common accounting method, the accrual method, includes accounts receivable when reporting income. In so doing, the firm would be paying income taxes on income not received.

Principle Six: Expense

In accounting **expense** is a reflection that assets have been used up in the process of, or for the purpose of, earning income. Most business expenses are obvious. Rent payments, staff salaries, and insurance premiums are expended in the process of earning income for the firm.

Some people confuse expense with liability because both denote something undesirable. However, in accounting they are not the same thing. Expense is *not* a liability. It is a bookkeeping entry indicating that property, usually in the form of cash, has been expended in the effort to earn income. For this reason accounts payable are expense items, not liabilities.

When is an expenditure not an expense? When it becomes an asset. For example, if Dunn and Sweeney decide to buy some land for $250,000, this is not an expense. Land is not used up, nor does it wear out through use. Instead of being an expense, this expenditure is considered a fixed investment in an asset because it is permanent. Therefore, the purchase price is not an expense. However, if Dunn and Sweeney decided to put a building on their land, and they were using pure cash accounting, the costs associated with putting up the building would be recognized as expenses at the time the expenditure of cash was made, even though the building will last for a long time.

Another example of an expenditure that is not an expense is when Dunn and Sweeney decide to buy computers for the firm. Even though office machines wear out as they are used, at the time of purchase they are intended to be used for more than one year and therefore are a fixed asset. However, as the equipment wears out with use its value declines. Since the definition of expense is the using up of assets to earn income, the cost associated with using up the asset is estimated, and only that cost is considered an expense. This practice of gradually writing off the cost of an asset as it is used up is called **depreciation.**

This chapter is not intended to take the place of courses in accounting, nor is it intended to replace the services of an accountant. It is merely intended to provide you with a basic understanding of accounting principles.

In summary, the six basic accounting principles are the following:

1. Entity
2. Profit
3. Time
4. Profits, property, owners' interest, and debt (PPOD)
5. Income
6. Expense

The Accounting Cycle

Accounting, like law, has its own language. Some accounting terms were presented in the preceding discussion of accounting principles. The terms presented here describe the bookkeeping routine known as the **accounting cycle.**

Bookkeeping   The process of recording, either by hand or with a computer, each financial transaction and organizing the information to be able to answer the PPOD questions is called **bookkeeping.** The books in which these transactions are recorded are the journal and the ledger.

The Journal   The book in which each transaction is written in chronological sequence to become a financial diary of the law firm is called the **journal.** To maintain a balance in the journal, each transaction requires at least two entries—a debit and a credit—so that assets always equal liabilities.

The Double Entry Requirement   **Double entry** bookkeeping requires at least two entries for each accounting transaction. In the journal each account that is affected by the transaction will be increased (debited) or decreased (credited). For example, when you purchase a typewriter for the office, the cash account is increased and the office equipment expense account is decreased.

The Ledger   The **ledger** has all the same information as the journal except it is sorted by account instead of by date. The process of copying journal entries into the ledger is called **posting.** Unlike the journal, the ledger contains all the *ALPIE* accounts (an acronym for the equation *Assets = Liabilities + Proprietorship* (owners' interest) + *Income − Expense*), the combined balances of which present a financial snapshot of the firm for the stated period.

The Trial Balance   In order to test the accounting equation to see that both sides balance, the bookkeeper prepares a **trial balance** after calculating the individual account balances for the period. If the equation does not balance, an error has been made either in entering a transaction or in addition or subtraction. Bookkeeping errors must be corrected at this point.

Closing Income and Expense Accounts   **Closing the books** is the process of giving zero balances to the income and expense accounts at the end of the fiscal year by transferring profit or loss to the proprietorship account. Only income and expense accounts (income statement accounts) are closed. The balance sheet accounts (assets, liabilities, and proprietorship) are not closed.

Statement Preparation   Preparing the income and expense statement and the balance sheet are the last steps in the accounting process. This means that the assets, liabilities, proprietorship, and profit information is put on the balance sheet statement and the income, expense, and profit information is put on the income statement. Together these statements put ALPIE in several formats to provide answers to the PPOD questions.

To summarize, here is the accounting cycle simplified:

1. Journal—a double-entry, chronological diary of transactions
2. Post—sorting journal entries into ledger accounts to form ALPIE
3. Trial balance—a chance to correct errors in entries or arithmetic
4. Close the books—giving income and expense accounts a zero balance and transferring profit (or loss) to the proprietorship accounts
5. Prepare statements—putting the information into the income statement and balance sheet form to answer the PPOD questions

The preceding discussion of the basic accounting principles and the accounting equation is summarized here for clarity and review of the process.

1. The accounting process, simplified, is the increasing and decreasing of individual accounts to reflect the principle of truth and balance.
2. The accounting equation is Assets = Liabilities + Proprietorship + Income − Expenses, or ALPIE.
3. The books, which contain identical information, are kept in two places: the journal sorts the information by date, and the ledger sorts the information by account.
4. Income and expense accounts are closed at the end of each accounting period in order to determine profits (or losses).

5. The accounting cycle is the process of recording information in the journal and ledger, closing the income and expense accounts, and preparing the income statement and balance sheet.

Accounting methods are used to measure the effectiveness of the entire law firm, or parts of it. For example, the litigation department and the corporate department could be set up as individual profit centers that are measured for profitability as units within the firm. Establishing individual profit centers within the firm can lead to more efficient management and higher overall profits by identifying, and reducing or eliminating, those less efficient departments that are being subsidized by the more efficient ones.

Accounting records are intended to be an arithmetical diary of events that show the financial condition of the law firm at any given moment. The managing partner(s) and the office manager are ultimately accountable for the financial condition of the law firm. Because of this accountability, it is important to point out the defects of the accounting process.

While accounting will identify, measure, record, and communicate financial information about an economic unit, accounting will not show the current market value of assets owned by the firm or the current value of an owner's equity. Accounting does not show all significant events that occur during the life of the firm—only those that affect the accounting equation. For example, the accounting process itself does not show the results of market research or internal changes in management, both of which may be critical to the firm's success. Further, because accounting is always done after the fact, it is never a truly accurate statement of the firm's financial condition. The balance sheet is always out of date when issued because the very next transaction changes the previous information. The value of accounting, therefore, is in its ability to show the economic progress of the firm over time and to provide information on which decisions can be made.

6–2   How to Read Financial Statements

On a daily basis a law office manager does not need to be informed about each bookkeeping transaction. The office manager does, however, need to be routinely informed about some key financial data. In very small law firms quarterly financial reports might be sufficient, whereas others will require monthly statements. The frequency with which financial reports are monitored is largely dependent upon how much money is flowing into and out of the firm.

What Kind of Information Should You Track?

Most managers are very interested in the amount of revenue coming into the firm. It is from revenue receipts that expenses, including salaries, are paid. Close monitoring of accounts receivable, then, would be a common occurrence in most firms. Managing partners and office managers often require weekly, if not daily, reports of income received.

Both managers and attorneys will no doubt be interested in reports of billable time, nonbillable time, and time spent on business development. Some firms might also be interested in tracking overtime hours or the productivity of individuals. In other words, each firm is unique in its financial report requirements. However, all managers and attorneys are interested in monitoring cash flow and in being able to compare one period's performance against another. This is where the financial statements are particularly helpful.

How Do You Organize the Information?

Once you determine what financial information you want to track and how often you are going to require reports, the next consideration is the form in which you will be able to effectively present the information to trigger action.

Raw numbers, such as total income or billable hours, on their own are often difficult to interpret. However, when the same information is presented as a percentage or ratio, most people are quickly able to make sense of it.

How to Interpret the Basic Financial Statements

The real value of financial statements is in their ability to help you predict the firm's future as well as to serve as a starting point for planning future actions. Financial ratios show the relationships among the various financial statement accounts by putting the numbers into perspective. For example, law firm A might have $1,567,878 of debt and annual interest charges of $195,985, while law firm B's debt is $10,767,983 and its interest charges are $1,432,142. The true burden of these debts and the firms' ability to repay them can only be ascertained by comparing the ratio of each firm's debt to its assets and its interest charges to the income available for payment of interest.

For most law office management purposes, ratios can be categorized into three groups: (1) liquidity ratios, (2) asset management ratios, and (3) profitability ratios.

Liquidity Ratios Law office managers and attorneys are concerned about one very important question: Will the firm be able to pay its debts as they come due? This question can be answered by relating the amount of cash and other current assets to the current obligations. There are two commonly used liquidity ratios that do this.

The firm's **current ratio** is computed by dividing current assets by current liabilities. Some of these numbers are found on the firm's balance sheet. For ratio analysis purposes, current assets normally include cash, marketable securities (the firm may have invested some of its profits), accounts receivable (only include those you are reasonably sure will be collected—not over 90 days old), and inventories (the estimated value of cases coming up for trial or settlement within six or twelve months). Current liabilities include accounts payable, short-term notes payable and any current payments due on long-term debt, accrued income taxes, and any other accrued expenses (usually compensation owed to partners).

If a firm is headed for financial difficulty it begins paying its bills slowly and building up bank loans. When current liabilities are rising faster than current assets, the current ratio will fall. This could mean trouble. The current ratio is the most commonly used measure of a firm's ability to pay its short-term obligations. To be useful, ratios are measured against the performance of other law firms. Ratio information is found in several resource reference guides at public libraries and business school libraries. One of the most reliable sources of this information is through your local commercial bank. Most commercial banks use an industry ratio guide published annually by Robert Morris Associates which contains information on law firms under the legal services category bearing Standard Industrial Code (SIC) #8111.

The current ratio calculation for Dunn & Sweeney at year-end 19xx is shown below.

$$\text{Current ratio} = \frac{\text{Current assets}}{\text{Current liabilities}} = \frac{\$700,000}{\$300,000} = 2.3 \text{ times}$$

$$\text{Industry average} = 2.5 \text{ times}$$

Dunn & Sweeney's current ratio is slightly below the industry average, but not low enough to cause concern. Since most of the firm's current assets could be converted to cash in the near future, it is highly probable they could be liquidated at close to their stated value, and the firm could pay off their creditors in full.

When using industry ratios, keep in mind that there are some well-managed firms that will be above the industry average figures and some other good firms that will be below it. However, if your firm's ratios deviate greatly from the industry average figures, this is a signal that further analysis is in order to find out why.

In addition to comparing your ratios with the industry averages, you will also want to compare them against your own previous years' ratios to determine whether the *trend* is upward or downward. Analyzing the trend, or determining why the numbers are going up or down, is one of the most useful financial tools to help you in future planning.

The second liquidity ratio is the **quick ratio,** sometimes called the acid test. The quick ratio is calculated by deducting inventory from current assets and dividing the remainder by current liabilities. Inventories, the backlog of cases currently pending, are the least liquid of the firm's assets. You might also consider deducting from current assets any of the accounts receivable of which you are uncertain about collecting. Doing so will give you a more accurate measure of the firm's ability to pay off its short-term obligations. This is the calculation for determining the quick ratio.

$$\frac{\text{Quick}}{\text{ratio}} = \frac{\text{Current assets} - \text{Inventory} - \text{Marginal A/R}}{\text{Current liabilities}} = \frac{\$400,000}{\$300,000} = 1.3 \text{ times}$$

$$\text{Industry average} = 2.1 \text{ times}$$

Dunn & Sweeney's quick ratio is considerably lower than the industry average, which could mean that too much emphasis is being placed on cases in inventory (which would not be generating current income), or that there are too many accounts with uncertain collectability, or that the firm is spending too much, or a combination of all of these. In any event, because of the disparity between the firm's quick ratio and the industry average, further investigation is indicated.

Asset Management Ratios   These ratios measure how effectively the firm manages its assets. The primary asset management tool with which you need to be familiar is determining how to calculate the number of days before a receivable is paid.

The firm's **average collection period** is the length of time that the firm must wait after sending a statement to receive payment. It is calculated by using the formula below:

$$\frac{\text{Average collection}}{\text{period (ACP)}} = \frac{\text{Average receivables [\$350,000]}}{\text{Annual fees/360 [\$3,000,000/360]}} = \frac{\$350,000}{\$8333} = 42 \text{ days}$$

$$\text{Industry average} = 57 \text{ days}$$

To calculate the average receivables number in the formula, add the receivables at the beginning of the year to the amount outstanding at year's end and divide by 2 [(beginning + ending)/2]. The annual fees figure would be the amount of total income received plus the amount of receivables outstanding at year's end, which is then divided by 360. Note that the financial community generally uses 360 rather than 365 as the number of days in the year for purposes such as these.

Here is another method for calculating the average collection period using a shorter time period than one year.

$$ACP = \frac{\text{Accounts receivable} \times 91 \text{ days (3 months)}}{\text{Fee billings last 3 months}}$$

Even though Dunn & Sweeney's average collection period of 42 days is less than the industry average, if the firm's payment terms call for payment upon presentation or within 30 days, the 42-day collection period indicates that the average client is not paying the firm's bills on time. If the trend in collection is rising and the firm's credit policy has not changed, this information would suggest taking steps to expedite the collection of accounts receivable.

Profitability Ratios Profitability is the net result of many management policies and decisions. When viewed together with the liquidity and asset management ratios, the profitability ratios provide another reflection of how the firm is operating.

The firm's **profit margin on income** (fees) is computed by dividing gross profit by total income from fees. The profit margin on income gives the profit per dollar of income and is stated as a percentage.

$$\text{Profit margin} = \frac{\text{Gross profit}}{\text{Income (fees)}} = \frac{\$120,000}{\$3,000,000} = 4\%$$
$$\text{Industry average} = 19\%$$

Dunn & Sweeney's profit margin is significantly below average, indicating that the firm's fees are relatively low or that its costs are relatively high, or both.

When reading any financial statement, the ratios will present a clearer understanding of the firm than just the numbers alone. Ratio analysis does have some limitations, however. If a firm has employed some window dressing techniques to make their financial statements look better, the ratios can be distorted. Also, different operating and accounting practices distort comparisons. Further, it is difficult to generalize about whether a particular ratio is good or bad. For instance, a high current ratio indicates a strong liquidity position, which is good, but it also could mean an excessive amount of cash in the bank, which is bad, because cash in the bank is a nonearning asset.

Using ratios mechanically and without thinking is dangerous. However, when used intelligently and with good judgment, ratios can provide useful insights into a firm's operations.

6-3   How to Develop Budgets

If there is any one financial area in which most law firms are remiss, it is in the area of developing budgets. For some unexplained reason, many people have the idea that the techniques used to improve a law firm's financial operations apply only to larger firms. The result of that thinking is that many small firms continue to operate in a confused state, worrying about whether they will survive from one year to the next. Fortunately, affordable technology and the caliber of law office managers have both improved to the point where successful management practices are now being applied to firms of all sizes.

Successful law firm management requires more than technology and competent administration. The most important element for success is a commitment from the lawyers that they want to be better managed and make more money. This commitment requires a willingness on the part of the lawyers to adopt a more businesslike approach to areas such as partner compensation, partner capital, and billing rates. Such a commitment also requires a change in mentality from an expense orientation to an income orientation. Without this two-part commitment from the partners, the office manager will find preparing and working with budgets difficult if not impossible.

Partner Compensation

Whatever budgeting system is eventually installed, whether manual or computerized, the system needs to have built into it the concept of an annual salary for the partners. The partners of every law firm with a history are generally able to predict, with a degree of certainty, the annual compensation of the partners. Spreading partner compensation evenly over the year, with periodic additions to recognize performance, enables the office manager to plan for cash flow needs over the course of the year. The management process cannot work effectively if the partners insist upon a random, on-demand partner compensation payment schedule. This is often the first hurdle smaller firms must overcome in the process of becoming professionally managed.

Partner Capital

The partners must also decide how the firm will raise cash to invest in technology, office space, and furniture. How much of the cash will be provided by the partners and how much will the firm borrow from the bank? Because cash flow budgets identify the amount of cash required to pay the partners and buy the assets necessary to provide client services, questions about partner capital must be answered before the budgets can be prepared.

Billing Rates

Preparing rate schedules that will yield the firm's desired profit results is a part of the budgeting process. Therefore, the partners must assess standard hourly fees, all other fees based on the firm's client mix, and the leveraging effect of associates and paralegals. Assuming that the partners have addressed the issues of partner compensation, capital, and billing rates, the rest of the budgeting process is relatively simple.

Steps in Preparing Budgets

First, a few words about budgets in general. They should not be prepared by accountants and they should not be set in stone. To be useful they need to be prepared by those who control the firm's finances, they should be able to provide the ability to compare actual numbers with the budgeted ones, and they should be revised as required. Perhaps you cannot predict the future, but you can get better control of it by creating budgets that are flexible enough to absorb the loss of a client, changes in interest rates, and all sorts of unexpected events.

Whether you do them manually, or use financial management software created specifically for law firms, you need to remember this accounting truism in preparing your budget: As fee income goes up, expenses will also increase. In other words, it costs money to make money.

Also be aware that all businesses are cyclical, even law firms. That means that in some months billings will be down because, for example, timekeepers are on vacation or because clients are postponing taking legal action until after the holiday. Accounts receivable will feel the impact thirty to ninety days later, depending upon the firm's average collection period.

Keeping all of the foregoing caveats in mind, here are the steps to preparing budgets for the law firm.

Step One: Estimate Gross Revenues You must first estimate the firm's gross revenues for the coming year. This step was confronted earlier in Chapter 2. You might want to review Section 2–2 at this time. Since Dunn & Sweeney takes a conservative approach in other matters, an income budget reflecting this attitude might look like Figure 6–2.

Figure 6–2 Income Budget

Partners (hourly)		
Number	2	
Average rate	$175	
Average hours	2000	
Total hours	4000	
Total gross		$ 700,000
Associates (hourly)		
Number	4	
Average rate	$110	
Average hours	1900	
Total hours	7600	
Total gross		$ 836,000
Paralegals (hourly)		
Number	2	
Average rate	$ 70	
Average hours	1400	
Total hours	2800	
Total gross		$ 196,000
Other Timekeepers		$1,000,000
Total Gross		**$2,732,000**

Step Two: Calculate Actual Billings and Collections After determining the firm's potential gross revenues for the year, the next step is to calculate the percentage of time that will actually be billed. This calculation makes adjustments for the reality that few timekeepers can bill at optimum levels of production.

The time to billing percentage can be ascertained based upon the firm's history in this regard. Typically this percentage will be in the 80 percent to 90 percent range. Dunn & Sweeney's time to billing percentage is 85 percent as shown in Figure 6–3.

Figure 6–3 Calculating Actual Billings and Collections

Billings	
Value of time for the year	$2,732,000
Time to billing percentage	85%
Budgeted billings	$2,322,200
Collections	
Value of budgeted billings for the year	$2,322,200
Collection percentage	90%
Budgeted collections	$2,089,980
Total budgeted collections	$2,089,980
Expense write-offs	(25,000)
Other income	30,000
Total income	$2,094,980
Less expenses	(1,204,350)
Net Income	**$ 890,630**

The second calculation is to determine the percentage of bills issued that will be paid. This calculation takes into account write-offs of bad receivables and the time delay of collections. Historical data will provide you with your firm's success record in collecting from clients. Hopefully, the percentage will be over 85 percent. Dunn & Sweeney have been able to collect 90 percent of bills issued. This calculation is reflected in Figure 6–3.

Note that some expense write-offs in Figure 6–3 were subtracted from the total budgeted collections. These write-offs are estimates of client-associated expense items that are not charged back to the client. Likewise, an estimate of other income includes amounts received from clients for copying expenses, telephone, and messenger services. After making these subtractions and additions, Dunn & Sweeney now have a budgeted total income of $2,094,980.

The final calculation required to estimate net income is to budget expenses. Although some people find estimating expenses a difficult task, it need not be one. In most law firms, about 80 percent of expenses are attributable to salaries, benefits, rent, and payroll taxes. These numbers are readily available. The remainder of the expenses are relatively insignificant. Therefore, you need only take last year's expenses and increase them by some reasonable percentage. Soon you will find that you are so good at estimating expenses that you will only miss the mark by a percentage point or two.

To arrive at the expense figure used in Figure 6–3, Dunn & Sweeney's employee salaries were estimated at $1,110,000 and other expenses were estimated at $94,350. After subtracting the expenses, the net income at Dunn & Sweeney is projected to be $890,630.

There are other methods you can use to budget expenses, such as calculating them as a percentage of gross fees, by lawyer, by department, or by billable hour. Regardless of the method you choose, the goal should be to spend more time estimating the expenses that are the biggest ones for your firm and the rest will take care of themselves.

Step Three: Develop Monthly Budgets The annual budgeted numbers can serve as an early warning to prevent the firm from getting into financial difficulties if they are put into a monthly budget format. Historical information showing your firm's cyclical variations will be of great benefit in preparing the monthly budgets. If the information is available, you should list billings and collections for each month for the past five years to avoid any unusual activity months that would skew your averages. If data is not available for the past five years, use whatever you have and keep in mind for the future that five years' worth of data is preferred to get the most accurate information.

Your monthly budget figures are calculated by using a percentage of total collections. To find this percentage figure, first divide the total for each month by the total of all months (the total for all January months, or $5,266, divided by $57,426, and repeat the process for each of the 12 months). Then, to find your monthly budget estimates, take each percentage times your total collection budget ($2,089,980 × 9.2% = $192,278). Figure 6–4 is Dunn & Sweeney's historical activity analysis for a three-year period with current year projections.

Figure 6–4 shows how collections and billings at Dunn & Sweeney varied over the three-year period. These variations are also used to compare budgets against the firm's actual results.

Monthly calculations are necessary to prevent you from finding out in December that the firm is 25 percent behind budget when that information was available in June.

Step Four: Net Income Budget   You now have enough information to prepare the net income budget, shown in Figure 6–5, using the cyclical collection information from Figure 6–4, and the estimated expenses, and expense write-off figures found in Figure 6–3.

Figure 6–4   Three-Year History of Collections and Billings

Collections (in thousands of dollars)

Month	19AA	19BB	19CC	Total	%	Budget 19XX
January	1483	1510	2273	5266	9.2	192,278
February	1379	1677	1754	4810	8.4	175,558
March	1654	1530	1906	5090	8.9	186,009
April	1484	1488	2113	5085	8.8	183,918
May	1492	1677	1874	5043	8.7	181,828
June	1429	1490	1545	4464	7.8	163,019
July	1552	1483	1612	4647	8.0	167,198
August	1344	1373	1654	4371	7.7	160,928
September	1330	1390	1356	4076	7.0	146,299
October	1601	1600	1495	4696	8.2	171,378
November	1373	1593	1526	4492	7.9	165,109
December	1501	1710	2175	5386	9.4	196,458
Totals	17622	18521	21283	57426	100.0	2,089,980

Billings (in thousands of dollars)

Month	19AA	19BB	19CC	Total	%	Budget 19XX
January	1517	1596	2145	5258	9.2	214,562
February	1443	1663	1856	4962	8.7	202,901
March	1507	1394	2100	5001	8.8	205,234
April	1408	1713	2254	5447	9.5	224,559
May	1394	1500	1975	4869	8.5	198,237
June	1220	1324	1590	4134	7.2	167,918
July	1636	1404	1557	4597	8.1	188,908
August	1376	1567	1326	4269	7.5	174,915
September	1515	1638	1225	4378	7.7	179,580
October	1542	1478	1520	4540	7.9	184,244
November	1418	1452	1678	4548	8.0	186,576
December	1538	1544	1984	5066	8.9	207,566
Totals	17514	18273	21210	57069	100.0	2,335,200

Figure 6–5 Net Income Budget

Month	Collections	Expense Write-Off	Other Expenses	Net Income
January	192,278	2083	100,363	89,832
February	175,558	2083	100,362	73,113
March	186,009	2084	100,363	83,562
April	183,918	2083	100,362	81,473
May	181,828	2083	100,363	79,382
June	163,019	2084	100,362	60,573
July	167,198	2083	100,363	64,752
August	160,928	2083	100,362	58,483
September	146,299	2084	100,363	43,852
October	171,378	2083	100,362	68,933
November	165,109	2083	100,363	62,663
December	196,458	2084	100,362	94,012
Totals	2,089,980	25,000	1,204,350	860,630
Other Income				+30,000
				$890,630

Step Five: Cash Flow Budget At this point you are probably way ahead of other small and midsized law firms in the budgeting process. However, the final step in the budgeting process, preparing the cash flow budget, is one of the most important steps. Yet too many firms pay too little attention to cash flow, with the result that partners must reduce their take-home pay, borrow from the bank, and remain in a cash-poor position.

The cash flow budget in Figure 6–6 takes the firm's cash objectives into consideration. For example, Dunn & Sweeney began the year with the following cash objectives:

- Maintain a checking account balance of at least $75,000.
- Pay partners full distribution of income by year's end.
- Reduce debt by at least $150,000 by year's end.
- Reserve $130,000 for capital assets.

Now that the firm's objectives are placed into the format for analysis expressed in Figure 6–6, and you can see an expected cash shortage of nearly half a million dollars, there are several key decisions to be made. Assuming that the firm wants to hold to its original objectives, how will the money be raised?

Figure 6–6 Cash Flow Budget

Balance at beginning of year	$ 46,987
Funds provided by:	
Net income	$890,630
Depreciation	110,000
Total funds provided	**$1,000,630**
Funds applied to:	
Capital asset reserve	$130,000
Debt repayment	150,000
Partner distribution (current year)	1,125,000
Total funds applied	**$1,405,000**
Excess (deficit)	($404,370)
Working capital balance	75,000
Cash shortage	**($479,370)**

How much will come from the partners and how much will be borrowed from the bank? What needs to be cut from the budget? Perhaps asset purchases can be delayed. Or debt might be paid at a lesser rate. Should partner distribution be reduced?

While there are many more pieces to the financial management process, most firms can go a long way toward a more sophisticated approach to managing finances with just these income and cash budgets.

6–4   Cash Flow Management

Individuals and law firms need cash to pay salaries and taxes, to buy fixed assets, and to pay debts. But generally, cash itself is a nonearning asset. Cash, sitting in most commercial checking accounts, earns no interest. Thus, the goal of cash management is to reduce to a minimum the amount of cash held necessary to conduct business and to invest the remainder in interest-bearing accounts.

There are some good reasons, however, to hold cash. One reason is to be able to transact business. Payments are made in cash and receipts are deposited into cash accounts. Cash balances associated with routine payments and collections are known as **transaction balances.** A **compensating balance** is the minimum checking account balance some banks require that you maintain on deposit as compensation for their services.

Other reasons for holding cash include to maintain a **precautionary balance,** a reserve for unpredictable fluctuations in cash flow, and a **speculative balance,** to enable a firm to take advantage of bargain purchases.

The cash budget is the means of determining cash needs. **Cash flow** is the actual net cash that flows into or out of the firm during some specified period. Cash flow is not the same as net income on the income statement. A more accurate distinction between cash flow and net income is that cash flow is real and net income is merely an accounting illustration of the firm's financial position. As illustrated by Figure 6–6, the accounting equation for determining cash flow is:

$$\text{Net cash flow} = \text{Net income after taxes} + \text{Depreciation}$$

Recognizing Cash Flow Problems

In managing cash flow it is critical to have an understanding of the sources of cash. For the law firm, the primary source of cash is client billings. But billings themselves are not sources of cash until the money is deposited into the firm's checking account. Some people want to overlook this fact and embark on spending programs based on billings instead of cash in the bank.

When decisions are made to spend money based on the profit and loss statement, or on increased client billings instead of actual cash balances, the rationale is that any lack of cash on hand is a temporary condition which will right itself.

The results of these actions usually include an increased use of trade credit, taking longer to settle accounts payable, or simply not paying bills. Firms that routinely experience cash flow difficulties sometimes find themselves limited to cash-on-delivery (COD) purchases from vendors—a most embarrassing situation for any law firm.

Lack of sound cash management practices can cause some firms to make frequent trips to the bank for last-minute deposits to meet payroll and cover tax payments. Sometimes the lawyers are required to cut, or skip, their own compensation. The red flag of warning should go up if your firm is experiencing any of these symptoms of poor cash management.

Typical Responses to Cash Flow Problems

When cash flow problems can no longer be ignored, responsive actions tend to be predictable. The first reaction is to eliminate all unnecessary overhead costs. In a law firm this usually means reducing administrative and clerical positions, which does nothing but increase the workload of those who remain and slow down the delivery of client services.

Employee benefits are the next line item to receive scrutiny, closely followed by other overhead expense items such as inventories of office supplies. The rationale behind this action is that increasing the deductible amount on insurance, for example, and maintaining only minimum supplies inventories will increase cash flow. These actions do little to increase the firm's cash flow, but they do greatly increase employee morale problems.

Next, attention is given to increasing billable hours by bringing in new clients. Or, in some instances of extreme reaction and unclear thinking, the firm might decide to bring in a new partner or associate with a built-in client base. Increasing billable hours might be a legitimate answer to cash flow problems, but doing so will also create more costs.

While these responses are predictable, they simply do not work. They are reactive responses to an existing, and often chronic, condition. Only proactive actions to eliminate the events that caused the cash flow crisis in the first place will have the desired long-term effect.

Components of Cash Flow Management

If cutting back on expenses and increasing billable hours is not the answer to cash flow, what is the answer? The answer to cash flow management is in managing the components. The components of cash flow management are accounts receivable, accounts payable, and practice management.

Managing Accounts Receivable   How do you know whether too much cash is tied up in receivables? A meticulous examination of your aged accounts receivable report and your average collection period will answer this question. How many clients pay within 30 days? How many take up to 90 days? How many are over 120 days past due? You should know exactly how much the firm's clients owe and when payment is expected. As checks are received, they should be posted to the clients' accounts so that at any time you can easily run a tape or a computer printout and know the status of accounts receivable.

Assuming that your agreement with clients is that bills are due when presented, or within 30 days, any accounts that are 30 days overdue require attention. This attention usually takes the form of the office manager making a telephone call to the client to see whether there is a problem with the bill or the service, and when payment might be expected.

As you examine your aged accounts receivable, pay particular attention to the client who has not paid anything on an account that is more than 60 days overdue. A call from the attorney might prompt payment. However, if there are a high number of these overdue accounts, the firm has a serious collection problem. The longer the time span between billing and payment, the less likely are the chances of being paid. There is an inverse relationship to the amount the client has invested in resolving their legal problem to the potential for collection problems. In other words, the less the client has invested in the outcome the more likely the firm is to have a collection problem. This is another reason why retainer fees are so important.

In most cases the firm will not collect on accounts that are more than 90 days overdue. To add to the difficulty in collecting these delinquent accounts, using a collection agency is not only impractical, but could also be dangerous. Incidences of malpractice claims are high after clients have been contacted by collection agencies.

Collection efforts, therefore, need to be focused on communicating expectations with the client from the beginning and in following the dos and don'ts of billing procedures discussed in Chapter 3.

Managing Accounts Payable   One basic principle of cash flow management is to get cash into your account as quickly as possible and pay it out as slowly as possible—not slowly enough to be delinquent in your payment of debts, but neither paying too far in advance of the due date.

The best cash flow management situation occurs when a firm has **synchronized cash flows,** or inflows coinciding with outflows, thereby allowing the firm to keep its cash balances required for day-to-day operation at a minimum. If your suppliers expect payment within 30 days of billing and clients are taking 45 days or more to pay their bills, cash flow is not synchronized.

Issuing statements on regular billing cycles and following up on delinquent accounts while holding payments until the last possible date will help keep cash flowing through the firm without the necessity of dipping into reserves or having to borrow from the bank.

Practice Management   An analysis of billable hours, individual attorney productivity, and income generated by area of specialization will provide information from which decisions can be made on where the firm should place emphasis to increase cash flow and profits.

Some types of cases, such as divorce, criminal, corporate, and tax, are often resolved in a relatively short period of time compared to personal injury litigation or product liability cases. When less time is required to resolve a legal matter, fees are usually collected more quickly. Thus, although an inventory or backlog of litigation cases with high fee potential might be attractive, only cash in the bank pays the bills.

Being free of cash flow worries requires that regular attention be given to the three components of cash flow management: accounts receivable, accounts payable, and practice management.

SUMMARY

6–1

The acronym PPOD (profits, property, owners' interest, and debt) answers the four accounting questions in which office managers and attorneys are most interested and summarizes the basic principles of accounting. The PPOD information is grouped into time periods and transferred to the balance sheet and income statement for purposes of comparison and analysis. The basic accounting equation is Assets = Liabilities + Proprietorship + Income − Expenses.

6–2

Accounting information by itself is not always helpful in determining the true financial position of the firm. When the numbers are put into percentage figures, or ratios, nearly everyone can make more sense from the information. Law office managers are particularly interested in the current ratio and the quick ratio, both of which answer the question of whether the firm will be able to pay its debts as they come due. The average collection period is critical to the firm's financial well-being. Determining the profit margin is the third financial management tool that helps the law firm make future planning decisions. When the firm's ratio is compared with the ratios of other law firms and with the ratios for prior periods, upward and downward trends are easily discerned.

6–3

The basic requirement for budget development is support from the attorneys and, in some cases, their willingness to adhere to a schedule of regular compensation payments. Questions must also be answered about how the firm will raise needed cash, the amount of excess money to be maintained in the operating account, and at what rate debt is to be repaid. The fundamental budgets required by most law firms are the income budget, the monthly budget based on annual collections and billings, the net income budget, and the cash flow budget.

6–4

A law firm needs cash to pay for routine transactions, to maintain a minimum checking account balance required by its bank, to establish a reserve for unpredictable fluctuations in cash flow, and to enable the firm to take advantage of bargain purchases. Ideally, the best cash flow management situation occurs when a firm has synchronized cash flow. This situation can only occur when accounts receivable are well managed. Law firms should pay particular attention to accounts that are nearly 60 days overdue on which no payments have been received. Issuing statements on a regular billing cycle and following up on accounts that are not paid when due are essential to managing cash flow.

REVIEW

Key Terms

accounting cycle
accounting equation
accounts payable
accounts receivable
assets
average collection period
balance sheet
bookkeeping
bottom line
cash flow

closing the books
compensating balance
current assets
current liabilities
current ratio
debt
depreciation
double entry
entity
expense

fiscal year
fixed assets
fixed liabilities
gross profit
journal
income
income statement
ledger
liabilities
net profit
operating account
owners' interest
partnership
precautionary balance
professional corporation
profit
profit margin on income
property
quick ratio
sole proprietorship
speculative balance
synchronized cash flows
transaction balance
trial balance
trust account

Questions for Review and Discussion

1. Use one or two sentences to describe each of the six basic accounting principles.
2. Define and explain the acronyms PPOD and ALPIE.
3. What is the difference between the balance sheet and the income statement?
4. Define the terms *income* and *expense* as used in accounting.
5. Why must law firms have a trust account?
6. List and explain the steps in the accounting cycle.
7. What is the difference between gross profit and net profit?
8. What are the formulas for computing current ratio, quick ratio, average collection period, and profit margin? What does each measure?
9. List the steps involved in preparing budgets for the firm.
10. What are the components of cash flow management?

Activities

1. Prepare a balance sheet, an income statement, an income budget, a monthly budget, and a cash flow budget based on your family's assets, liabilities, income, and expenses.
2. Sweeney's son decided to work as a court messenger and process server while on summer break from college. He was allowed to use a desk and telephone at Dunn & Sweeney's offices at no charge, but he had to rent a car for two months at $250 per month, spend another $250 each month for gas and insurance, and have business cards printed for $35. By working long hours seven days a week, he was able to take in $3,500 during his summer break. What was his profit or loss?

   Income from services $_____
   Total expenses $_____
   Profit (or loss) $_____

   Note that on accounting statements loss figures are enclosed in parentheses.
3. Explain the difference between a statement about profits "for the year ending December 31, 19xx" and a statement that property is owned "as of December 31, 19xx." *Hint:* One statement covers a specific period and the other reports a condition at a given date. Which one is the given instant in time? Explain the meaning of this statement: "Every balance sheet of an ongoing business is out of date by the time it is prepared."
4. Using the information presented on page 137 in the section entitled "Profitability Ratios," determine how much Dunn & Sweeney's net profit before taxes will have to increase to put them on par with the industry average.
5. Using the information presented on pages 136–137 in the section entitled "Asset Management Ratios," determine how much additional cash Dunn & Sweeney would generate if the firm could reduce its average collection period from 42 days to 30 days, with all else held constant.

CHAPTER 7   Personnel Management

OUTLINE

7–1   How the Times Have Changed
    Culture Defined
    Cultural Changes and Employees
    Employment at Will
    Federal Legislation
    History of EEO Legislation
    Creating a Safe and Healthful Work Environment
7–2   Creating Personnel Policies
    The Need for Policies
    How to Write Personnel Policies
7–3   Factors in Employee Compensation
    Factor 1: Compensation Objectives
    Factor 2: External Economic Conditions
    Factor 3: Internal Considerations
7–4   Guidelines for Hiring Personnel
    How to Define the Job and the Position
    How to Find Qualified Applicants
    How to Conduct an Interview
7–5   Methods of Evaluating Employee Performance
    Management by Objectives
    Coworker Evaluation of Performance
    Management Performance Evaluation
7–6   How to Increase Employee Job Satisfaction
    Find Ways to Enrich Each Job and Position
    Try the Team Approach
    Consider Adjustments in Work Schedules

COMMENTARY

Dunn & Sweeney has adopted a progressive attitude toward managing one of the firm's most valuable resources—its employees. You have been asked to bring the firm up to date in this area by writing job descriptions and personnel policies, providing guidelines for new-hire interviews and performance evaluations, as well as reviewing the firm's compensation program and suggesting ways to increase employee job satisfaction.

OBJECTIVES

In Chapter 6 you learned the fundamental principles of accounting, how to prepare the basic budgets for a law firm, how to read a financial statement, and how to control cash flow. After completing this chapter, you will be able to:

1. Define *culture.*
2. Explain the impact of culture on a law firm.
3. Describe the impact of recent cultural changes on employee attitudes.
4. Discuss the effects on employers of antidiscrimination legislation.
5. Explain the reasons for developing personnel policies.
6. Discuss the relationship between job worth, employee worth, and wages.
7. Describe the content of a job description.
8. Outline the steps involved in hiring and interviewing staff personnel.
9. Describe methods of evaluating employee performance.
10. Describe ways to enrich or redesign staff jobs in the law office.

7-1   How the Times Have Changed

The way in which an organization functions is affected not only by how well it is organized and managed, but also by shifts in cultural forces and the resulting legislation.

Culture Defined

Generally speaking, **culture** is the behavior patterns and values of a society or social group. These behaviors, as well as the accompanying attitudes, beliefs, and values, are learned from others. They are socially transmitted and vary from one individual to the next based, in large part, upon input received while growing up.

Values are programmed into us by family members, friends, teachers, and the electronic media. In addition, where we grow up—rural, suburban, or urban environments in the north, south, east, or west regions of this country, or in other countries—has an impact on our value systems. Everyone is subconsciously aware of the differences in value systems held by people from various regions and nations. Another critical component in our value programming is our family's income, which has a direct impact on us as we develop. How you feel about money and material possessions is likely to be a reflection of your family's economic system during your value programming years.

Employees bring their cultural values into the firm. Therefore, a law firm functions within the cultural system of the society in which it is located. **Corporate culture,** however, is more than just a reflection of social values; it is a set of basic assumptions held by the firm's founders about success and the way life "ought" to be, based on the founders' value systems. With the passage of time these assumptions may or may not have been modified. The current firm's beliefs, values, and behaviors are a blending of the founders' assumptions and the firm's subsequent experiences.

To get the feel for the differences in corporate culture, spend some time going around to different law firms and soak up the culture. Temporary positions are a good way to do this. You will notice differences in the way people dress, the jargon they use, the way clients and employees are treated, and individual mannerisms. You will also notice the more subtle indications of the firm's culture, such as who talks to whom, what groups have formed, which people go to lunch or take breaks together, and how employees relate to bosses.

Corporate culture is also reflected in the location of the office building, its design, and its furnishings. The building gives both employees and clients a message about the beliefs and values of the firm. The furnishings and office layout reflect where the firm has been and where it is going. Some firms choose a modern, high-tech decor while others are more traditional in appearance. A firm that believes open communication and close working relationships are important will reflect this belief by having more open spaces and fewer doors. Conversely, one that discourages personal involvement among employees will have individual offices with doors that are frequently closed.

Corporate culture is important—to the individuals working in the firm and to the overall success of the firm. Since culture is a reflection of the past, changes in the environment in which the firm operates often require significant modifications of the firm's culture—and change is never easy. The question facing most law firms today is not whether the culture will change, but how to manage the changes.

Cultural Changes and Employees

Whether they are partners in the firm, members of the management team, or part of the support staff, every person in the firm brings his or her own attitudes, beliefs, values, and customs to the workplace. Reactions to work assignments, leadership styles, compensation, and benefit plans are influenced by culture—which is continually changing. Human resource (HR) policies and procedures must be adjusted from time to time to cope with these changes. Examples of cultural changes affecting the workplace are the recent unprecedented changes that have occurred in the area of employee rights.

Employment at Will

The **employment at will** doctrine holds that, in the absence of a collective bargaining agreement or other written contract, either the employer or employee has the right to terminate their relationship at any time without reason or cause.

The employer's rights to fire at-will employees is subject to certain restrictions imposed by federal laws, such as Title VII of the 1964 Civil Rights Act and the Fair Labor Standards Act, as well as by laws enacted by a number of states.

In general the courts have recognized that grounds might exist for overturning discharges of at-will employees in cases where a termination violated a public policy, such as when an employee is fired for filing a workers' compensation claim or refusing to commit perjury; when a termination breaches an implied contract, such as being retained as long as the work was performed satisfactorily; or when a termination breaches the covenant of good faith and fair dealing, such as being arbitrarily dismissed after years of satisfactory service.

In an attempt to be prepared if the employer is subsequently hit with a wrongful discharge claim, many employers include a disclaimer on job application forms stating that employment with the firm is an at-will arrangement that can be terminated by either party at any time. Other firms have employees sign employment at will agreements, have a written policy statement spelling out their employment relationship, conduct regular performance appraisals, keep employee files up to date regarding any disciplinary actions taken, and conduct an exit interview, including a written explanation of why the employee is leaving. Figure 7–1 is one sample of an employment at will agreement.

Figure 7–1 Employment at Will Agreement

In consideration for my employment by Dunn & Sweeney (Employer), I agree to conform to any and all rules and regulations which are currently in existence or which may hereafter be adopted or promulgated by Employer. I understand that these rules and regulations, including those relating to employee benefits, may be changed, withdrawn, or added to by Employer at any time, at Employer's sole discretion and without any prior notice to me.

I further acknowledge that notwithstanding any such rules and regulations, my employment is, and is intended to be, at-will and may be terminated at any time, with or without cause, without prior notice, by either myself or Employer. The at-will nature of my employment shall not be modified or affected in any way by any employee benefits, including pension or retirement benefits, now or hereafter offered, extended, or made available by Employer.

Dated: _____

_____
Employee Signature

Federal Legislation

Over the past few decades, federal legislation has changed the rules for employers by granting employees specific rights. Some of these laws include the right to equal employment opportunity, equal pay for men and women performing essentially the same job, a safe and healthful work environment, and the right to privacy in the workplace.

Equal employment opportunity (EEO), or the employment of individuals in a fair and nonbiased manner, and **affirmative action,** an attempt to correct past discriminatory practices by recruiting minority group members, have received unprecedented attention from the media, the courts, and legislators during the past 30 years. These legal mandates require employers to comply with the laws and their administrative guidelines. Failure to comply subjects employers to the risk of litigation, invites negative public attitudes, and damages employee morale.

Equal employment opportunity is not only a legal issue; it is also an emotional issue. The topic is of concern to everyone regardless of sex, race, religion, age, national origin, color, or position in the organization. The culture of the firm will determine how it reacts to these topics.

History of EEO Legislation

Although some people had always been concerned by discriminatory employment practices, nondiscriminatory employment became a national social concern in the mid-'50s and early 1960s. Three factors in particular contributed to the growth of public awareness: (1) a growing body of laws and regulations covering discrimination; (2) changing attitudes regarding employment discrimination; and (3) published studies highlighting the economic problems of women, minorities, and older workers.

The public had been aware of discriminatory employment practices as far back as the early 19th century. The first Civil Rights Act was the 14th Amendment to the Constitution, enacted in 1868. It extended to all individuals the right to enjoy full and equal benefits of all laws regardless of race. However, job discrimination was a widely accepted practice then, and the Civil Rights Act did little to change these discriminatory practices.

More specific federal policies began to emerge in the 1930s and 1940s. Still suffering from the aftershocks of the stock market crash and the Great Depression, Congress enacted the Unemployment Relief Act in 1933, which prohibited employment discrimination on account of race, color, or creed. This was still not enough to stop discriminatory practices.

In 1941 Franklin D. Roosevelt issued Executive Order 8802, which established the Fair Employment Practices Committee. The committee was to ensure that every American citizen, "regardless of race, creed, color, or national origin," would be guaranteed equal employment opportunities with firms that had World War II defense contracts. However, the committee was given no power to enforce the executive order, so, as might be expected, they could do little to resolve employment discrimination problems.

During the Truman, Eisenhower, and Kennedy presidencies, other federal legislative efforts were made to resolve inequities in employment practices. But these early EEO efforts had few positive outcomes primarily because the regulatory agencies were given no enforcement power. Also, the laws often failed to specify what actions were considered discriminatory or to offer any methods of correction. However, the lack of positive outcome to these early EEO efforts can be attributed in large part to the fact that employers covered by the acts (typically, defense contractors) were asked to voluntarily comply with EEO legislation. In the absence of compulsory compliance, employers often violated the laws without punishment. Nevertheless, these early executive orders and laws laid the groundwork for passage of the Civil Rights Act of 1964.

The Civil Rights Act of 1964   Title VII of the **Civil Rights Act of 1964** (as amended) prohibits discrimination in hiring, training, promotion, pay, fringe benefits, or other conditions of employment. Discrimination is prohibited on the basis of race, color, religion, sex, or national origin. Hourly workers, supervisors, professional employees, managers, and executives—all are covered by the law. Section 703(a) of Title VII of the Civil Rights Act states that:

> It shall be an unlawful employment practice for an employer:
> 1. To fail or refuse to hire or to discharge any individual, or otherwise to discriminate against any individual with respect to his compensation, terms, conditions, or privileges of employment because of such individual's race, color, religion, sex, or national origin; or
> 2. To limit, segregate, or classify his employees or applicants for employment in any way which would deprive or tend to deprive any individual of employment opportunities or otherwise adversely affect his status as an employee because of such individual's race, color, religion, sex, or national origin.

The Civil Rights Act of 1964, as amended by the Equal Employment Opportunity Act of 1972, extends this legislation to include discrimination against people with physical disabilities. All employers with 15 or more employees are covered by these two acts. Five groups of people are specifically protected under Title VII. They are African-Americans, Hispanics, American Indians, Asian–Pacific Islanders, and women. While all groups are not specified under Title VII, their lack of inclusion does not mean that it is legal to discriminate against other groups not specifically set out.

The Civil Rights Act of 1964 also established the Equal Employment Opportunity Commission (EEOC) to administer and enforce the law. There are, however, certain types of employers who do not have to comply with Title VII regulations. They are all-male or all-female schools, or schools serving one religious group; federal and state employment systems; the District of Columbia; Indian tribes; and elected officials and their personal staffs in state and local governments.

One significant change resulting from the 1972 amendment was to bar classification or labeling of "men's jobs" and "women's jobs." Only then did newspapers eliminate the "Help Wanted: Female" and "Help Wanted: Male" categories from the classified section. Until that time, positions for secretaries, nurses, and stewardesses were found under "Help Wanted: Female" while almost all other positions were advertised for males. Today, not only do we find men working as nurses and flight attendants; they also work in law firms as paralegals, word processors, secretaries, and receptionists.

It is important to note that the law does not require employers to hire, promote, or keep workers who are not qualified to perform their job duties; it does, however, give both employers and employees the opportunity to find the best-qualified person for the job. And employees may still be rewarded differently provided that such decisions are not based upon race, color, sex, religion, or national origin.

The Equal Pay Act of 1963   The **Equal Pay Act** was passed to amend the Fair Labor Standards Act (FLSA) and was designed to prohibit discrimination in pay, fringe benefits, and pensions based upon a worker's gender. Specifically, employers cannot pay members of one gender less than that paid to members of the other gender for jobs requiring substantially the same skill, effort, and responsibility under similar working conditions and in the same organization. Employers do not violate this law when wage differences are based on seniority, merit, or incentive pay plans. But an employer must not base wage differences on gender alone, and minimum wage and overtime policies must be applied equally to both men and women.

No discussion of equal pay is complete without mentioning the subject of **comparable worth.** The concept underlying comparable worth is that jobs requiring comparable knowledge, skills, and abilities should pay at comparable levels. There are two views on this subject. One is that it is discriminatory to have a situation in which jobs of equal worth have unequal levels of compensation. For example, does the job of gardener (typically male) require more knowledge, skill, and ability than that of a secretary (typically female)?

Another view on the subject of comparable worth is that supply and demand creates the disparity in pay, not discriminatory action by employers. Historically, the truth is "female" jobs are paid at a lesser rate than "male" jobs. According to the U.S. Department of Labor, women today are still being paid approximately 30 percent less than men in all job categories.

As mentioned earlier, men are entering jobs traditionally held by women largely as a result of EEO and affirmative action requirements. This can only benefit women in the long run, since men are often more willing to assert themselves, thereby creating changes in these positions once held only by women. Some positive changes include higher wages, better working conditions, and improved job status. Only time will tell the outcome of the changes now taking place in the workplace regarding comparable worth. However, until it is resolved this issue certainly will be one of ongoing interest to both men and women.

Age Discrimination in Employment Act of 1967   The **Age Discrimination in Employment Act (ADEA),** as amended, prohibits specific employers from discriminating against a person 40 years of age or older in any area of employment, including selection, because of age. Employers covered by ADEA are those with 20 or more employees; unions with 25 or more members; employment agencies; and federal, state, and local governments. The only exception to ADEA is where age is a **bona fide occupational qualification**

(BFOQ); in other words, an older person might reasonably be excluded from consideration as a model for teenage fashions. Likewise, it is also reasonable to expect department stores to hire female models for women's fashions and for a professional football team to hire male locker-room attendants.

The BFOQ exception does not apply to race or color, and the courts have construed the concepts narrowly. Any organization claiming a BFOQ must prove that sex, religion, age or national origin is a *business necessity*, a practice that is necessary for the safe and efficient operation of the organization.

Pregnancy Discrimination Act of 1978   Prior to 1978, many women were forced to resign as soon as their pregnancy was known without disability benefits or maternity leave. If they returned to work with the same employer, these women were often given lower paying and lower status jobs—if they were rehired at all.

The EEOC put a stop to these punitive practices concerning childbirth. The **Pregnancy Discrimination Act** amends the Civil Rights Act of 1964 by stating that pregnancy is a disability and that pregnant employees are to be treated the same as any employee with a medical condition. Employers cannot deny sick-leave days for morning sickness or pregnancy-related illnesses. Furthermore, accrued seniority, reinstatement, and payment under existing health insurance plans and sick-leave policies must be applied to disability due to pregnancy, miscarriage, abortion, childbirth, and recovery from childbirth in the same manner as any other temporary disability.

Equally important to career-minded women, it is illegal to discriminate in hiring, promoting, or terminating women because of pregnancy. Evaluation is to be based solely on ability to perform the job. In addition, pregnancy leave dates are now established by the woman and her doctor and are based on the pregnant individual's ability to work. Some women work right up to the time of delivery and return to work after a short recovery period.

Americans with Disabilities Act of 1990   The **Americans with Disabilities Act of 1990 (ADA)** is the single most important piece of antidiscrimination legislation to be enacted since the Civil Rights Act of 1964. The ADA prohibits discrimination against people with disabilities in the use of public services, transportation, public accommodations, and telecommunication services. In addition, the ADA prohibits discrimination against qualified applicants with disabilities in employment.

Effective July 1992, this new law applies to all employers who have 25 or more employees for each working day in each of 20 or more calendar weeks in the current or preceding year. In July of 1994, this law will include all employers with 15 or more employees.

Specifically, the ADA prohibits employers from discriminating against any qualified applicant with a disability with regard to job applications, hiring, promotions, discharge, compensation, training, and any other terms, conditions, or privileges of employment. Also prohibited is the use of nonjob-related qualification standards, employment tests, or selection criteria that would tend to screen out individuals with disabilities. A qualified applicant with a disability is defined as an individual who, with or without "reasonable accommodation," is able to perform the "essential functions" of the job. The employer is free to determine the essential job functions.

The Americans with Disabilities Act defines a person with a disability as one who has a "physical or mental impairment that substantially limits one or more major life activities (such as caring for yourself, walking, speaking, hearing, and working), a record of such impairment, or who is regarded as having such an impairment."

Designed to protect those who are currently disabled and those who have completely or partially recovered from a disability or illness, this law would apply, for example, to an employee who has undergone successful treatment for a life-threatening illness or who was badly disfigured in an accident.

Sexual Harassment   During the decade of the 1980s there were enough reports of sexual harassment by both women and men to indicate that the problem is widespread. In one federal government study as many as 70 percent of the women interviewed reported being victims of sexual harassment experiences.

According to the EEOC guidelines on sexual harassment, any "unwelcome advances, requests for sexual favors, and other verbal or physical conduct of a sexual nature" constitute **sexual harassment** when submission to the conduct is used as a basis for employment conditions. The conduct is also illegal when it interferes with the employee's work performance or creates an "intimidating, hostile, or offensive working environment."

Harassing behavior can be subtle or obvious. For example, if a supervisor promoted a worker based on the acceptance of an after-work date, that conduct is clearly illegal. An example of another form of sexual harassment is a case in which a female Los Angeles Police Department officer's locker was broken into by her male counterparts to tape a magazine centerfold inside the door with a photo of the female officer's face replacing the centerfold's face. Yet another type of sexual harassment can occur when a supervisor frequently touches a subordinate or makes inappropriate comments on appearance.

Sexual harassment is a difficult issue to define because actions that are offensive to one person might not be considered offensive by another. Jokes, suggestive remarks, and catcalls may be harassment. It depends on the viewpoint of the individual. The key word in the EEOC guidelines is "unwelcome." It is important to note that men are also harassed by female supervisors and coworkers. However, men are less likely than women to discuss the incident with others and men rarely make a formal complaint.

Employers are required by the federal government's *Uniform Guidelines* to prevent the sexual harassment of either female or male employees. According to the EEOC, an employer is guilty of sexual harassment when the employer knew or should have known about the unlawful conduct and failed to take action. Furthermore, employers are also accountable for the harassing behavior of nonemployees, such as clients or salespeople, when they allow them to sexually harass employees.

In cases where charges were proved, the EEOC-imposed remedies have included back pay, reinstatement of position, payment of lost benefits, interest charges, attorney's fees, and, in some instances, criminal charges where there was physical involvement. Damages may be assessed against both the employer and the harasser. Figure 7–2 is an example of a written policy statement on sexual harassment.

Creating a Safe and Healthful Work Environment

The **Occupational Safety and Health Act of 1970 (OSHA)** was designed to protect the safety and health of employees. Some organizations have a more structured safety awareness program than others. This is largely dictated by the working environment. At the very least, a basic safety awareness program

Figure 7–2   Sexual Harassment Policy

> SUBJECT: Sexual Harassment
>
> PURPOSE: To stress the firm's strong opposition to sexual harassment and to identify the complaint procedures available to victims, as well as the disciplinary actions that could be imposed for sexually harassing conduct or behavior.
>
> GUIDELINES:
>
> **1.** It is illegal and against the firm's policy for any member of the firm, male or female, to harass another member of the firm by: making unwelcomed sexual advances or favors or other verbal or physical conduct of a sexual nature a condition of employment; using the submission to or rejection of such conduct as the basis for or as a factor in any employment decision affecting the individual; otherwise creating an intimidating, hostile, or offensive working environment by such conduct.
>
> **2.** Creating an intimidating, hostile, or offensive working environment may include such actions as persistent comments on a person's sexual preferences or the display of obscene or sexually oriented photographs or drawings.
>
> **3.** The firm will not condone any sexual harassment by any member of the firm. Everyone will be subject to severe discipline, up to and including discharge, for any act of sexual harassment they commit.
>
> **4.** Anyone who feels victimized by sexual harassment should report the incident to their supervisor immediately. If the person's supervisor is the source of the alleged harassment, the person should report the problem to the supervisor's superior. In the event the matter cannot be handled internally for some reason, the local office of the Equal Employment Opportunity Commission should be contacted for further advice and guidance.
>
> **5.** All complaints of sexual harassment will be carefully investigated including questioning anyone who may have knowledge of either the incident in question or who may have experienced similar problems. All findings will be documented.
>
> **6.** No person will be subject to any form of retaliation or discipline for pursuing a sexual harassment complaint.
>
> Effective date: 10/1/90

Source: Adapted from The Bureau of National Affairs, Inc., Washington, D.C. (1990). Reprinted with permission.

should include training in first aid and CPR (cardiopulmonary resuscitation), how to evacuate the premises in an emergency, standard operating procedures for office equipment, and good housekeeping practices.

Because of the public's growing awareness of good health practices in general, factors in the work environment affecting health are receiving more attention. Air and water pollution occurring throughout the world has made us more conscious of our immediate environments; articles in newspapers and magazines have contributed to exposing the potential dangers at work.

Common Office Hazards   Some of the more common health hazards at work include chemicals and toxic substances; dust, smoke, fumes, and asbestos; various types of gases, mists, and vapors; excessive noise; extreme temperatures, which contribute to respiratory ailments; and infectious diseases.

Office workers may be subjected to hazards such as cuts, trips, falls, electrical shock, fires, and noise. However, among all the hazards in office environments, air pollution may be the worst. Air pollutants come from building materials, furniture and furnishings, duplicating fluids, typewriter cleaners, tobacco smoke, photocopier toners, rubber cement, correction fluids, and other items commonly found in offices. Contributing to the "sick" building syndrome are asbestos ceilings, sealed windows, and inadequate ventilation systems. Stale and germ-infested air is recirculated rather than exchanged for fresh air in many newer buildings.

Smoking in the Office   One of the most controversial office pollution subjects is smoke from cigarettes, cigars, and pipes. Studies linking passive (other people's) smoke to disease and health, as well as irritation from smoke getting in their eyes, noses, throats, and clothes, have nonsmokers demanding a smoke-free working environment. The costs of smoking extend beyond personal health concerns. Property and equipment require more maintenance in smoking environments, and health insurance premiums often cost more for smokers. Recognizing the problems and concerns caused by people smoking, many offices have adopted a smoke-free policy.

Video Display Terminals   Another source of office health problems in recent years is the video display terminal (VDT) now being used by millions of workers. When VDT equipment is not designed properly, maintained, or used appropriately, a number of health problems can occur. These problems can include visual difficulties, muscular aches and pain, job stress, and radiation hazards. The risks of exposure to VDT radiation have not been resolved, and miscarriages, birth defects, reproduction problems, and cataract formation have been attributed to VDT use.

The firm can help protect the health of employees by providing training and education on the proper use of equipment, involving employees in workstation design, and encouraging frequent rest periods.

Drugs and Alcohol   The federal **Drug-Free Workplace Act** of 1988 requires federal grant recipients to establish a drug-free workplace. Under the provisions of the law, it is illegal for employees to manufacture, distribute, dispense, possess, or use a controlled substance while at work.

Drug or alcohol use is essentially a personal problem that spills over into the workplace, affecting job performance. The number of people who are addicted to either or both of these substances continues to grow at an alarming rate. It is estimated that absenteeism and loss of productivity resulting from substance abuse cost organizations tens of millions of dollars each year—and the amount is rising.

Drug and alcohol problems may be found at all levels of any organization, including law firms. Symptoms might include excessive absenteeism, tardiness, unexplained absences from the work area, an unusual number of telephone calls, and frequent and lengthy visits to the washroom. Changes in mood during the day, unsteady gait, and trembling hands are also signs of drug or alcohol problems.

Each firm needs to outline a recommended course of action for anyone who is found to be in violation of its drug and alcohol policy. Actions can range from providing medical and counseling assistance at the firm's expense to dismissal. It is widely recognized that the payoff for better health is not only for the individuals but also for the firm in terms of increased efficiency, improved morale, and other savings.

AIDS and Other Life-Threatening Illnesses   In recent years employers have been faced with employment-related issues surrounding acquired immune deficiency syndrome (AIDS) and other life-threatening illnesses. One of the main questions has been whether termination of a person with AIDS or another life-threatening illness violates federal and state handicap discrimination laws. Most states' fair employment laws prohibit employer discrimination against the handicapped, and in many of these states, employees suffering from AIDS or any other life-threatening illness are protected under the antidiscrimination laws.

Among other things, antidiscrimination laws prohibit an employer from refusing to hire an otherwise qualified applicant solely on their past or current medical history, nor can an employer require a worker with AIDS to take mandatory leave. In addition, most states have privacy laws that protect the confidentiality of medical information. An employer who releases information about an employee's medical condition may be open to a lawsuit for slander or defamation of character.

Privacy of Employees   The 1974 **Privacy Act** pertained almost exclusively to records maintained by federal government agencies, but a subsequent report of the Privacy Protection Study Commission to the President in July 1977 influenced private employers to implement guidelines for maintaining personnel files. Subsequently, many law firms developed privacy programs. The recommended voluntary privacy guidelines include the following:

1. Tell employees what records are maintained and, if requested, permit them to see and copy all of the material, with the exception of certain management records.
2. Allow employees to correct, amend, or supplement any records that an employee or former employee believes to be inaccurate; or explain why the corrections or amendments are not made.
3. Avoid using an applicant's or employee's arrest record unless required by law.
4. Do not release information about an employee without that individual's consent, and state only employment dates, positions held, and salary.

Compliance   Some of the employee rights laws pertain only to employers who receive federal government contracts or federal funds or who have a certain number of employees. Other employee rights laws have been adopted by individual states and cities and extend to private employers. While some law firms in some states may not be legally bound to abide by these laws pertaining to employee rights, most employers recognize that to attract and retain good employees it is in the firm's best interest to follow the established guidelines. To obtain a copy of the fair employment laws for your state, contact the state office for the Department of Labor.

7–2   Creating Personnel Policies

Some people in management make policy decisions on an as-needed basis, relying on personal hunches, their own likes and dislikes, or their feelings toward the individual involved. That is a risky way of managing personnel. Eventually people who prefer to manage this way find that this ad hoc style of decision making not only is time-consuming but can cause unhappiness among employees.

The Need for Policies

Any law firm with more than a half dozen employees should have a policy handbook. All employees are sensitive to differences in treatment, no matter how slight, and nothing impairs employee morale and efficiency more quickly than a display of favoritism in decision making. Personnel policies not only lessen the opportunity for partiality in decision making, they also make the decision-making process faster and more consistent throughout the firm.

How to Write Personnel Policies

The formulation of personnel policies should be a cooperative effort among the firm's top management, the office manager/administrator, and the human resources manager. Not only must the policies be consistent with the firm's objectives; they must also be compatible with current economic conditions and societal trends as well as comply with federal, state, and local laws and regulations regarding employer-employee relationships.

At the very least, your firm's policy manual should answer the questions most frequently asked by employees about compensation, holidays, benefit programs, leaves of absence, and any other critical issues that might affect morale or result in legal problems because they are not addressed. Typically, policies are effective on the date they are issued and remain in effect until they are rescinded or changed. Therefore, it is a good idea to put an effective date on each policy.

Written personnel policies can serve as a valuable aid in orienting and training new personnel as well as in answering routine questions. However, in recent years personnel policy statements and employee handbooks have assumed the force of a legal contract between employer and employee. Employers will refer to policy statements as the basis for their personnel actions, and employees may refer to the firm's failure to adhere to established policies as a violation of their rights. It is important, therefore, that personnel policies be developed only after considerable thought has been given to the ramifications of the policy's content.

Additionally, it is a good idea to consult a legal expert in the field of labor relations before you issue policy statements to employees. However, you will also find extensive published material on this subject at your local law library, your local public library, and through professional associations. (Figure 7–2 shows a sample policy, on sexual harassment, adapted from personnel policy materials developed by The Bureau of National Affairs, Inc.)

Here are some suggestions of subjects you might want to include in your policy manual:

- Equal opportunity statement that a person's religion, age, sex, national origin, race, or color will have no part in hiring, promotion, pay, or benefits decisions.
- Definition of probationary period, during which a new hire can be dismissed without cause, and indication of when benefits will start to accrue.
- Definition of work hours in terms of workweek, time allotted for lunch and breaks, and cutoff time for pay periods.
- Definition of overtime pay.
- Establishment of vacations, holidays, personal leave absences, jury duty, bereavement, sick leave, and disability leave terms.

These suggestions are only a few of the items you will want to consider for your firm's policy manual. Others could include a dress code, hiring of relatives, safety rules, and causes for and methods of discipline. When developing your personnel manual, keep in mind that the goals of your manual should be to keep all employees informed about the firm's rules and regulations and to provide management with backup support when they are required to enforce the policies.

7–3 Factors in Employee Compensation

Employees entering the work force today are more vocal than their predecessors in expressing concerns about the quality of work life and the psychological benefits derived from their work. Even though these are major issues for today's workers, it is doubtful that many of them would continue working without being paid. So, for obvious reasons, compensation is a key part of personnel management.

For the employee, wages are a tangible reward for service. For the employer, wages are their single greatest expense. Therefore, it is essential that the firm have a sound compensation program to motivate employees yet keep labor costs at an acceptable level. Here are the factors you need to consider when evaluating your firm's compensation program.

Factor 1: Compensation Objectives

The firm's compensation program should contribute to its overall goals and objectives through the effective utilization and management of the firm's human resources. Some law firms believe in compensating employees at or above the high end of the wage range in order to be able to choose from the best talent available. Other firms take a more conservative approach to compensation, hoping to attract employees who are motivated by needs other than money.

As discussed earlier, the firm's philosophy toward employees affects decisions in many areas—but nowhere is this impact more evident than in the way the employees are compensated.

Factor 2: External Economic Conditions

In developing a compensation policy the firm must consider some external economic conditions, including (1) conditions of the labor market, (2) wage rates for the area, and (3) cost of living.

Labor Market Conditions Supply of, and demand for, qualified labor is reflected by the labor market. When demand for skilled labor is high and supply is low, not only do wages rise but recruiting employees becomes extremely difficult.

In the legal profession the supply of attorneys and paralegals has grown at an unprecedented rate in recent years, with supply exceeding demand in some areas, thus keeping wages low. At the same time, the supply of legal secretaries and legal word processors has continued to drop, while demand for these skills is at an all-time high. The basic economic laws of supply and demand explain why legal secretaries are being paid more than paralegals in many areas—there are simply fewer of them and their skills are very valuable.

Area Wage Rates The firm's wage structure should provide rates that are in line with those being paid by other firms in the area. If a firm's wage rates drift above existing area levels, labor costs, as a percentage of total expenses, may become excessive. This could result in the firm going out of business. On the other hand, if they are allowed to drop below area levels, the firm will encounter difficulty in recruiting and retaining competent personnel.

Every industry and profession conducts wage surveys—usually on an annual basis. This information is then published by trade groups or professional associations. For example, starting salaries for graduating attorneys are widely published in business newspapers and periodicals. The Association of Legal Administrators conducts annual wage and benefit surveys covering all personnel in the law firm, including partners, and provides the information to their membership. Salary information is also available to paralegals and legal secretaries through both local and national paralegal associations and legal secretaries associations. Employment agencies and personnel recruiters (commonly known as "headhunters") are also reliable sources of information about prevailing wage rates in their geographical areas. In addition, your state's Department of Labor gathers wage, salary, and employee benefit statistics on a quarterly basis and can provide you with current information for your area.

Cost of Living Factors Inflation makes it necessary to adjust compensation rates to keep up with purchasing power. In times of runaway inflation, **cost-of-living adjustments (COLA),** an index that considers the rate of inflation and its impact on purchasing power, are usually made on a quarterly basis. At other times, these adjustments are made annually. COLA adjustments are based on changes in the **consumer price index (CPI)**—a measure of the average change in prices over time in a fixed "market basket" of goods and services, including food, clothing, shelter, fuels, transportation fares, charges for medical services, and other day-to-day goods and services. COLA and CPI figures are compiled and published by both state and federal Departments of Commerce.

As a basis for establishing pay rates, CPI has value. For example, the cost of housing in some areas is far greater than in others, so employers must pay more to attract employees to these areas. However, caution must be applied in using CPI figures as a basis for subsequent wage increases. Quite simply, it is inequitable. A COLA of $.50 represents a 10 percent increase for an employee earning $5 per hour ($.50/$5.00 = 10%), but only a 5 percent increase for one who is earning $10 per hour ($.50/$10.00 = 5%). Under this system, where is the employee incentive to take on more responsibility?

Factor 3: Internal Considerations

Internal factors that influence wage rates include (1) the worth of the job to the firm, (2) the employee's relative worth, and (3) the employer's ability to pay.

Job Worth One internal factor influencing wage rates is the worth of the job to the organization. Without a formal compensation program, firms rely heavily on the labor market and the subjective opinions of people to determine the worth of the job. Larger firms with formal compensation programs are also likely to rely on a job evaluation system as well to aid in wage rate determination.

It is beyond the scope of this text to address all of the components, which might include education and years of experience, in determining which jobs or positions should be paid more than others. However, it is important to note that attorney time and paralegal time are regularly billed to clients. Therefore, the relative worth of these billable hours to the firm should be taken into consideration when establishing wage rates.

Employee's Worth   After determining the worth of the position to the firm, the next step in determining compensation is to evaluate the employee's relative worth to the firm in terms of meeting the job requirements. This determination can be made after reviewing the employee's performance and comparing performance against established goals. Those employees who are contributing toward achieving the firm's goals and are meeting or exceeding the job requirements can be recognized through promotion and various incentive systems.

Merit raises are a common reward for performance. But, as with COLA, they have their problems. If merit raises are truly based upon merit, or superior performance, they must be determined by an effective performance appraisal system that distinguishes between those employees who deserve the increases and those who do not. Too often, merit raises lack credibility with employees because the relationship between performance and any raise is not well defined. Many so-called merit raises are granted automatically, thus rewarding employees more for showing up than for being productive on the job.

Ability to Pay   All employers simply cannot afford to pay the same wages and benefits. There are differences in ability to pay, for example, between the public sector and the private sector. In the District Attorney's office, a public sector employer, the amount of pay and benefits for paralegals and other employees is limited by the funds budgeted for this purpose and by the taxpayers' willingness to provide them.

In a private law firm, pay levels are determined by the amount of fees generated and by the profits a firm can derive from the services they provide. Thus, the productivity of a firm's employees and its ability to invest in labor-saving equipment play a large part in determining pay levels.

Of course, economic conditions and competition will also significantly impact the rates a firm can afford to pay. Although for the most part the practice of law tends to be recession-proof, a severe economic downturn can reduce income the same way that pressure from competitors might. In these situations firms have little choice but to reduce wages and/or lay off employees, or go out of business.

Until the past decade, private law firms seemed to be immune to the whims of the economy, and most lawyers, due to the quality of their personal and business relationships with their clients, did not concern themselves much with competition from other firms. However, in the past ten years the profession has witnessed not only the loss of loyalty from clients but the total demise of some firms. Here are the factors that will influence your firm's compensation program:

- Factor 1: Compensation objectives
- Factor 2: External economic conditions
- Factor 3: Internal considerations

7-4 Guidelines for Hiring Personnel

Recruiting, scheduling appointments, and interviewing can consume many billable hours for even a small law firm. Therefore, adding new staff is an expense for the firm from the moment the decision is made. In an attempt to select the most appropriate person for the job, the firm must rely on the completeness and accurateness of the job description and the acumen of the person conducting the interview.

How to Define the Job and the Position

A **job** is defined as a group of related activities and duties that are similar in nature. A **position** refers to different duties and responsibilities performed by only *one* employee. For example, in a law firm two paralegals (two positions) may be involved in doing research for several attorneys, but both of them have only one job (doing research).

A job represents different things to the employee and the employer. For most employees, a job provides their primary source of income and determines their standard of living; in some cases, a job also determines their social status. On the other hand, to the employer a job represents a way for the firm to achieve its goals. Since a job consumes a rather significant portion of our lives, job satisfaction results when both the employee and employer are satisfying their needs.

The process of determining the responsibilities, duties, and tasks for each job and describing how these are to be performed is called **job design.** This information, together with the position title and to whom the position reports, is called a **job description.**

Typically, a job description is composed of at least three parts: the job title, the job identification section, and a job duties section. In addition to giving psychological importance and status to the position, the job title should provide some indication of the duties involved and should indicate its relative level in the firm's hierarchy. For example, Junior Paralegal implies that the job occupies a lower level than Senior Paralegal. Avoid using job titles such as Paralegal I and Paralegal II, since most people would have difficulty distinguishing one job from the other.

Included in the job identification section are such items as the location of the job, the person to whom the jobholder reports, a payroll or code number, or any other identification information. The job duties section contains statements covering the duties and responsibilities of the job, usually arranged in order of importance. A sample job description for a legal administrator is presented in Figure 7–3.

Every member of the staff in your law firm should have a job description so that individual jobs and the relationship between jobs in the firm can be assessed from time to time to ensure efficiency. When the duties of each job are clearly defined, it is less likely that some jobs will be neglected and others duplicated. Further, written job descriptions make the selection process easier for both the employer and the employee. Too many employees accept a position, only to find later that it was not as represented in the interview process because the interviewer did not have an accurate description of the job or the position.

Figure 7–3 Job Description

JOB TITLE: LEGAL ADMINISTRATOR

JOB SUMMARY:

The LEGAL ADMINISTRATOR manages the planning, marketing, and business functions, as well as the overall operations of the law firm. He or she reports to the managing partner or the executive committee and participates in management meetings. In addition to general responsibility for financial planning and controls, personnel administration (including compensation), systems, and physical facilities, the legal administrator identifies and plans for the changing needs of the firm, shares responsibility with the appropriate partners for strategic planning, practice management and marketing, and contributes to cost-effective management throughout the firm.

JOB DUTIES AND RESPONSIBILITIES:

1.   Prepares plans, forecasts, budgets, profitability analyses and financial reports. Supervises the accounting functions including billing and collections. Controls cash flow, banking relationships, investments, tax planning, tax reporting, trust accounting, payroll, pension plans, and other financial management functions.
2.   Recruits, selects, places, orients, and trains support staff. Evaluates, motivates, counsels, disciplines, and terminates support staff. Administers benefits and insurance programs.
3.   Negotiates office space lease, plans and designs space. Purchases inventory, office equipment, and vendor services. Supervises reception/switchboard services, telecommunications, mail, and messenger services.
4.   Prepares strategic and tactical plans for business development, risk management, quality control, and organizational development including making policy.
5.   Forecasts business opportunities, plans development activities and marketing for legal services, and enhances the firm's visibility and image in desired markets.

JOB REQUIREMENTS:

1.   Familiarity with legal or other professional service organizations, and experience managing business operations including planning, marketing, financial and personnel administration, and management of professionals.
2.   Ability to identify and analyze complex issues and problems in management, finance, and human relations and to recommend and implement solutions. Ability to manage office functions economically and efficiently, and to organize work, establish priorities, and maintain good interpersonal relations and communications with lawyers and support staff.
3.   Possess demonstrated supervisory and leadership skills as well as excellent skills in written and oral communication. Demonstrated willingness and ability to delegate.
4.   Graduation from a recognized college or university with major course work in business administration or finance, or comparable work experience.

How to Find Qualified Applicants

Once you have an up-to-date description of the job and the position to be filled, your next step is to locate qualified applicants. There are many resources available to help you in your search.

Newspaper Advertising   Placing an ad in the newspaper is one of the most commonly used resources to find qualified applicants. While newspaper ads will typically provide you with the greatest number of applicants, generally more than half of those responding are not qualified for the advertised position. To read through the resumes and determine which ones are qualified may take more time than anticipated.

Personnel Agencies Private employment agencies are another source for applicants. Your firm will pay a fee to the agency for their help in finding an applicant if the applicant is subsequently hired by the firm. Personnel agencies earn their fee by advertising jobs, preselecting, interviewing, and testing hundreds of people to find only qualified applicants for you to interview. Using an agency can save you many hours of time sifting through resumes and returning telephone calls from people who do not possess the skills you are seeking.

Professional Associations Most of the local chapters of professional associations, such as the National Association of Legal Assistants, the Association of Legal Administrators, the Legal Assistants Management Association, and others, have an employment chairperson who is responsible for placing announcements of vacant positions in their newsletters or publications. Usually there is no charge for these announcements and you will reach a qualified audience.

Employee Referrals Recommendations from employees are another way to find possible applicants. Some firms reward the employee who recommended a hired applicant with a bonus in their paycheck or a gift certificate to a good restaurant or department store.

Educational Institutions Typically, educational institutions are a source of young applicants with formal training but lacking full-time work experience. If your firm is willing to provide closely supervised training during the first few months on the job, staying in touch with the placement counselors at the educational institutions in your community can provide you with an excellent resource for office staff personnel.

You may decide to use one or all of these methods to find your pool of qualified applicants. Once you have identified several applicants with potential, the next step is to interview those you have selected.

How to Conduct an Interview

The primary reason to conduct an interview is to collect enough information about the applicant so that you can rationally determine whether the candidate can do the job as described and whether he or she will be a good fit in your firm. To be able to make this determination, you will need to find out about background, employment skills, personality, and potential in general as an employee with your firm.

No doubt there will be a number of questions you would like to ask in the interview that the Equal Employment Opportunity Commission (EEOC) and many state agencies have determined to be discriminatory. Since many of these questions seem like natural ones to ask, many interviewers are nonplussed when told that their questions are not permitted.

Interview Questions You Cannot Ask Here is a list of some of the questions that are improper in an interview because of the potential to discriminate:

- Are you married? What is your spouse's name? What does your spouse do for a living?

- Do you have children? How many children do you have? How old are your children?
- What is your maiden name? Have you ever been known by any other name?
- Do you have any physical defects, illnesses, or disabilities? Have you had any recent or past illness or operations? What was the date of your last physical exam?
- Have you ever been arrested? (You can ask if the person has ever been convicted of a misdemeanor or felony, but each conviction should be judged on its own merits with respect to time, circumstances, and seriousness.)
- When did you attend high school or grammar school? When did you graduate from high school or grammar school?
- Do you have a legal driver's license? Do you have a car? What kind of car do you have?
- What is your date of birth? How old are you?
- What are your hobbies? What organizations do you belong to?
- What church do you belong to? What holidays do you observe?
- Who would we contact in case of an emergency? Who would you give as a credit reference?
- What salary earnings do you expect?

The EEOC Point of View   Only questions that deal with the applicant's ability to perform the job are permissible under the EEOC guidelines. Therefore, it is not proper to ask any question about a person's family responsibilities, since these matters do not directly affect job performance.

Because it is against the law to discriminate based on age, no questions may be asked that might lead you to draw a conclusion about the applicant's age, such as when and where did you go to school? Likewise, no questions may be asked about the applicant's religious affiliation, holidays observed, or memberships in organizations or clubs.

Inquiring into an applicant's arrest record, credit references, or ownership of a car has been determined by the EEOC to have no bearing, in most cases, on whether the applicant can perform the job. In addition, the EEOC has determined that questions of these kinds tend to discriminate against certain minority groups. Likewise, asking about a person's health or disability can open up the possibility of claims of handicap discrimination.

Finally, asking the applicant what salary earnings are expected might be viewed as discriminatory in the event the applicant is not aware of the current wage rate for the position and understates expectations, or if the applicant was underpaid in a previous position.

How to Get the Information You Want   When you are in doubt about any interview question, remind yourself that only questions pertaining directly to the applicant's current ability to perform the job are permitted. There are, however, many permissible ways to find out an applicant's potential job performance and dependability. For instance, instead of asking about family life and responsibilities, you may ask what hours the applicant is able to work, if the applicant is able to work overtime or on weekends without advance notice, and if he or she is able to attend work regularly.

Instead of asking about owning a car, you may ask how the applicant will get to work every day. You may also ask whether the applicant would have any difficulty in performing the job as it is currently described or whether special accommodations would be needed, instead of asking about any physical disabilities.

To determine whether the person will "fit in" at your law firm, ask the applicant for a self-description. Open-ended questions usually elicit a wealth of information about the applicant's life-style and personality and will help you gauge how well the person will do with the other people in your firm. Some other suggestions of open-ended questions you might ask include: "What is the major motivator in your life?" and "What aspects of your last job did you like best and what did you like least?" To determine the applicant's problem-solving ability, you might try: "Tell me about the last time you had a difficult problem on your job (or a difficult boss to work for, or a difficult research project), and tell me how you solved it and what was the result."

Once the applicant has been hired, the firm is entitled to know about the person's family and background for insurance purposes, as well as whom to notify in case of an emergency and the relationship of that individual to the employee.

Choosing the best employees for your firm is a subjective decision. You must rely on open-ended questions and your people-reading skills to support your decision, not illegal questions.

7–5 Methods of Evaluating Employee Performance

Nearly every employer and employee recognizes the importance of objective feedback on job performance. But despite good intentions, many employees feel their performance evaluations are not as fair or constructive as they could be. The most frequent complaints from employees include the following:

- No real discussion took place and the employee had little opportunity to participate.
- No specific issues were addressed.
- Ratings were sometimes inconsistent with performance.
- No information was given on how to improve.

Three points of view are involved in evaluating employee performance: the employee's, the employer's, and the court's. For employees, performance evaluation issues center around self-respect, growth, challenge, accomplishment, freedom, security, and financial recognition of productivity.

On the other hand, employers are concerned about whether they have the support and cooperation from their employees to achieve the firm's goals and objectives, and whether they have the authority to terminate an employee who is not performing or who is otherwise undermining its goals.

In wrongful termination lawsuits the courts are interested not only in the methods used to document performance evaluations but also in what measures were taken to correct any disciplinary matters. Employers can infer from recent court decisions that a balanced system is preferred—one that outlines specifically what an employee must do to improve performance and keep his or her job. Furthermore, many courts recommend a review system that identifies on an ongoing basis what the employee must do to keep the job. Failure to disclose the standards against which the employee is being measured is viewed negatively by the court.

To satisfy all three points of view, employers need to evaluate employee performance through a process that encourages employees to become more involved in the feedback process. Here are some methods for making the evaluation process a two-way dialogue instead of a one-way dictum.

Management by Objectives

Management by objectives (MBO) is both an evaluation tool for translating organizational goals into specific, individual objectives and a method for measuring the relative worth of an individual employee to the organization. A departure from the more traditional approach, in which supervisors alone established goals for subordinates, MBO seeks to evaluate employee performance based on success in achieving goals established jointly with supervisors. Further, under MBO all efforts are focused on the goals to be achieved by the employee rather than on the activities performed or the personality traits of the employee.

Steps in Designing an MBO Program   A successful MBO program requires four steps: (1) establishment of individual employee objectives based on the firm's goals; (2) measurement of results for purposes of evaluation; (3) communication between management and employee; and (4) rewards based on individual effort and results.

Step 1: Establish individual employee objectives. Begin with a meeting between management and employee where the two discuss objectives for the employee, both from management's perspective and from the employee's. The objectives discussed should not only benefit the firm; they should also contribute to the professional growth of the employee.

After discussing both the firm's objectives and the employee's, reach an agreement on both specific short-term (six months or less) objectives and long-term (one year or more) objectives. Whether short- or long-term, objectives must be clearly stated and can be neither too difficult nor too easy to attain. If the goals are too hard to achieve, the employee is likely to give up. On the other hand, if the goals are too easy, they will not motivate or provide feelings of accomplishment once reached. Then, assign each objective a priority, since reaching some goals may be more important than others.

Step 2: Establish a method to measure each goal. To do so, each goal must be specified in exact terms. For instance, how would you measure a paralegal's goal to "increase billable hours over the next three months"? A measurable goal would be to "increase billable hours over the next three months by 10 percent without increasing normal work hours."

It is important that goals be established jointly by management and employee, not only to coordinate the firm's goals with the employee's, but to make sure they are realistic and attainable. In addition, when employees are given an active role in determining their own success on the job, the degree of commitment to success is positively affected. On the other hand, when management does not take an active interest in the goal setting process, the employee may feel that management has little interest in personal development or in evaluating performance in general.

Step 3: Set a specific time for review and evaluation of goals. The evaluation discussion should be constructive—not a forum for placing blame or finding fault. To get away from the report-card tone of the session, management should assume the role of a coach instead of a judge, and the employee should openly express his or her concerns. Assuming that the goals were clearly defined, measurable, and reasonably attainable, the review session should be mutually rewarding. The last part of this session should be devoted to establishing new goals for the next period.

Step 4: Reward individual efforts. Once the performance review has been completed and documented, management needs to find ways to reward exceptional performance. While money is widely recognized as one way to reward employees, it is not the only way. Many employees are also rewarded with opportunities for career advancement, public recognition for performance, respect, additional challenges and responsibilities, and more freedom to make decisions in matters directly concerning them, such as benefits and work hours. Figure 7–4 is one sample of an MBO evaluation form.

In summary, here are the steps in an MBO performance evaluation:

1. Establish short-term and long-term goals.
2. Establish a method to measure each goal.
3. Set a time for review and evaluation of goals.
4. Reward exceptional performance.

Coworker Evaluation of Performance

Some firms, particularly those where teams are formed, are asking staff members to evaluate each other. Coworker evaluations serve the purpose of getting input from several sources, not just from management's perspective, and are thus more likely to present a true evaluation of the worker's contribution to achieving the team's goals as well as the firm's goals.

After the individual coworker evaluation forms are collected and the results tabulated, a meeting is held between the supervisor and employee to discuss the results of the evaluation and areas of improvement. A copy of the tabulated results, along with notes pertaining to new goals set between management and employee, is placed in the employee's personnel file. The completed individual evaluation forms are destroyed after tabulation. Figure 7–5 is one form of a coworker performance evaluation form.

Management Performance Evaluation

In recent years management too has recognized some benefits from making the performance evaluation a two-way process. The usual performance review system is from the top down, without any input from employees about management's performance. But many firms are recognizing that today's employees respond positively to opportunities to evaluate management when there is no fear of reprisal. Since management rarely has the time or the inclination to give feedback to each other on some of the issues covered by the evaluation form, the information provided from this type of evaluation is often welcomed. Figure 7–6 is one form used by employees to evaluate management's performance.

The best performance evaluation systems are those that allow the firm to take into consideration the individual contribution of each employee, and to recognize that contribution and reward the employee appropriately based on performance.

7–6 How to Increase Employee Job Satisfaction

Today's workers strive for greater balance in their lives—a more holistic lifestyle—and many firms are altering their attitudes and personnel policies to help them achieve their goals. Here are some methods you can use to increase employee job satisfaction.

Figure 7–4 Performance Appraisal Form

PERFORMANCE APPRAISAL

GENERAL INSTRUCTIONS

During the months of October and November, annual performance appraisal discussions are conducted for all salaried exempt and non-exempt employees. To ensure an effective link between pay and performance, the performance appraisal discussion must be completed for each salaried employee prior to completion of the annual merit review.

This form is used to facilitate the discussion. The performance appraisal process provides both the employee and management with an opportunity to:

1. Clarify employee's roles and responsibilities;
2. Evaluate employee's accomplishments related to last year's performance objectives;
3. Discuss employee's strengths and areas for improvement;
4. Establish employee's performance objectives for next year;
5. Briefly discuss empoyee's career interests and developmental activities (detailed career development planning is accomplished on the employee's anniversary date); and
6. Assess specific factors as reflected by employee's past performance.

PROCEDURE

EMPLOYEE

1. Review last year's performance appraisal focusing on last year's performance objectives for use in this year's evaluation.
2. Complete Sections 1 and 2 (can be typed or printed).
3. Submit to management.

MANAGEMENT

4. Review last year's performance appraisal, concentrating on last year's performance objectives.
5. Review employee's comments in Section 1.
6. Complete management comments in Section 1 by concurring/clarifying and elaborating on employee's self-assessment of performance in Section 2.
7. Review employee's self-assessment of performance in Section 2.
8. Provide management assessment of performance by commenting in Section 3.
9. Schedule performance appraisal interview with employee, discussing each item on form.
10. Sign form, obtain employee's acknowledgment signature and next level management signature.
11. Provide employee with copy of completed and signed performance appraisal.
12. Forward original to SBU/FSU administrator.

SBU/FSU ADMINISTRATOR

13. Ensure accountability of performance appraisal for each salaried employee.
14. Forward original to Career Resource Center for filing.

Note: During this process, the Career Resource Center will be available to assist employee and management. In addition, management may request participation in a Performance Planning and Appraisal Workshop by contacting the Career Resource Center.

Performance Appraisal

Section **1**

Review Period:		
	From	To

Name		Employee No.	Job Title		Job Code

Dept No.	Dept Name	SBU/FSU	Division	Component
				MDAC

Employee Comments

1. **Job Duties:** Describe current job responsibilities.

2. **Accomplishments and Strengths:** Describe recent job accomplishments and summarize work-related strengths. (Include those related to previously set performance objectives.)

3. **Areas for Improvement:** Areas that when strengthened will result in performance improvement in current position.

4. **Performance Objectives:** Identify job-related performance objectives in your present assignment. (These will be evaluated in next year's performance appraisal.)

5. **Career Interests*:** Describe the type of work that you would like to do within short range (3-5 years) and your long-range career goals.

6. **Development Actions and Plans*:** Describe development actions accomplished and plans for the future.

Management Comments

Employee Signature	Date

*Detailed career development planning is documented annually on your anniversary date

Figure 7-4 *continued*

Figure 7–4 *continued*

Section 2 — Employee — *Provide a Self-Assessment for Each Category*

Section 3 — Management — *Describe Employee's Performance for Each Category*

Category	Employee's Comments	Management Comments
1. Job Knowledge/Technical Capability To what extent does employee possess the knowledge/capability to perform job functions?	1.	1.
2. Work Output To what extent does employee accomplish the job? (Consider accuracy, duration, and thoroughness.)	2.	2.
3. Dependability Consider whether employee completes his or her assignments on time with a minimal need for follow-up. Are attendance and punctuality satisfactory?	3.	3.
4. Communication To what extent does employee communicate effectively (verbal and written)? Consider how well employee communicates/listens in up/down communication link.	4.	4.
5. Creativity and Originality To what extent does employee see new, usable and different ways to carry out his or her duties?	5.	5.
6. Interpersonal Relationships Consider how well employee relates with peers, superiors, and subordinates.	6.	6.
7. Leadership Consider how well employee evaluates and utilizes subordinates and inspires the group to a team effort. If not in leadership position, what has employee exhibited to indicate leadership potential?	7.	7.
8. Five Keys to Self-Renewal: Describe employee's involvement. Examples of involvement are described below: 1. **Strategic Management** — Knowledge of company's long-range goals, problems, and opportunities. Supports/suggests methods for pursuing strategic management goals. 2. **Human Resource Management** — Establishes personal goals in support of organization needs. Seeks opportunities for self-development. Challenges and coaches subordinates. Provides opportunity for subordinates to pursue developmental goals. Supports equal opportunity objectives. 3. **Participative Management** — Nurtures team-oriented climate. Contributes to decision-making process at each opportunity. Solicits support and subordinate involvement. 4. **Productivity Improvement** — Suggests/encourages productivity improvement efforts. Actively participates in Quality/Productivity initiatives. Effectively utilizes organizational resources. Exhibits cost consciousness in daily activities. 5. **Ethical Decision Making** — Observes and promotes MDC code of ethics. Demonstrates ethical behavior in daily activities.	8.	8.

Additional Space

Comments — Employee

Comments — Management

Management Signature	Date	Next Level Management Signature	Date
Employee's Acknowledgement	Date	Project Review (If Appropriate)	Date

Figure 7–5 Staff Evaluation Form

Staff Member: _____ Date: _____

Evaluation Period: From _____ To _____ Hire Date: _____

Rate performance according to this scale:
  5—Outstanding (rarely equalled)
  4—Very good (unusually well done)
  3—Satisfactory (normal expectancy)
  2—Less than expected (needs improvement or inconsistent)
  1—Unsatisfactory (unacceptable)
  n/a—Not applicable or No basis for evaluation

	Rating	Comments
Technical Knowledge and Job Performance		
1. Demonstrates knowledge of technical job requirements, procedures, and principals appropriate to job level.		
2. Maintains accuracy and quality in written materials and workpapers.		
3. Accepts responsibility for and follows through on assignments.		
4. Completes assignments on time.		
5. Organizes and plans work effectively by setting and following priorities.		
6. Initiates solutions to problems.		
7. Achieves chargeable hour goals.		
8. Maintains appropriate level of professionalism with clients and coworkers.		
9. Shows enthusiasm and a positive attitude toward assigned work.		
10. Meets standards for hours worked, attendance and punctuality.		
Communication and Interpersonal Skills		
11. Works towards building positive relationships with other personnel.		
12. Assists coworkers as needed.		
13. Communicates well orally.		
14. Communicates well in writing.		
15. Exercises good judgment in handling problems.		
16. Keeps supervisor informed of workload.		
17. Maintains regular contact with clients and provides updates on work-in-process.		
18. Represents the firm well in client contacts.		
Supervisory Skills		
19. Assists staff in their development.		
20. Provides direction and feedback.		
21. Demonstrates ability to effectively manage and utilize personnel.		
22. Works toward developing teamwork among self and personnel.		
23. Delegates effectively.		

Figure 7–5 *continued*

	Rating	Comments
Personal Characteristics/Attributes		
24. Exhibits professional appearance and good personal grooming.		
25. Maintains a positive attitude.		
26. Seeks opportunities for personal development.		
27. Demonstrates maturity and good judgment.		
28. Exhibits self-motivation.		
29. Displays ability to maintain confidentiality.		
30. Demonstrates evidence of one who cares.		

Major strengths are:

Strengths could be used more effectively by doing the following:

Areas needing improvement are:

Improvement could result by doing the following:

Find Ways to Enrich Each Job and Position

Clearly defined jobs will increase job satisfaction. But when a job ceases to provide challenge or opportunities for growth, it can become a grind. **Job enrichment** refers to one common approach to breaking monotony by redesigning the job. The usual ways of enriching a job are to build into it more planning and decision-making authority, increase autonomy and responsibility, and give the employee more control over the outcome. Because job enrichment results in a more exciting job for the employee, job satisfaction and productivity tend to increase while employee turnover and absenteeism decrease.

It is important to emphasize that job enrichment is not a panacea for other problems such as dissatisfaction with pay or not getting along with the boss. In fact, if employees already feel they are overworked and underpaid, job enrichment will backfire. They will see it as being asked to do even more for the firm without any apparent benefit to them. While job enrichment has great motivational potential in a law office, it is not for everyone. Some employees simply do not want additional responsibility or authority and are satisfied with performing only those duties specified in their job description.

Try the Team Approach

One approach to job enrichment is to make jobs more interesting and responsible by organizing teams. Typically, the team approach to job enrichment works this way. Each partner/shareholder in the firm would be "captain" of a team consisting of one or two associate attorneys (or law clerks), two or more paralegals, a word processor, and a secretary. The entire team would regularly meet each Monday morning or Friday afternoon for the purpose of

Figure 7–6 Upward Evaluation Form

Evaluatee: _____ Position: _____

Evaluation Period: From _____ To _____

Rate performance according to this scale:
  5—Outstanding (rarely equalled)
  4—Very good (unusually well done)
  3—Satisfactory (normal expectancy)
  2—Less than expected (needs improvement or inconsistent)
  1—Unsatisfactory (unacceptable)
  n/a—Not applicable or No basis for evaluation

	Rating	Comments
Technical Knowledge and Job Performance		
1. Demonstrates knowledge of technical job requirements, procedures, and principals appropriate to job level.		
2. Properly plans and controls caseload.		
3. Accepts responsibility for and follows through on assignments.		
4. Completes assignments on time.		
5. Organizes and plans work effectively by setting and following priorities.		
6. Initiates solutions to problems.		
7. Displays integrity, objectivity, and a high standard of ethics.		
8. Maintains appropriate level of professionalism with clients and coworkers.		
9. Shows enthusiasm and a positive attitude toward assigned work.		
10. Respectful of commitments, obligations, and responsibilities of others.		
Communication and Interpersonal Skills		
11. Works towards building positive relationships with staff.		
12. Assists other personnel as needed.		
13. Communicates well orally.		
14. Communicates well in writing.		
Approach to Client Relations		
15. Exercises good judgment in handling problems.		
16. Represents the firm well in client contacts.		
17. Makes himself/herself available to clients.		
18. Offers timely client services.		

Figure 7–6 *continued*

	Rating	Comments
Supervisory Skills		
19. Assists staff in their development.		
20. Provides direction and feedback.		
21. Demonstrates ability to effectively manage and utilize personnel.		
22. Works toward developing teamwork among self and personnel.		
23. Delegates effectively.		
24. Is trustworthy and conscientious.		
25. Makes appropriate decisions.		
26. Attempts to involve lower level staff in making decisions.		
27. Demonstrates maturity and good judgment.		
28. Acts as a positive role model for other personnel.		
29. Seeks out and accepts feedback on performance.		
30. Demonstrates evidence of one who cares.		

Major strengths are:

Strengths could be used more effectively by doing the following:

General comments:

giving case status updates to team members. Keeping each other informed serves the purpose of facilitating work flow, project scheduling, and time management. But perhaps the greatest benefit from the team approach is the service provided to clients. Where there are teams, a client can talk to any member of the team and get the information he or she wants with one phone call.

In larger firms several teams can be organized, usually by area of specialization, and the megafirms might have several teams in the same division. Work teams often participate in after-hours activities such as softball, bowling, tennis, and golf, with the intraoffice teams competing against each other. Many firms have found that forming teams to get the work done not only increases client satisfaction, but also promotes employee loyalty to the firm and feelings of goodwill toward coworkers.

Consider Adjustments in Work Schedules

Altering the normal workweek of five 8-hour days is another form of job design. Giving employees increased control over the hours they work can contribute to productivity and morale. Some of the more common ways of altering work schedules include the *four-day workweek, flexible working hours,* and *job sharing.*

In the four-day workweek the number of days in the workweek is shortened by lengthening the number of hours worked per day. Some law firms have found many advantages to this, including a larger pool of job applicants and a reduction in absenteeism, turnover, overtime, and commuting problems. Of course, employees benefit from a reduced number of workdays too. They have an extra day for personal matters and leisure activities, extra time to spend with family members, and a reduction in commuting costs.

Among the disadvantages of a four-day workweek is fatigue, which begins in the seventh hour. However, with adequate planning and acceptance from management, the four-day workweek can benefit both the employee and the employer.

Flexible working hours, or *flextime,* permits employees to choose daily starting and quitting times, provided that they work a set number of hours per day or week. Typically with flextime, employees are given considerable latitude in scheduling their work and lunch periods, but there is a "core period" during the morning and afternoon hours when all employees are required to be on the job.

By allowing employees greater flexibility in work scheduling, tardiness and absenteeism can be reduced. Not only do employees gain more job satisfaction by being in control of their time, they are more productive on the job. Flextime helps reduce traffic congestion during peak commuting hours and, in most cases, actually reduces commuting time. Firms offering this benefit have also found personnel recruiting to be easier.

Job sharing is a relatively new concept whereby arrangements are made for two part-time employees to perform a job that otherwise would be held by one full-time employee. Job sharing is particularly suited to the needs of families and older workers, both of whom represent the fastest growing segments of the nation's labor pool.

A benefit to job sharing for employers is that part-time employees can be scheduled to conform to peaks in the daily work load, which can result in cost savings. Employees benefit from having time off during the week to take care of personal needs and are less likely to be absent from work when scheduled.

There are two common problems with the job sharing concept. One is that the firm may not want to orient and train a second employee. This can be solved by allowing two current employees to share a job. It worked quite well in one firm where two paralegals gave birth within weeks of each other and, instead of hiring two replacements, the firm extended the offer to job share after the births. Another problem is what to do about benefits for part-time employees. By permitting employees to contribute the difference between benefit costs for a full-time employee and the pro rata amount for a part-timer, this problem is reduced.

Job satisfaction is limited only by the creativity of the individuals and the firm. Whether it is approached conservatively or from a sky-is-the-limit perspective, today's law firms must be innovative and flexible enough to attract employees from a dwindling qualified labor pool. In summary, here are three methods used to increase employee job satisfaction:

1. Find ways to enrich each job and position.
2. Try the team approach.
3. Consider adjustments in work schedules.

SUMMARY

7-1

Behavior patterns and societal values are reflected in the corporate culture of a law firm. The antidiscrimination legislation enacted in recent years is one example of how the values of society have an impact on corporate culture. Starting with the Civil Rights Act of 1964, as amended, which prohibits discrimination based on sex, race, religion, national origin, or color, subsequent acts prohibit discrimination based on pregnancy, age, or physical handicap or disability. In addition, employers are now required to protect employees by providing a safe and healthful work environment and by maintaining employee privacy on the job and to outsiders. In less than three decades there have been many major changes in the workplace due to shifts in the value systems of individuals who make up our American culture.

7-2

Personnel policies give structure to the law firm as well as provide management with written decision-making guidelines to ensure that all employees are treated impartially. Policies should reflect the firm's objectives as well as be compatible with current economic conditions and societal trends. The firm's policy manual can answer the employees' most frequently asked questions and provide support to management when the rules need to be enforced. Because a policy manual could be construed by the courts as an agreement between employer and employee, consulting with an expert in labor law is advisable when formulating personnel policies.

7-3

An employee compensation program must contribute to the firm's overall goals through the effective management of human resources as well as provide employees with a monetary reward for their efforts on behalf of the firm. In developing a compensation policy the firm must take into account external economic factors, such as conditions of the labor market, wage rates, and cost of living for the area, as well as internal factors, such as how much the job means to the firm, the employee's relative worth, and the firm's ability to pay. Recognizing that jobs have different meanings to employers and employees, the goal of any compensation policy must be to reflect these differences equitably.

7-4

Finding and hiring employees requires considerable effort and can consume many hours. The process begins with an up-to-date, clearly written job description that accurately reflects the duties and responsibilities of the position as well as the requirements for potential applicants. Qualified applicants can be found from a variety of sources, including newspaper advertising, personnel agencies, professional associations, employee referrals, and educational institutions. Once a pool of qualified applicants has been located, the next step is to interview those who are likely candidates for the position. Attention and care must be taken during the interview to not ask questions the EEOC has found to be discriminatory and to still get the information you want from the candidate. Only questions that pertain to the candidate's ability to perform the job as described are legal ones.

7-5

Feedback on performance is important to all employees. Improvement in job performance and professional growth can be enhanced through the information obtained during the review. There are several methods used to evaluate employee performance. The trend in recent years has been to involve the employee in a two-way dialogue instead of receiving input from management only. Management by objectives (MBO) is the most widely known method used for this two-way review process. Other employee performance evaluations are between coworkers who evaluate each other and upward evaluations, where staff members evaluate management performance. All of these methods, or similar ones, have been successfully implemented by many firms and provide an invaluable source of information to both employees and management.

7-6

Recognizing that many employees are seeking a more balanced life-style, employers are finding ways to increase employee job satisfaction through job enrichment programs. By increasing responsibility, authority, and autonomy on the job, employees feel more in control of their jobs and usually are more satisfied with their work. Some firms have found that the formation of teams increases not only employee satisfaction but client satisfaction as well. Other firms have found that adjusting work schedules and job sharing have decreased absenteeism and increased productivity, loyalty, and morale. When management and employees work together to find creative solutions to increase job satisfaction, everyone benefits.

REVIEW

Key Terms

affirmative action
Age Discrimination in Employment Act
Americans with Disabilities Act
bona fide occupational qualification
Civil Rights Act of 1964
comparable worth
consumer price index
corporate culture
cost-of-living adjustments
culture
Drug-Free Workplace Act
employment at will
equal employment opportunity
Equal Pay Act
job
job description
job design
job enrichment
management by objectives
Occupational Safety and Health Act
position
Pregnancy Discrimination Act
Privacy Act
sexual harassment

Questions for Review and Discussion

1. How would you define *culture?*
2. What impact does the culture of a society have on a law firm?
3. What has been the impact of recent cultural changes on employee attitudes toward work?
4. When Chrysler Corporation announced a layoff of 1,500 mid-level managers due to a decline in auto sales, it simultaneously announced plans to hire 2,000 new college graduates. Do you think Chrysler may be discriminating in any way according to the EEO guideline? Explain.
5. Why do law firms need personnel policies?
6. Explain the relationship between wages, job worth, and employee worth and how they affect a firm's compensation program.
7. What items should be included in a job description?
8. As personnel manager for your firm, what steps would you take to fill employee staff positions?
9. Would you prefer to receive a pay raise based on an MBO or similar evaluation or on COLA? Explain.
10. List some ways to enrich any job.

Activities

1. Write your own job description as it is now. Then make a list of ways to redesign and enrich your job. Now, rewrite your new job description.
2. Research sexual harassment litigation in your state and present your findings to the class.
3. Contact your state office of the Department of Labor and obtain a copy of the Fair Employment Laws guidelines. Present an outline of the guidelines to the class and take a class survey regarding compliance.
4. Conduct an interview with a classmate for a new paralegal position in your firm.

PART THREE

THE INTANGIBLE

LAW OFFICE

MANAGEMENT SKILLS

Chapter 8
Communication Skills and the Law Office Manager

Chapter 9
How to Be a Leader

Chapter 10
Managing Groups

CHAPTER 8   Communication Skills and the Law Office Manager

OUTLINE

8–1   How Communication Breaks Down
        Elements of Effective Communication
        Barriers in Effective Communication
8–2   Communicating without Words
        Body Language
        Decoding Nonverbal Communication
8–3   How to Become an Effective Listener
        Effective Listening Techniques
8–4   How to Give Constructive Feedback
        Positive Feedback
        Negative Feedback
8–5   How Communication Flows within the Firm
        The Formal Networks
        The Informal Networks

COMMENTARY

After several months as the office manager at Dunn & Sweeney you can see that progress has been made in several areas. The plans for new office space are coming along, several new money-saving procedures you suggested have been implemented, and the firm has budgets for the first time. Everything seems to be going quite well. Yet from time to time you feel that you are having difficulty communicating with your coworkers. Just yesterday one member of the staff angrily rebuked you for not having told her of a new procedural policy that caused her to have to put in some overtime hours to correct the error. After checking your notes, you find that she was present at the meeting during which the new procedures were discussed and to which everyone agreed. Sometimes your suggestions at partners' meetings are met with a blank look from one or two of the attorneys and you are not sure you are getting through to them. And next week you must begin the staff's annual performance evaluations.

OBJECTIVES

In Chapter 7 we learned that personnel management is influenced by many factors such as culture, legislation, job design, compensation, and giving feedback on performance. After studying this chapter, you will be able to:

1. Define the terms *communication* and *effective communication*.
2. List the six elements in the communication process.
3. Explain the purpose of feedback.

4. Identify common barriers to effective communication.
5. List the elements of nonverbal communication.
6. Describe the impact of culture on the decoding process.
7. Explain the techniques for effective listening.
8. Describe the purpose for and common forms of constructive feedback.
9. List the four elements of constructive feedback.
10. Describe the purposes of both the formal and informal communication networks.

8–1   How Communication Breaks Down

Communication, or the transfer of information between two or more people, is a process composed of six elements: a sender, the message, the channel used to send the message, a receiver, feedback from the receiver, and context. The communication process is a circular one and when illustrated might look like the sequence shown in Figure 8–1.

Elements of Effective Communication

Communication is especially important in the practice of law. Being an *effective* communicator is an essential skill for success for both law office managers and lawyers. How do you know when you are communicating effectively? When the receiver understands the *intent* and *content* of the message sent by the sender, effective communication has occurred.

Communication takes place in two ways. One way is when the initiator of the communication, or the **sender,** makes a *conscious decision* to express an emotion or thought to another person—the receiver. The other way communication occurs is through an *unconscious action* that the receiver observes and reacts to.

Thus, communication is based on either a conscious or unconscious act that conveys meaning, or a **message.** Messages are either **verbal,** consisting of words either spoken or written, or **nonverbal.** Nonverbal messages are contained in the sender's eyes, face, body movement, positioning, physical appearance, tone of voice, and in the **context** (time and place) of the communication.

Figure 8–1   The Communication Process

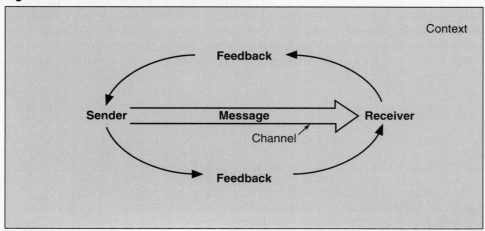

Two of the most commonly used **channels,** or ways by which messages may be communicated, are written and oral. Court documents, letters to clients, interoffice memoranda, and file notes are communication channels frequently used in a law office. Telephone calls, client interviews, staff meetings, and lunchroom conversations are also frequently used channels over which messages are sent and received.

Messages are either intentionally or unintentionally directed to a **receiver,** usually a person or a group of people. The receiver must be paying attention to the sender and be ready to receive the message or no transmission will take place.

Feedback begins with the listener's response to your message. A puzzled expression may indicate that the message was not clearly understood. An inappropriate action would also reflect a communication problem. After the message has been given and acted upon, with either a verbal response or an action, it is your turn to provide feedback. Feedback in this case would tell the employee that his or her response to your message was either correct or incorrect, and it may take the form of praise or reprimand.

Barriers in Effective Communication

Since communication takes place nearly all the time, either verbally or nonverbally, you need to recognize some of the barriers likely to occur in the process that can cause a breakdown in communications.

Sender Barriers   The worst assumption a sender can make is that the intent and content of the message were received and interpreted as the sender intended. Here are four common erroneous assumptions about communication often made by message senders:

1. People communicate only when they have consciously chosen to do so.
2. All messages are verbal.
3. Words have intrinsic meaning and everyone understands what they mean.
4. Most receivers are good listeners.

In reality you are communicating all the time, and a good part of the time you may not be aware of the nonverbal cues you are passing along. When your words and actions are in conflict, the receiver is faced with the dilemma of sorting through your mixed message.

Some message senders assume that because they speak the same language as the receiver, the meaning is clear by virtue of the words themselves. However, words mean whatever a person wants them to mean and are thus subject to individual interpretation. You need to recognize that message receivers are not passive receptacles of information and are likely to respond in unpredictable ways based on how they interpret a message. The most effective communicators, then, are those who take the time to develop rapport with their receivers to gain a better understanding of their perceptions, attitudes, and motivations.

Message Barriers   The receiver of a message may not interpret the communication as the sender intended because their points of view differ, the message is too vague, or words were used that have multiple definitions or transcend the receiver's vocabulary.

Consider the word *bar*. Does the word imply a piece of wood or metal? Or does it imply a barrier or obstacle, as in "to bar entry"? Is the implication a place where liquor is served, or does it refer to the division in a court between the bench and the rest of the courtroom? Or is the reference to the legal profession or to lawyers collectively, as members of the bar? A dictionary will list about 50 different meanings for this three-letter word. Because words can have multiple and sometimes conflicting meanings, your message should be constructed so the words are construed according to your intention.

Often messages are made more confusing by the use of jargon, such as "legalese," colloquial expressions, and slang words, or by using red-flag words that trigger an immediate emotional response, usually a negative one, in the receiver. Words that fall into these categories cause a receiver to "tune out" (a colloquial expression) the message. For example, to refer to a mature woman as a girl in a conversation with another woman indicates that the sender is insensitive to the receiver. And words such as *feminist, communist,* and *welfare,* are likely to evoke strong emotional reactions in some people when used in certain contexts.

Similarly, body language and behavior can support or contradict the sender's verbal message, thereby creating another barrier in understanding. For example, sitting on the edge of your chair indicates interest in the person or subject, and nodding the head indicates agreement (in our culture, but not in some other cultures). Failing to attend a meeting will contradict a professed interest in it, and arriving late to work several days a week may be interpreted as not being satisfied with your job.

Channel Barriers The two most common ways to deliver a message are either orally or in writing. If the sender makes an inappropriate choice in selecting the channel to convey the message, misunderstanding may occur. For example, it would be inappropriate for the county clerk to regularly convey all instructions for filing documents over the telephone; the chance for error is too great, and it is time-consuming. Likewise, it would not be appropriate for you to review the performance of an employee only in writing without having a personal discussion.

Unfortunately, within each channel there are many possibilities for misunderstanding. Sometimes oral messages do not get through because the sender talks too fast or too slowly, uses words incorrectly, fails to emphasize important points, slurs words, or speaks with a heavy accent.

According to psychologist Albert Mehrabian's study of communication ("Communication Without Words," *Psychology Today* [September 1968]), 38 percent of the impact of your message is dependent upon the manner in which the words are spoken, or **vocalics.** The way you express words may have a greater impact on the message than your behavior or your use of nonverbal cues.

A speaker's *vocabulary, pronunciation, dialect, voice pitch, rate of speaking, inflection,* and *fluency* are all channels of communication and can have a decisive impact on whether you get your message across. For example:

- If a person's message is inundated with slang words or if his or her vocabulary is limited, the message may not be taken seriously or may be misunderstood.
- If a speaker's dialect, a deep southern accent for instance, encounters the unconscious prejudice of the listener, the message may be blocked.
- If the speaker has a high-pitched, shrill voice, his or her tone may penetrate the listener far more than the message the sender is trying to convey.

- If a speaker speaks too fast or too slowly, chances are the message will miss its mark.
- If a message is relayed in a monotonous inflection, or, at the opposite extreme, in a singsong pattern, the listener may become either bored or distracted.
- If a message is interrupted by the speaker's lapses into too many *ums*, *ers*, *ya'knows*, the message's impact is diluted.

Listeners can draw many conclusions from the vocalics of the message sender. In addition to detecting emotions, many listeners are able to tell when someone is lying or attempting to deceive them by the vocalics. However, it is important to recognize that in drawing conclusions based on vocal characteristics alone, the listener is engaging in a form of stereotyped thinking; that is, broader characteristics are attributed to an individual based on specific traits, and conclusions about that person's message may be in error.

The principles that guide oral communication are applicable to written messages as well. For both channels of communication, it is essential that your thoughts are well-organized and clearly expressed.

Context Barriers When and where the communication takes place can affect the outcome. For example, if you choose to approach an employee about a problem in her performance while she is preparing to leave for the day, your message may miss its mark. On the other hand, choosing a more opportune moment, when she is prepared to listen, may produce the desired result.

Receiver Barriers Your receiver's unique values, attitudes, and belief systems color the meaning he or she attaches to your message. Each of us filters messages through our own unique value system and makes judgments based on that system. The result of our individual cultural experiences can be a communication bias known as **stereotyping,** which is the process of attributing certain characteristics to individuals based on their group membership or socioeconomic status. Stereotyping can have a profound effect on both your sending and receiving communication behavior.

Another receiver-based barrier might be poor listening skills. The average message sender speaks at the rate of about 120 words per minute; but the brain of the receiver is able to handle about 480 words per minute. No wonder poor listening is a common communication problem. Most listeners are not listening. They are forming responses, jumping to conclusions, making judgments, or thinking about other things.

Finally, if the receiver does not share the same viewpoint on the subject matter as the sender, the message might be misunderstood. Opinions on political issues, employees' rights, or membership in a group might unconsciously create a barrier to communication between the sender and the receiver.

Feedback Barriers Your feedback to an employee's action is, in its own right, a message as well. Effective feedback should reflect a timely response to the employee's reaction to your original message. If feedback is not specific or fairly immediate, its value may be lost, leaving the employee in the dark as to whether he or she interpreted your message correctly. For this reason, effective managers praise or reprimand as soon as possible. Also, if your feedback is not specific enough, its relationship to your original message or directive will not be understood. For example, "Nice job on the Adams brief" is more effective as praise than "Nice job."

8-2 Communicating without Words

Without opening your mouth, you have communicated volumes of messages to others. The way you look, the way you act, and the way you take care of yourself provide receivers with an impression of you that is often more powerful than words alone could create. There is truth in the axiom that you never get a second chance to make a first impression. Furthermore, an impression once made is often difficult to change.

Albert Mehrabian's study has shown that only 7 percent of the impact a message has on others comes as a result of the words used. His findings further indicate that of the remaining 93 percent of message impact, 38 percent comes from tone of voice and inflection, and the remaining 55 percent is attributed to physical behavior, or body language.

Body Language

One conclusion of Albert Mehrabian's study, and many others that examine the body as a communication tool, might be that actions do speak louder than words. Each of us communicates a message to others from our face, eyes, body, clothing, gestures, and touch.

The Face   Facial expression is often the most trustworthy indicator of emotions such as happiness, sadness, anger, surprise, contempt, disgust, interest, concern, and embarrassment. We have come to rely on the face to provide us with insight into a person's character. For example, some people are described as having an honest face or a strong chin as an indication of their character, while others might have narrow, shifty eyes. Or we might make presumptions about a person from a scar on the cheek or a broken nose.

A moustache, beard, or goatee on a man might suggest either nonconformity or conformity, depending on the times and the context; or they might suggest a lack of openness, an attempt to hide behind the facial hair. A tendency toward meticulousness might be presumed from well-groomed facial hair, while unkemptness might suggest a lax attitude.

The Eyes   Eye contact, or the lack of it, can provide information about the person's feelings, character, and culture. In our culture a direct glance—that is, maintaining eye contact with the other person about 60 percent of the time—is often interpreted as honesty, friendliness, interest, and a desire for feedback. But a person who stares or glares at you is usually thought of as threatening and aggressive, while someone who avoids eye contact might be perceived as uninterested, embarrassed, ashamed, or submissive. The lack of eye contact might simply be a cultural trait, however.

The Body   How many times have you drawn conclusions about a person based on their posture, height, weight, and skin color? Many people assume, for example, that tall people are good leaders and that fat people are friendly.

How you hold your body is also subject to a variety of interpretations. Do crossed arms mean that the person is defensive, defiant, or withdrawn? Are hands on the hips a sign that you are goal oriented (know what you want), or that you are ready for a fight? Leaning back in your chair with hands clasped behind your head might be interpreted as a sign of smugness or superiority, while slouched posture might be an indication of defeat or submissiveness.

Clothing   The clothing you choose is likely to disclose three things about you: behavior, values and attitudes, and how you earn your living. An immaculate dresser is likely to be a careful person who pays attention to detail, and a person in hiking boots probably enjoys the outdoors. A person with old-fashioned values is likely to be found wearing more traditional styles, while wearing excessive jewelry might be a sign of materialism.

What you choose to wear during working hours often tells others much about what you do for a living. A blue-collar worker's clothes are typically functional, chosen to help him do the job. A white-collar worker, on the other hand, usually chooses more formal attire considered appropriate for business.

Gestures   The movements you make with your hands, fingers, arms, and legs can serve to clarify, amplify, or emphasize your verbal message. Pointing to a chair while offering someone a seat or nodding in agreement while someone else is speaking are routine gestures. Pounding on a desk in anger or slamming the door are gestures that display emotion or are used for effect.

Other types of gestures, known as *emblems,* can even replace a verbal message. Just about everyone knows the meanings of the thumbs up or thumbs down gesture, the upward extension of the middle finger, and a wave of the hand to a friend.

Touch   In our culture physical contact between business associates is limited. Here the handshake is often the only form of touch used in the business environment. The handshake is at once a greeting and sign of acceptance. Failure to offer your hand to someone who is expecting it may be seen as a sign

Figure 8–2   Nonverbal Cues

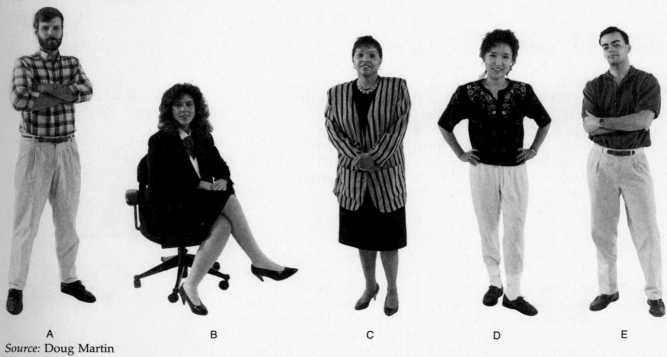

A   B   C   D   E

Source: Doug Martin

of rudeness or unfriendliness. At the other extreme, a compulsive handshaker who shakes your hand upon arriving, leaving, and passing you on the street might be exhibiting a strong need for acceptance.

Since so much is read into the handshake, the way you shake hands is important. A tight, vise-grip style might indicate a zest for life, a desire to dominate, or an intent to inflict physical or emotional pain. A limp grasp, on the other hand, might be interpreted as a sign of insecurity or negativity.

Decoding Nonverbal Communication

Some people are better at decoding nonverbal messages than others. Those who are capable of interpreting nonverbals with a high degree of accuracy are people who do not rely on just one cue but look at all the cues being given. Those who know how to decode effectively know that the context in which the nonverbal message is taking place must be considered. They are also aware of their own biases and prejudices and recognize the necessity to put them aside when interpreting the nonverbal messages of others. Study the five photographs in Figure 8–2 and look for nonverbal cues. After spending a few minutes studying the photographs, complete the assessment in Figure 8–3.

Figure 8–3 Nonverbal Message Assessment

		Circle Your Selection
1.	The most intelligent person is	A B C D E
	The least intelligent person is	A B C D E
2.	The hardest worker is	A B C D E
	The most lax worker is	A B C D E
3.	The one who likes to party is	A B C D E
	The one who prefers being alone is	A B C D E
4.	The one with the most money is	A B C D E
	The one with the least money is	A B C D E
5.	The warmest person is	A B C D E
	The coldest person is	A B C D E
6.	The one likely to be a leader is	A B C D E
	The one least likely to be a leader is	A B C D E
7.	The most sexualy active person is	A B C D E
	The least sexually active person is	A B C D E
8.	The most assertive person is	A B C D E
	The least assertive person is	A B C D E
9.	The most trustworthy person is	A B C D E
	The least trustworthy person is	A B C D E
10.	The most happy, content person is	A B C D E
	The least happy, content person is	A B C D E

Source: Adapted from *The Communication Experience in Human Relations*, Lyle Sussman and Sam Deep (Cincinnati: South-Western Publishing Co., 1989). Reprinted with permission.

As you made your assessments of the people in the photographs, how did you feel? What, if anything, did you do that was different from your usual nonverbal assessment of others? Which nonverbal cues do you think are the most obvious?

How can you become more aware of your nonverbal messages? One of the easiest ways is to catch yourself off guard in a mirror whenever you can, or have someone videotape you on several occasions walking across a room, standing and talking with another person, or sitting down while carrying on a conversation. Other ways to learn about your nonverbal messages is to be consciously aware of how you are using gestures, posture, and tone of voice while you are communicating, or ask a friend to give you feedback on your nonverbals.

Since the major impact of your message is likely to be interpreted from the nonverbal cues you are sending, your ability to communicate effectively is largely dependent upon your successful use of nonverbal cues.

You can evaluate your communication skills using the self-assessment guide in Figure 8–4 to determine the extent to which you might be contributing to a breakdown in communication.

8–3   How to Become an Effective Listener

The goal of effective listening is for the listener to have an accurate understanding of the message at the end of the conversation. To achieve this goal, an effective listener is one who actually hears and understands what is being said rather than assumes what is said. Effective listening skills can be learned and are as essential to the communication process as the words you use or the nonverbal cues you send.

Effective Listening Techniques

In order to become an effective listener, you must actively participate in the conversation in ways that are designed to keep the communication flowing rather than to shut down, turn off, or put the other person on the defensive. Here are some of the techniques you can use to become an effective listener.

Be an Active Listener   An active listener is one who shows involvement with the speaker by maintaining eye contact; has appropriate, alert, open body language, indicating an interest in the speaker's comments; concentrates on what the speaker is saying; responds with comments such as "I see" and "Uh-huh" or an affirmative nodding of the head; and restates or summarizes parts of the conversation for clarity and to signify an accurate understanding of the message.

Active listeners are aware that words have different meanings to different people and that to understand the speaker's message individual biases, prejudices, and past experiences must be recognized and put aside. Only when listeners can develop empathy for a speaker by putting themselves in the speaker's shoes will true understanding take place. You must know where the speaker is coming from before you can understand the message.

Reduce or Eliminate Distractions   Distractions come from a variety of sources. One source is the environment itself, such as when a radio is playing

Figure 8–4   Communication Effectiveness Self-Assessment

Rating Scale: 4—I always do this.
                 3—I often do this.
                 2—I sometimes do this.
                 1—I seldom do this.
                 0—I never do this.

_____ **1.** When I have something to say, I am open and honest about my need to say it.

_____ **2.** I communicate with an awareness that the words I choose may not mean the same thing to others.

_____ **3.** I recognize that the message I receive may not be the one that was intended.

_____ **4.** Before I communicate, I ask myself questions about who the receiver is and how that might affect the reception of my message.

_____ **5.** While I communicate, I look for indications that I am understood.

_____ **6.** My messages are brief and to the point.

_____ **7.** I do not use jargon with those who might not understand it.

_____ **8.** I avoid using slang words and colloquial expressions with those who may be put off by them.

_____ **9.** I do not use red-flag words that may upset or distract the receiver.

_____ **10.** I recognize that how I say something is as important as what I say.

_____ **11.** The nonverbal messages I send conform to the meaning I want to get across.

_____ **12.** I give careful consideration to whether my message would be best understood by the receiver in a meeting, over the telephone, or in writing.

_____ **13.** I form opinions about what others say based on what I hear them saying instead of on what I think of them as a person.

_____ **14.** I make a genuine effort to listen to ideas with which I don't agree.

_____ **15.** I look for ways to improve my listening skills.

_____ **Total Score**

How to Interpret Your Score

Score

50–60   Were you really being honest? If so, you are an extremely effective communicator who almost never contributes to any misunderstanding.

40–49   For the most part you are an effective communicator who only contributes to break downs in communication once in awhile. The goal of this assessment is to move everyone up to this level.

30–39   You are an average communicator and are responsible for your share of any misunderstandings.

20–29   Many people (at least those who are honest) fall into this category. While things could be worse, there is much room for improvement in the way you communicate. The goal of this assessment is to move you to a higher category.

10–19   You are a frequent source of communication problems and you will benefit from additional communication exercises and paying attention to their implications for you personally.

0–9   Your honesty is commendable and you need to work on your effectiveness as a communicator.

Source: Adapted from _The Communication Experience in Human Relations_, Lyle Sussman and Sam Deep (Cincinnati: South-Western Publishing Co., 1989). Reprinted with permission.

too loudly or when the door to your office is left open, signaling that drop-in visitors are welcome. Ringing telephones, poor ventilation, temperatures that are too hot or too cold, or physical barriers between the speaker and listener, such as a desk, are also environmental distractions to effective listening.

Another source of distractions that prevent the listener from active listening is the listener's own biases, prejudices, and defensive reactions, which often keep the message from getting through.

In the perfect communication environment listeners would also be able to get beyond the speaker's accent, mannerisms, and appearance, suspending judgments and giving full attention to the speaker's message. But to remain totally objective and rise above all the inevitable distractions takes more skill than that possessed by most listeners.

Let Others Do the Talking   You cannot hear what the other person has to say if you are doing all the talking. The more talking you do, the more likely you are to convince the other person that you think what you have to say is more important than what they have to say. The result is that they will no longer want to talk to you. Likewise, when you interrupt others you are telling them that your thoughts are more important than theirs.

Good listeners do just that—they listen. They do not attempt to control or manipulate the conversation by jumping in with unasked-for advice, nor do they deflect the conversation to call attention to themselves by recalling similar situations. Good listeners also avoid the temptation to fill up the air space when the speaker has paused to collect thoughts or catch a breath. "Dead air" should be a concern only in radio or television, not in interpersonal communication.

Pay Attention to Nonverbal Cues   Since the words themselves have relatively little impact on the message and are subject to individual interpretation for meaning, effective listeners pay attention to the speaker's tone of voice, placement of emphasis, speed of delivery, pitch, and volume for clues to the speaker's feeling about the topic.

Voice inflection adds emphasis to certain words, while increased speed in delivery might indicate anxiety or slowing down could be a sign of reluctance to discuss the topic. A high pitch or loud volume could be a sign of stress or emotional intensity.

Of course, the speaker's face, eyes, posture, gestures, and general appearance will tell you about the person's overall attitude and feelings. You want to be especially aware of the relationship between the nonverbal and the verbal messages. If they are not supporting one another and instead are sending mixed messages, you will want to ask the speaker for clarification.

Develop Effective Listening Skills   Poor listeners are those who think that the speaker is solely responsible for getting the message across to the listener. Effective listeners, on the other hand, realize that communication is a two-way process requiring effort on both parts to reach understanding. Here are the four steps to becoming an effective listener.

Step 1: Learn to *concentrate.* Shut out both the external and internal distractions and open yourself up to actually hearing the message. You must be determined to understand what the other person is saying.

Step 2: Probe for better understanding by asking for clarification. "I'm not sure I understand." "Please repeat that." "Is this what you mean?"

Step 3: Reflect the speaker's comments to extend and amplify as a way to gain understanding. "This is what I heard you say. . . . Is that what you meant?" "If that is true would it mean that . . . ?"

Step 4: When you think you have heard and understood the message, *summarize* it by paraphrasing and giving feedback to the speaker. This is the process that allows you to determine whether you have indeed understood the message. "This is what you want me to do . . . ." "I think I understand how you feel. You are feeling . . . ." If your impression of the conversation accurately reflects the speaker's intent, then you have succeeded in being an effective listener.

In summary, here are the techniques that can help make you an effective listener:

1. Be an active listener.
2. Reduce or eliminate distractions.
3. Let others do the talking.
4. Pay attention to nonverbal cues.
5. Develop effective listening skills.

8-4   How to Give Constructive Feedback

Providing feedback is an integral part of the communication process. Without feedback there is no way for employees to gauge their performance. Positive feedback serves not only as praise but as encouragement; negative feedback, on the other hand, can be interpreted not only as a reprimand, but as a guide to improve performance.

Positive Feedback

Nearly everyone can remember getting silver or gold stars for their work in kindergarten or grade school. Those stars provided us not only moments of happiness and joy but motivation to get more stars as well. Unfortunately, most of us have not seen a gold star since grade school.

Have you ever wondered why some people are so remiss in handing out a few words of praise, or positive feedback, when they know that something so insignificant as a foil star can produce such a great return? Is it that they have forgotten the feeling associated with positive recognition? Or is it that they just feel uncomfortable when giving a compliment?

Some people feel that it is unnecessary to give praise for doing the job that is expected. As long as the performance is satisfactory, nothing needs to be said about it. Other people tend to believe that the stick is more motivating than the carrot. In other words, punishing the behavior you don't want is more productive in the long run than rewarding the behavior you want. Still other high achievers think that everyone can and should live up to the same lofty expectations they have for themselves. Since this is virtually impossible, there is never any performance good enough to be praised.

Drs. Kenneth Blanchard and Spencer Johnson wrote a best-selling book called *The One-Minute Manager* (New York: Morrow Press, 1987) for the purpose of providing a new way to get positive behavior results through one-minute praisings and one-minute reprimands. Here are their simple, yet powerful, suggestions.

1. Establish and write down a few clearly stated goals with measurable performance standards.

2. Then catch people doing things *approximately* right and encourage the continuance of that behavior with a few words of specific praise. "Nice job" will not do. Specific praise would be "Jack, you did a great job on getting all those exhibits assembled and marked on time. Thanks." Do not wait for people to do things exactly right before offering praise, or you might never get the chance to praise someone. Instead, give people a verbal star for doing things approximately right.

3. A short, quick reprimand is appropriate when an employee is found to be falling short of the performance standards. Reprimands are focused on behavior, not the individual. "Jack, I'm really disappointed that you failed to meet the deadline on the Smith case. You are a good paralegal and capable of meeting established deadlines. I know you feel bad about missing the deadline too and will do better next time."

By keeping both praise and reprimand short, you make both expressions more powerful.

Negative Feedback

Few, if any, people enjoy being criticized. Yet critical feedback is a part of life and is necessary for growth. It can be an effective way to improve performance and provide the receiver with the necessary information to change undesirable behavior.

It is important for you to keep in mind that you cannot change the behavior of another person. Only they can make the decision to change. You can, however, provide them with the information from which *they* will decide whether or not to make a behavior change.

Some general ideas about criticism by Hendrie Weisinger and Norman Lobseng in their book *Nobody's Perfect* (New York: Stratford Press, 1981) are designed to put criticism in a new perspective. The authors point out that the word *criticism* is a derivative of the word *critique*, and one definition of *critique* is "to give information." If you were then to look at criticism only as providing information, you can gain a better understanding of its usefulness in interpersonal skills, whether you are giving it or receiving it.

People rarely regard criticism as an evaluation process. The typical response to criticism is defensiveness, the protective armor put on to shield us when our imperfections have been discovered. However, when criticism is presented appropriately and explained as an information-giving device, there is a greater likelihood that it will produce the desired results.

Some people provide negative feedback more skillfully than others. But if the receiver remembers that he or she is free to choose how much importance to give the information and how to respond to it, critical feedback can lead to closer relationships and better performance. Furthermore, the appropriate response to the person who gave you this important information is "Thank you."

Elements of Constructive Negative Feedback   To be constructive and achieve the desired results, negative feedback should be provided as soon as possible after the incident to which it refers and be focused only on that particular incident. However, the person giving the feedback should be aware of his or her own emotional state at the time and the intent of the feedback. If the giver is highly emotional and intends only to put down, humiliate, or embarrass the receiver, then no action should be taken until the giver is more in control.

All feedback should be specific and descriptive of the incident, not simply reflecting the giver's evaluation or judgment. Most importantly, constructive negative feedback will pertain to situations or events over which the receiver has some control to make changes. If the receiver is criticized for faults or shortcomings over which he or she has no control to make changes or is unable to act upon, that person will only become frustrated by the giver's feedback.

Weisinger and Lobseng's formula for giving constructive negative feedback is:

1. *Be descriptive.* Constructive feedback describes specifically the situation or behavior. It is not evaluative or judgmental; it is focused on behavior and not the individual.
2. *Show empathy.* Feedback should indicate understanding, concern, and respect for the person and express your feelings about the situation or that person's behavior.
3. *Be specific.* Clearly state the specific situation or behavior you want to see changed. If you are vague, most receivers will pay no attention to your requests.
4. *State consequences.* State the positive consequences should the receiver choose to accept and act on the feedback. Also state the negative consequences on which you are prepared to follow through if the receiver chooses not to act in response to your feedback.

Because giving constructive feedback requires thought and skill, Weisinger and Lobseng suggest using this model to script (write out) feedback.

1. Start by describing the situation or behavior you want to see changed. Begin your statement with the word "When," not "You." ("You" statements have aggressive undertones and most people become defensive when a "You" statement is directed toward them.) "When/When you/ When I/When we . . ."
2. Next, express your feelings using an assertive "I" statement. "I feel angry/sad/confused/happy/frustrated . . ." You might also show empathy by saying, "I understand why you . . ."
3. Then describe the behavior you want to see and use an "I" statement here too. "I prefer that you . . ." "I want you to . . ."
4. Do not forget to state the positive and negative consequences associated with action or inaction. "If you . . . then I/we . . ."

The following example demonstrates Weisinger and Lobseng's feedback model in action:

> When you are continually late for work, I feel disappointed and upset. I understand that sometimes unforeseen things happen that cause everyone to be late once in awhile. But you have been late three times this week, which leads me to think that you may not take your job seriously. We need you and depend on you. I want you to take responsibility for getting to work on time beginning right now. If you are willing to show us that you are serious about your career with us, then we will be able to continue thinking of you as a valuable member of our staff. If you choose not to take responsibility for getting to work on time every day then we will have to find someone to replace you.

In this example the receiver of the message has enough information to decide what action to take and is also aware of the consequences if the decision is to take no action. This constructive feedback model allows the receiver to stay in control and to retain a sense of personal power. The message is not a put-down, and it is neither insulting nor embarrassing since it only deals with facts and behavior.

One last suggestion when giving negative feedback: After you have stated the consequences, ask the receiver for feedback by saying, "What do you think

Figure 8–5 Critical Feedback Assessment

Read the following statements of critical feedback. Then indicate the missing elements of constructive feedback in the blank next to each statement.

1. You are always complaining about everything and it upsets me. _____

2. You have a bad attitude. _____

3. All you need to do is work harder and you will succeed. _____

4. Get real! Life isn't fair! _____

5. Everyone here likes working with you. I just wish you had more skills. _____

6. Your clothes don't reflect the image of this firm. _____

7. Too bad your brief was full of typing errors. Otherwise, it was okay. _____

8. Others would probably take you more seriously if you were taller. _____

9. Why are you so sensitive? _____

10. You are one of the best paralegals in the firm. It is not like you to overlook checking the citations in a brief. I know something must have been bothering you. Tell me what happened. _____

about this?" Or, "How do you feel about what I have said?" Or, "Do you think you can do what I asked you to do?" Questions like these allow the receiver to take part in the discussion and to negotiate with you if the receiver thinks you are being overbearing or asking for too much. The more feedback that takes place between the giver and the receiver, the more likely you are to be able to resolve any issue to your mutual satisfaction. Try your understanding of critical feedback skills by referring to Figure 8–5.

8–5   How Communication Flows within the Firm

The communication process within a law firm is much like the communication process between individuals. The sender puts a message into the communication channel with the expectation that it will reach the receiver who will interpret the message and eventually provide feedback to the sender.

One major difference, however, between organizational communication and interpersonal communication is that the firm has two additional channels to use for sending messages. These channels into which an oral or written message is placed are called communication **networks,** systems of person-to-person relationships through which information flows in the firm. There are two types of communication networks: formal and informal.

The Formal Networks

Perhaps the best way to describe the firm's formal communication network is that it is management's idea of who should communicate with whom in order to get the job done. It is the official communication that travels through the structured organizational network.

In a small firm the formal networks are so simple they are barely noticeable. For example, when Samuel D. Jones, Esq., was a three-person law firm, making a decision to purchase new equipment was easy—the secretary told the lawyer, who placed the order or told her to go buy what she needed. As the firm grew to become Jones, Smith, Jordan, Cohen & Savalas, so did the complexity of the purchasing system. Now the secretary expresses her desires to the office manager, who sends a memo to the administrator, and the matter may then become an agenda item for decision by the executive committee.

Within firms information flows through the formal networks in several ways—downward, upward, and horizontally.

Downward Communication Information that flows from higher to lower levels in the organization is called downward communication. Some of the most common forms of downward communication include memos and reports, policies and procedures, and firm newsletters.

This top-down communication is important in the law firm since the better informed employees are about goals and expectations, the more likely they will be able to achieve them. However, too many managers fail to recognize the importance of including an explanation for why a task is necessary when giving instructions, or they fail to give thorough instructions. Failure to be specific or to provide an explanation can lead to misunderstanding, frustration, and confusion for employees.

Unfortunately, because employees usually receive so much downward communication, they tend to be selective about the information they want to see or hear, and ignore the rest. No matter how good the communicator is, there always seems to be a certain number of individuals who fail to get the message.

Upward Communication Upward communication occurs when messages flow from lower levels in the firm to higher management. Typically, upward communication includes suggestions for making improvements, unsolved work problems, reports on what employees are doing, or readings of the morale pulse of the organization.

Upward communication provides management with feedback on the accuracy of downward communication as well as how decisions are being received. In addition, by listening to the concerns of employees, management can prevent new problems and resolve old ones.

Law firm management will benefit from encouraging and paying attention to upward communication; otherwise they might find themselves in a surprise situation, such as several people quitting at the same time!

Horizontal Communication Horizontal communication takes place between members of a firm with equal power—partner to partner or secretary to secretary, for example. Typical horizontal communication is for the purpose of coordinating tasks, solving problems, resolving conflicts, sharing information, or building rapport.

The Informal Networks

While the formal networks are the official communication channels in the firm, it is the informal network, often referred to as the **grapevine,** that is the real workhorse of law firm communication. You can be sure that the grapevine is in operation wherever there are more than two people working together—the law office is no exception!

Informal communication takes different forms involving different sorts of people. For example, several secretaries overhear another mention she is going to quit; they learn the news a week before she tells her boss. Or two newly hired associates discover during orientation that they share a common interest in using computers, so they begin meeting regularly for lunch to share ideas. Consider also the ambitious junior partner who strikes up a friendship with the senior partner's secretary and consequently seems to know just the right time to get the boss's ear on matters concerning career advancement.

The Importance of Informal Networks Many people consider informal contacts, such as those just mentioned, to be the most important means of communication within any firm. In fact, some studies have concluded that as much as 90 percent of what goes on in a firm has nothing to do with formal events. Even if this figure is overstated, there are several reasons why these informal communication links are not to be discounted.

One reason is the tremendous amount of information that results from these communication links. Some attorneys, for example, will spend a great amount of time talking to people (inside and outside the firm) they do not need to deal with in order to do their jobs, such as secretaries, paralegals, receptionists, and clerks. Why do they bother to cultivate relationships with these people? No doubt the answer lies in the information these people have. It is a well-known fact that secretaries and receptionists are every firm's unofficial information gatekeepers whose power and influence are not to be underestimated. Attorneys also recognize that paralegals and court clerks have a wealth of knowledge and information that might be useful someday.

Informal networks are important too because of the speed with which information is passed around. While a memo is being typed and duplicated, its contents can be spread throughout the firm with a series of telephone calls.

Some communication experts believe that between 80 and 90 percent of the information heard on the grapevine is true. But the receiver must take responsibility for distinguishing between truth and rumors. Rumors are statements that cannot easily be verified and are based on emotional issues. Typically, messages having great emotional impact are more likely to be distorted. One way to stop a rumor is not to pass it along the grapevine.

Some law firms do everything possible to encourage constructive interaction among employees, and many successful people go to great lengths to develop strong informal networks both inside and outside the firm. You can develop your own informal network by communicating with a variety of people, including those within your firm, those who are members of your professional associations, those who work for the courts, messengers, and investigators. Treat everyone you meet with respect, and don't be afraid to ask questions when you find a knowledgeable source of information. Establishing your own communication network will not only help you succeed in your career but will also provide you with valuable sources of information.

SUMMARY

8-1

Communication is an important management function involving the transfer of information between two or more people. There are six elements in the communication process: a sender of the message, the message itself, the channel used to send the message, the context of the message, a receiver, and feedback. To be effective, both the intent and content of the message must be understood by the receiver. Therefore, both the sender and the receiver are responsible for making sure the message is understood, and both rely on feedback to clarify messages. Some common barriers to communication are subjective interpretations of words, poor choice of time and place, environmental distractions and cultural conditioning, poor listening habits, and stereotyping. Likewise, your vocabulary, pronunciation, dialect, fluency, pitch, emphasis, inflection, and rate of speech can have a direct impact on effective communication.

8-2

Research indicates that 93 percent of communication occurs without the use of words. Voice tone and inflection account for 38 percent of nonverbal communication, and 55 percent is attributed to physical behavior, or body language. The face, eyes, body, clothing, gestures, and touch speak volumes to others about your beliefs, attitudes, and values. Decoding nonverbal communication requires attention to several cues and depends on the ability to set aside personal biases in interpreting information.

8-3

An effective listener must have an accurate understanding of the message at the end of the conversation. Effective listening is a learned skill that requires the application of certain techniques, such as actively taking part in the communication process by maintaining eye contact, exhibiting appropriate body language, concentrating on the speaker's comments, and restating or summarizing the speaker's comments for clarity and to ensure accurate understanding. Further, by reducing or eliminating distractions, letting others do most of the talking, and paying attention to the nonverbal cues of the speaker, the effective listener will be able to hear and understand both the intent and content of the message.

8-4

Feedback is an integral part of the growth and development process. Positive feedback, more commonly known as praising, is too often withheld in favor of attempting to motivate by punishment rather than through reward. Giving constructive negative feedback, or criticism, is also a part of the manager's job. To be constructive, negative feedback should be descriptive, show empathy, be specific, and state consequences.

8-5

Communication in law firms flows through both the formal and informal networks. The formal network is used to convey messages from top management downward to employees; suggestions and problems flow upward from lower levels to higher levels in the firm; and horizontal communication takes place between people of equal status for task coordination, problem solving, and building relationships. The informal network, often referred to as the grapevine, tends to be remarkably accurate and fast and is the source of most unofficial information in the firm.

REVIEW

Key Terms

channels
communication
context
feedback
grapevine
message
networks
nonverbal
receiver
sender
stereotyping
verbal
vocalics

Questions for Review and Discussion

1. What is the difference between communication and effective communication?
2. What are the six elements in the communication process?
3. Why is feedback important to the communication process?
4. What are some of the common barriers to effective communication?
5. What are the elements of nonverbal communication?
6. What is the cultural impact in the communication decoding process?
7. List the techniques for effective listening.
8. What is the purpose of constructive feedback and what two common forms are most often associated with constructive feedback?
9. If negative feedback is to be constructive, what elements must be present?
10. What is the purpose for the formal and informal communication networks?

Activities

1. This activity is designed to illustrate the use of vocalics and emotion in communication. One person will be the message sender and all the rest will be receivers. The sender will think of and convey one of the following emotions—anger, fear, happiness, surprise, or sadness—using only his or her voice by counting aloud the numbers one through ten, with his or her back to the group. The sender will not announce to the receivers which emotion he or she is trying to convey, so the only nonverbal cues the receivers will have are the sender's vocalics. Since the words themselves have no meaning, the receivers will listen to the vocalic cues and decide if the sender is angry, fearful, happy, surprised, or sad. If time permits, ask for several volunteers to be message senders to emphasize the differences in vocalic cues. Time required: 15–45 minutes.

2. To test concentration ability, select two people to stand before the group to simultaneously read paragraphs from different printed materials, such as a newspaper, textbook, or similar source. At a signal from the instructor, they begin to read at the same volume until the instructor tells them to stop—about two minutes. The listeners are to choose which person they will listen to before the reading begins. After the readings have ended, the listeners will summarize, in writing, the message communicated by the person they chose to listen to.

   After the summaries are complete, the two readers are given new material to read. This time the listeners are instructed to concentrate on the speaker they have chosen to listen to and to apply good listening skills, such as leaning forward in the chair, maintaining eye contact, blocking outside noise, or doing whatever they believe will allow them to listen better. When the second readings have ended, the listeners will summarize what they heard. Then compare and discuss this activity and what they learned about listening techniques and skills. Time required: 20–30 minutes.

3. Form groups of two. Have each member of the pair recall, or make up, a communication problem they experienced, or are now experienc-

ing, at work, at school, or in a personal relationship. The speaker tells the problem to the listener and asks for feedback. The listener should pay attention to the common barriers in communication and employ effective listening techniques to make sure the intent and content of the communication are understood. The listener should keep in mind that effective listening does not mean coming up with a solution to the problem. Rather, effective listeners are more likely to be good counselors and coaches who provide enough feedback for the speaker to formulate his or her own solutions. Time required: 15–20 minutes.

4. Take the statements of criticism found in Figure 8–5 and make them into constructive feedback statements. Script out (write down) your new statements. You will need to make up some of the information in order for the statements to conform to the model. It is important, however, that you follow the format of the feedback model. That is, begin with a "When" statement and then follow with an "I" statement to express your feelings and to show empathy. Then use another "I" statement to describe the behavior you want to see, and state the consequences. Include both a positive consequence and a negative consequence for each statement.

CHAPTER 9   How to Be a Leader

OUTLINE

9–1   Leadership Styles
  Autocratic Leadership
  Developmental Leadership
  Situational Leadership
9–2   Leadership Attitudes
  Theory X Attitude
  Theory Y Attitude
  Derived X Attitude
9–3   Motivation
  Maslow's Need Theory
  Herzberg's Two-Factor Motivation Theory
  Modern Motivation Problems
9–4   Power and Its Impact
  Position Power
  Personal Power
  Office Politics

COMMENTARY

After several months as Dunn & Sweeney's first office manager you know that some people in the firm can always be counted on to do an exceptional job. They usually have a good attitude and are liked by just about everyone. On the other hand, one or two staff members have difficulty in meeting any deadline—including getting to work on time—and while at work, their attitude is clearly one of doing just enough to get by. You know that part of the office manager's unwritten responsibilities is to be a leader and motivate the staff. But having tried to lead by example, you are finding yourself overworked, exhausted, and on the edge of burnout while everyone else seems to be going about business as usual. Your frustration is mounting as you realize they are not getting the message.

OBJECTIVES

In Chapter 8 you learned that communication skills are an integral part of the management process. After studying this chapter you will be able to:

1. Define leadership and leadership styles.
2. Name three of the most common leadership styles.
3. List the characteristics of the most common leadership styles.
4. Describe the Theory X and Theory Y leadership attitudes.
5. Discuss the impact of attitude on leadership.
6. Illustrate how human needs affect motivation.
7. Discuss Maslow's theory and Herzberg's theory of motivation.
8. List common motivation problems faced by today's office manager.

9. Describe the difference between defensive behavior and abnormal behavior.
10. Explain the functions of power and politics in leadership.

9–1 Leadership Styles

While there are many definitions of **leadership,** the term for our purposes refers to an attempt to influence others to achieve specific objectives because they want to, not because they have to. Leadership is an interpersonal process and does not rely on formal authority to get things done. Leaders can be found throughout the law office—among the staff as well as the lawyers. They are the individuals who are held in high esteem and have the respect of others in the firm, even though they are not always liked. Because the law office manager is a highly visible person throughout the firm, she or he is usually considered a leader and often is indirectly responsible for leading the firm toward its goals.

Your **leadership style,** then, is the patterns of behavior that are associated with you as a leader. These patterns of behavior include your attitude toward yourself and others, how you communicate, and your skill as a manager in achieving goals. Generally speaking, a leader feels more comfortable with a particular leadership style and tends to use it consistently. However, because of this tendency, your leadership effectiveness will vary from one situation to the next depending upon the followers. To assess your assumptions about people, their work, and motivation refer to Figure 9–1.

There is no doubt that the law firm's performance is tied to the quality of its leadership. An unskilled leader can destroy morale and efficiency while a strong leader can transform a lackluster group into a successful organization.

Autocratic Leadership

Some leaders tend to be **autocratic,** or authoritarian, by relying on their authority and the power of their position to get things done. Autocratic leaders usually think they know what they want and express those wants as *direct orders* to others. Autocratic leaders are typically so concerned about keeping control that they will structure all work situations for others, who merely do what they are told. No independent thinking or creativity is allowed when an autocrat is in charge.

The autocratic leader believes that people have very little ambition, will try to avoid responsibility, and want to be told what to do at all times. You will not hear from an autocrat unless something is wrong because these leaders are not interested in anyone else's ideas; they will provide you with all the information you need.

Historically, many people have believed that management has the right to make decisions and issue commands with the expectation that they will be obeyed without question. This outdated yet prevalent viewpoint of leadership considers interpersonal influence unnecessary. Having authority is what counts. However, there are at least a couple of major problems with this approach to leadership in today's law firms. One is that employee expectations have changed as the values of society have changed; another is that in the legal profession, where a basic requirement for all jobs is above-average intelligence and the ability to think, the autocratic style of leadership will create morale and productivity problems.

Figure 9–1 Leadership Style Assessment

Place a check mark in the appropriate column for each of the following statements before reading the explanation for this assessment. For best results, read each statement only once and mark the column. There are no right or wrong answers—only your answers. Think of people in the general sense, not specific individuals, as you read each statement.

	Strongly Disagree	Disagree	Agree	Strongly Agree
1. Almost everyone could improve his/her job performance quite a bit if he/she really wanted to.	____	____	____	____
2. It is unrealistic to expect people to show the same enthusiasm for their work as for their leisure activities.	____	____	____	____
3. Even with encouragement, very few people show the desire to improve themselves on the job.	____	____	____	____
4. Given enough money, people are less likely to worry about things such as status and recognition.	____	____	____	____
5. When people talk about wanting more responsibility, they really want more money and status.	____	____	____	____
6. Most people don't like to make decisions on their own so it is difficult to get them to assume responsibility.	____	____	____	____
7. Being tough with people will usually get them to do what you want.	____	____	____	____
8. A good way to get people to do more work is to crack down on them once in a while.	____	____	____	____
9. A leader's prestige is weakened if he/she has to admit he/she was wrong.	____	____	____	____
10. The most effective leader is one who gets results regardless of the method used with people.	____	____	____	____

(continued)

If your assessment in Figure 9–1 is way out at the autocratic end of the scale—that is, a score somewhere between 52 and 60—you are probably having difficulty as a leader. You tend to be high-handed in dealing with people and apparently feel that most people do not possess any initiative of their own; that they have to be watched very carefully or they will take advantage of you and the firm. You believe that these people have nothing of value to contribute to a group endeavor, that they are motivated by selfishness, and that you must control all their activities or the work will not be done. An MBO (management by objectives, see Chapter 7) approach to job enrichment will not work in this environment.

Developmental Leadership

The opposite of the autocratic leader is the **developmental leader.** This leadership style not only provides people with the opportunity and encourage-

Figure 9–1 *continued*

	Strongly Disagree	Disagree	Agree	Strongly Agree
11. It is too much to expect that people will do a good job without prodding.	___	___	___	___
12. The leader who expects people to set their own performance standards will probably find they don't set them very high.	___	___	___	___
13. Most people don't use much creativity and ingenuity on the job because they don't have much of either.	___	___	___	___
14. One problem in asking for ideas from others is their perspective is too limited to make their suggestions practical.	___	___	___	___
15. It is human nature for people to try to do as little work as they can get away with.	___	___	___	___
Total for each column	___	___	___	___
Above column total	(× 1)___	(× 2)___	(× 3)___	(× 4)___

Grand total (add the four products together) ___

Scoring:

1. First total the number of marks for each column and place your answer on the line at the bottom of each column. The totals for all four columns should be 15.
2. Then multiply the number in each column as indicated. For example, multiple the total for the Strongly Disagree column by 1; the total for the Disagree column by 2, and so on.
3. Add up the four products to get your grand total. Your answer will be somewhere between 15 and 60.

Interpretation: If your score is 60------------------------30----------------------15

Your style:	Autocratic	Developmental
Often called . . .	Boss	Leader
Motivates from	Fear	Inspiration
Supervision is . . .	Close	General

Source: Adapted from *What Managers Need to Know*, Roger Fritz (Naperville, Ill.: Organizational Development Consultants, 1988). Reprinted with permission.

ment to excel in performance; it also looks upon people as enjoying their work and eager to accept responsibility. This leadership style leads to staff participation in setting objectives and taking part in some of the decision-making processes, especially those that will affect them directly.

Developmental leaders will consider the ideas of others even when they conflict with their own. They recognize that people learn from making mistakes and will allow a reasonable margin for error while holding consistently high expectations. These leaders encourage people to reach out in new directions, help them understand the objectives of their job, and set goals with them, not for them.

One of the most successful uses of developmental leadership in the law office occurs when all the staff members are asked for ideas and input when the firm decides to update its computer technology. Many people feel threatened by computers or are resistant to learning how to use a new piece of equipment or a new program. However, when these reluctant learners are directly involved in the process of gathering information, talking with vendors, and expressing their ideas, the result is more likely to be enthusiasm for change rather than fear.

If your assessment in Figure 9–1 placed you way out on the developmental leadership end of the scale—that is, your score was somewhere between 15 and 20—you too may be in trouble as a leader. This is because you are too permissive in your leadership style and do not have an adequate sense of the need for controls. You have difficulty in holding people accountable for their agreed-upon standards of performance.

Of course, it is rare to find either the autocratic or developmental leadership style in its pure state. No doubt your assessment in Figure 9–1 falls somewhere along the line from pure autocrat on the one hand to pure developmental leader on the other. But if your score fell in the 30 to 33 range, you could also be in trouble as a leader. It depends on how you got your score. A careful reading of the assessment questions will indicate that all of them really say the same thing in a different way. You should not have many "strongly agree" and "strongly disagree" answers, which offset each other. Check marks in these columns indicate an inconsistency in your behavior, which is not the type of behavior attributed to a leader. Of course, the individual circumstances surrounding any situation will dictate what you will do at any given moment. But remember, it is the general pattern of behavior that you have developed over time that determined your score on the leadership continuum.

Situational Leadership

By now it should be obvious that one leadership style will not be the most effective approach in all situations. The **contingency approach** to leadership, as developed by Ohio State University theorist and psychologist Fred Fiedler and later expanded by management experts Kenneth H. Blanchard and Paul Hersey into the **situational style,** recognizes that there is no one best way to influence people. Rather, the leadership style a person uses with individuals or groups is largely dependent upon the situation and the readiness level of the people the leader is attempting to influence to perform a particular task.

As discussed earlier, autocratic leaders tend to be task-oriented, or concerned only with getting the job done, while developmental leaders are more relationship-oriented, showing concern for others' feelings. Fiedler's contingency approach to leadership found that the decision to emphasize tasks or relationships in a situation depends upon the degree of trust and confidence placed on the leader by the group members or the individual, the simplicity or complexity of the task, and the leader's ability to reward or punish. (See *A Theory of Leadership Effectiveness* [New York: McGraw-Hill, 1967].)

Fiedler's research suggests that a task-oriented approach works best when focusing on the task is preferable to focusing on relationships. The task-oriented approach works either when the task is highly structured and the relationship is good between the leader and followers, such as when you call on staff members to help get out a large mailing; or when the relationship is extremely poor, the task is unstructured, and the leader lacks power, such as when morale is low and a job no one wanted to do has been dumped on you to complete against an impossible deadline. In both of these situations, focusing on the task at hand and not on relationships will get the job done. In the first example, no focus on relationships is required because the staff respects you and will help you out. In the second example, focusing on relationships instead of the task would serve no useful purpose.

In Hersey and Blanchard's situational model the maturity level of followers is an important consideration when deciding whether to place emphasis on tasks

Table 9-1 Personal Characteristics of Effective Leaders

Superior intelligence	Emotional maturity
Sense of purpose in life	High resistance to stress
Self-confident	Empathy towards others
Favorable self-image	Seeks responsibility
Task completion oriented	Creative and venturesome
Decisive and intuitive	Good time management
Organized and energetic	Highly motivated
High level of personal integrity	Excellent communication skills
Problem solvers not problem avoiders	Able to tolerate frustration and delay

Source: Adapted from *Human Behavior in Organizations*, 3rd ed., J. Clifton Williams and George P. Huber (Cincinnati: South-Western Publishing Co., 1986). Reprinted with permission.

or relationships. (See *Management of Organizational Behavior* [New Jersey: Prentice Hall, 1988].) In this model the term *maturity* has little to do with chronological age. Instead, maturity refers to the employee's level of motivation, his or her willingness to take responsibility, and the amount of knowledge and experience the employee has in a given situation. For example, a young, ambitious, well-trained paralegal might be more mature than a bored, complacent attorney. It is important to note when considering maturity that a person might have a low maturity rating in one situation and a high rating in another.

According to the situational model, an immature follower needs close supervision and task-oriented leadership. But as the level of maturity increases, less guidance is required and social relationships can be emphasized. Eventually, when a mature employee is functioning at the highest level, only an occasional comment is necessary.

There are as many different leadership styles as there are leaders. Which one is best? The one that works for you. You will take and use the parts of the various leadership styles with which you feel comfortable and that produce results. No matter which style you choose or how you apply it, never underestimate the intelligence of those you are leading. Remember that there are no leaders without followers. (Table 9-1 presents some of the characteristics of effective leaders.)

9-2 Leadership Attitudes

We have already discussed the style of an autocratic leader, which presumes a superior-inferior attitude and relationship between leader and followers. The developmental and situational leaders, on the other hand, encourage interpersonal relationships as well as getting the job done. No discussion of leadership is complete, however, without including the Theory X and Theory Y attitude concepts developed by Douglas McGregor, former Professor of Industrial Management at MIT, and their affect on managerial effectiveness.

Theory X Attitude

McGregor noticed that, in general, managers tend to have either a positive or a negative attitude toward their subordinates. The label he used for those managers who take a pessimistic view of workers is **Theory X.** An X manager believes that most employees dislike work and will avoid it whenever they can; and, because most people dislike work, they have to be pushed, closely supervised, and threatened with punishment to get them to do their jobs. X managers also believe that most people are basically lazy, lack ambition, avoid responsibility, and have security as a major goal because they are self-centered and have little concern for the organization.

Theory Y Attitude

Theory Y managers, on the other hand, believe that workers who are allowed to experience some personal satisfaction in their work will do more than is expected of them. Y managers think most people consider work as natural as play or rest, and that a person's attitude toward work is a reflection of their experiences with it. According to Y managers, punishment does not motivate employees. Instead, Y managers believe that employees are motivated when they are informed of the firm's goals and their role in achieving those goals. In addition, Y managers expect that most people will not only seek out but be willing to accept responsibility and challenges when they are allowed to be imaginative and creative in their work.

Which of these two sets of attitudes seems to fit your general perception of others? If your attitudes fall more into the Theory X category, you fit the pattern of the traditional, autocratic manager. On the other hand, a Theory Y attitude is reflective of the newer, more positive assumptions held by an increasing number of today's managers. The assessment guide in Figure 9–2 is one more way to evaluate your style and attitude toward others.

Derived X Attitude

Reality, however, is neither all X nor all Y. This brief discussion of McGregor's theories runs the risk of implying that you are either one type or the other. In reality, most people are sincerely interested in being effective leaders, and many have adopted the more positive attitude toward workers. Unfortunately, some have also been "burned" in the process, causing a shift in attitude from a Y position to what is called the **Derived X,** or the *I've-Been-Burned Theory*

A Derived X manager is one who worked hard to provide job-enriching responsibilities and opportunities for personal growth, only to have others fail in their efforts or take advantage of the situation. Managers who get burned have usually failed to correctly size up the people with whom they are working. They gave them either too much or too little responsibility, direction, and autonomy. Or they completely misread their attitude and motivation cues. With good reason, a Theory Y manager who has been burned a few times will be reluctant to place too much trust in others in the future.

Why are these points of view and theories important to you as a law office manager? Many psychologists have concluded that there is validity in the phenomenon known as the **self-fulfilling prophecy**—that one person's attitude and expectations can influence the behavior of others. If your attitude is one of superiority, being the boss and having all the answers, you probably do not expect others to extend themselves for you or to achieve great things for themselves—and they won't. If, on the other hand, you consider all others as equals, as worthwhile contributors, wanting to achieve and excel, you will find yourself the leader of a group that will follow you just about anywhere.

Figure 9-2 Attitude Assessment

	Yes	No
1. I will accept others' ideas even when they differ from my own.	___	___
2. My instructions or procedures should always be followed as issued.	___	___
3. Before I proceed with an important policy change, I try to get the support of people working for me.	___	___
4. The image of authority should be presented by people in authority in the way that they dress, communicate, and conduct themselves.	___	___
5. It's best to let people implement your instructions the way they think best.	___	___
6. I like to rule with an iron fist because doing so provides direction and guidance.	___	___
7. I treat everyone as my equal.	___	___
8. The suggestions I receive from others are rarely very good since they do not have the range of experience or the perspective necessary to see things the way I do.	___	___
9. I rarely change the duties of others without first talking it over with them.	___	___
10. A good manager gives complete, detailed instructions of how things should be done to get them done correctly.	___	___
11. I accept suggestions from others and often use their ideas.	___	___
12. Consulting others in important decisions is a time-waster when you want results.	___	___
13. A good way to manage is to have regular staff meetings during which you solicit ideas.	___	___
14. I often do things my own way. It cuts down on time loss and frustration, and things get done faster, better, and more efficiently that way.	___	___

Scoring: Add odd-numbered "yes" answers to even-numbered "no" answers.

    10 or more = developmental style with a Theory Y attitude
    5 or less = autocratic style with a Theory X attitude

Source: Adapted from *What Managers need to Know,* Roger Fritz (Naperville, Ill.: Organizational Development Consultants, 1988). Reprinted with permission

In summary, here are the views of Theory X and Theory Y managers:

Theory X Managers Believe	Theory Y Managers Believe
• People inherently dislike to work.	• Work is as natural as rest or play.
• People lack ambition and will avoid responsibility.	• People want to be self-controlled and self-directed.
• People are seeking only security and want to be led.	• People not only accept but seek responsibility.
• Managers motivate with control, direction, and force.	• People are self-motivated.

The difference between these two managerial perspectives is described further in Table 9-2.

Table 9-2 Managerial Attitudes

Ineffective—Theory X Oriented	Productive—Theory Y Oriented
People work best when scared. Make them feel insecure and afraid.	Let people see how their work can help them achieve personal goals.
Give people half a chance and they'll mess things up.	Get people actively and intelligently involved in their work.
If you want something done right, do it yourself.	Don't manage people, manage individuals.
Do it my way or else.	Differences generate ideas.
Don't rock the boat.	Hear what others think.
Wait long enough and things will take care of themselves.	I don't have all the answers.

Source: Adapted from *The Critical Edge: How to Criticize Up and Down Your Organization and Make It Pay Off,* Hendrie Weisinger (Boston; Little, Brown & Co., 1989). Reprinted with permission.

9-3 Motivation

Why do some people eagerly take on each day with energy, ambition, and a positive outlook while others seemingly sleepwalk through their lives? Why are some people motivated by challenging assignments while others respond to money? The answer to both of these questions is a complex one based on individual human needs. These **needs** result from lacking something in our lives or from feeling deprived. They drive us toward a goal or provide the incentive to find a way to fill the void we are experiencing. What drives you toward satisfying your needs may be quite different from what will work for someone else, but the process is the same and it is called motivation. **Motivation** is the process of energizing behavior toward satisfying needs.

Maslow's Need Theory

The major proponent of **need theory** was psychologist Abraham Maslow, who proposed that all humans have levels of needs, which can be illustrated in the form of a pyramid and categorized as either physiological or psychological. (See Figure 9-3.)

Starting from the base of the pyramid, these needs are basic physiological or survival needs, such as the need for air, food, water, shelter, and clothing. Safety or security needs form the next level in the pyramid and include those things that make you feel physically safe and emotionally secure, such as to be free from physical harm and fear, or to have a savings account. On the middle level of the needs hierarchy Maslow placed social needs, such as belonging to groups and forming interpersonal relationships. Then comes the need for self-esteem and ego satisfaction, including self-respect, respect from others, recognition, and status. At the top of the hierarchy is the need to self-actualize, the level at which you are preoccupied with self-fulfillment, focusing on personal growth and opportunities to realize your full potential as a human being.

Maslow believed that once a need has been sufficiently satisfied, that need will no longer motivate you. Instead, you will be motivated by the next level of needs. For example, once you are able to provide a roof over your head and put food on the table, then you will concern yourself with the quality of the safety of the neighborhood and putting money aside to satisfy your other needs. Once

Figure 9–3 Maslow's Need Hierarchy

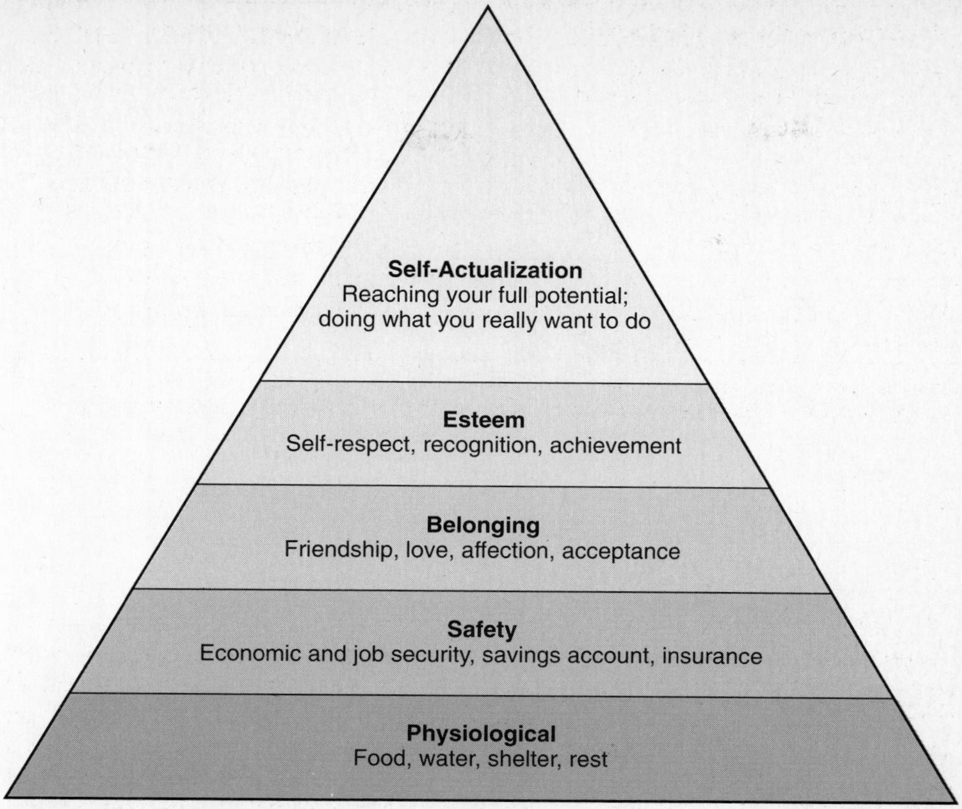

Source: Adapted from *Human Behavior in Organizations*, 3rd ed., J. Clifton Williams and George P. Huber (Cincinnati: South-Western Publishing Co., 1986). Reprinted with permission.

your needs are sufficiently satisfied at these levels, you will then be able to strive for the higher-level needs of social acceptance and making a contribution to society.

Needs affect motivation in many ways. For example, if your career and professional needs are being met on the job, then you are no doubt a highly motivated employee. If your needs are not being met in the workplace, you are probably continually frustrated and in frequent need of a morale boost. Furthermore, if your goals are incompatible with your needs—for example, your goal is to be independently wealthy by the time you are 40 years of age, but meeting the basic physiological needs of your family requires that you work for someone else with little opportunity to acquire great wealth in that time frame—the result may be a low level of motivation. In other words, you will do just enough to keep your job and will spend a great deal of time daydreaming.

While working with highly motivated people is much easier and more enjoyable than working with those who are less motivated, sometimes the best action a leader can take is to help others define realistic and achievable goals that will, in turn, improve their motivation. You cannot motivate someone else; but leadership does include being able to help others motivate themselves by recognizing their needs and determining how the job can help them meet those needs. Think about the needs *you* have had over the past month relating to your job and categorize them according to the five levels of Maslow's hierarchy outlined in Figure 9–4.

Figure 9–4 Does Your Job Meet Your Needs?

Using the five levels of Maslow's hierarchy, categorize the needs you have had over the past month relating to your job. Fill in the blanks, then place a line on the continuum to indicate to what degree this category of needs has been satisfied over the past month.

My PHYSIOLOGICAL needs are: _____

How my job or employer helps me to meet my needs (e.g., employer provides salary): _____

Degree of need satisfaction: Low Degree   High Degree
                               0% _____ 100%

My SAFETY/SECURITY needs are: _____

How my job or employer helps me to meet my needs (e.g., employer provides benefits plan): _____

Degree of need satisfaction: Low Degree   High degree
                               0% _____ 100%

My SOCIAL needs are: _____

How my job or employer helps me to meet my needs (e.g., employer provides softball league): _____

Degree of need satisfaction: Low Degree   High Degree
                               0% _____ 100%

My SELF-ESTEEM needs are: _____

How my job or employer helps me to meet my needs (e.g., employer provides recognition dinners): _____

Degree of need satisfaction: Low Degree   High Degree
                               0% _____ 100%

My SELF-ACTUALIZATION needs are: _____

How my job or employer helps me to meet my needs (e.g., employer provides job training): _____

Degree of need satisfaction: Low Degree   High Degree
                               0% _____ 100%

All needs cannot be completely satisfied all the time. Hypothetically, Maslow described the average person this way:
        85% of physiological needs satisfied
        70% of safety/security needs satisfied
        50% of social needs satisfied
        40% of self-esteem needs satisfied
        10% of self-actualization needs satisfied

How do you compare with Maslow's hypothetical average? _____

Table 9–3   Herzberg's Two-Factor Theory

Maintenance-Hygiene Factors (Dissatisfiers)	Motivators (Satisfiers)
Pay	Recognition
Benefits	Personal respect
Supervision	Challenging work
Employee rules and policies	Responsibility
Bonuses	Authority
Coworkers	Creativity

Herzberg's Two-Factor Motivation Theory

A different motivational theory was proposed by another psychologist, Frederick Herzberg, after studying job attitudes and conducting a series of interviews in the Pittsburgh area. Herzberg thinks that what was traditionally thought to motivate—money and good supervisors, for example—instead are demotivators. Although many managers think people "should" produce at higher levels when they receive the rewards they have been promised, Herzberg believes that the things employees take for granted actually create more dissatisfaction with the job than satisfaction and therefore do not motivate. (See *Work and the Nature of Man* [Cleveland: World Publishing Co., 1966].)

The two-factor idea is that job factors fall into one of two categories: they are either *motivational factors* or *maintenance-hygiene factors*. (See Table 9–3.) Motivational factors are job turn-ons that encourage you to do your best. Because these turn-ons are focused on job content, they occur at the time the work is performed and make it rewarding in and of itself. For example, researching and writing a brilliant brief is satisfying and motivating to a paralegal.

On the other hand, maintenance or hygiene factors are job stay-ons, and while they will encourage you to stay on the job, they do not necessarily motivate. Hygiene factors can keep you from being dissatisfied with your job, but by themselves they cannot motivate. The term *hygiene* is used by Herzberg in its preventive and environmental sense. For example, good quality drinking water is necessary to prevent disease but it does not cure disease.

Working conditions and pay are two examples of hygiene factors. A satisfactory work environment will usually maintain a certain level of employee complacency, as will competitive salaries. However, neither factor is motivational. Without a competitive rate of pay, for example, the firm will not be able to attract top talent. But no matter what the rate of pay is, it will never be enough. When was the last time you heard someone complain because they were being paid too much?

Herzberg contends that hygiene factors are necessary to keep people on the job and provide some level of satisfaction, but that only the motivators will encourage you to do your best. In other words, you are motivated by your accomplishments, or job content, more than by the maintenance factors. As a way to assess your own motivators, refer to Figure 9–5.

Job turn-ons include the following:

- Achievement
- Recognition
- Creativity
- Responsibility
- Personal growth
- Advancement opportunities

Figure 9–5   What Motivates You?

Circle the number that indicates how much each of the following factors affects your job satisfaction.

	Very Little				Very Much
1. Feelings of achievement/success on the job	1	2	3	4	5
2. Recognition for outstanding performance	1	2	3	4	5
3. The specific work I am doing	1	2	3	4	5
4. Responsibility	1	2	3	4	5
5. Career advancement opportunities	1	2	3	4	5
6. Opportunities for personal growth	1	2	3	4	5
7. The firm's policies and procedures	1	2	3	4	5
8. The firm's supervisory practices	1	2	3	4	5
9. Personal relationships with coworkers	1	2	3	4	5
10. The working environment	1	2	3	4	5
11. Salary	1	2	3	4	5
12. Job status	1	2	3	4	5
13. Security of position	1	2	3	4	5
14. Relationship with my boss	1	2	3	4	5

The following are some job stay-ons:

- Salary and benefits
- Working conditions
- Job status
- Rules and policies
- Coworker relationships
- Job security

Modern Motivation Problems

In the past two decades the proliferation of tranquilizing drugs and the reduction of mental institutions has resulted in many people with personality disorders now receiving outpatient treatment and continuing to work. In most cases their employers and coworkers are unaware of the seriousness or nature of their personality problems. Law firms now regularly cope with an ever-increasing variety of personality disorders, including alcoholism and drug abuse, as though they were routine medical problems. In addition, law office managers regularly must deal with other common on-the-job personality disorder problems, such as excessive absenteeism, tardiness, withdrawal, and personality conflicts.

Why are these personality disorders motivation problems? They are not motivation problems in the positive achievement-oriented sense previously discussed. Rather, personality disorders are defensive reactions and abnormal behaviors motivated by the need to survive. Self-preservation is an inherent, inborn instinct and survival is *the* primary motivator for all species. Since people with personality disorders know of no other way to survive, they are often defensive and exhibit abnormal behavior.

Defensive Behavior Nearly everyone has felt defensive at one time or another. When someone is coming toward you with a raised fist or when you are being unfairly criticized, you are naturally going to do whatever is necessary to protect yourself. You put up a defense with actions or words. A **defensive reaction** is a way of thinking that cushions the blow resulting from your immediate inability to overcome an obstacle or barrier that has been placed in your path. Defensive reactions allow you to maintain a positive self-image, which you desperately need to do, since while you are being attacked it is difficult for you to see yourself as acceptable and worthwhile. Here is a breakdown of the most common defensive reactions you need to be familiar with.

1. Rationalization. Rationalization is an excuse. It is an ego-defense mechanism that allows you to avoid taking responsibility for your behavior. For example, you fail to complete an assignment on time and insist that the problem was caused by other people who continually interrupted your train of thought.

2. Fantasizing. More than an occasional daydream, fantasizing is a defense mechanism that reduces stress caused by frustration. Instead of actively working toward turning dreams into reality, excessive dreamers prefer to live in a fantasy world. Fantasizers will regularly play the lottery, for example, but have difficulty in getting to work on time three days in a row.

3. Projection. Another ego-defense mechanism, projection is blaming others for your own shortcomings. For example, an attorney lectures you on your inability to meet deadlines when the problem was caused by her poor time management habits.

4. Aggression. Aggressive behavior, a common reaction to stress, is the indiscriminate attacking of real or imaginary sources of frustration, such as shouting at a secretary for something over which he or she has no control. For the most part, this type of behavior is self-defeating and counterproductive, since the typical reaction to aggressive behavior is either defensive behavior or withdrawal. Rooted in insecurity, aggressive behavior is exhibited in a number of ways, from physical violence to treating staff members in a condescending, overbearing, threatening, and demeaning manner.

5. Scapegoating. This is a form of aggressive behavior used against those who cannot fight back instead of being directed toward the source of frustration. For example, a law office manager who has had a particularly bad day at the office may go home and yell at the kids and the dog.

6. Repression. When certain unpleasant ideas or memories cause conflict, we tend to blot them from our consciousness in an attempt to raise our self-esteem. This is exemplified by office managers who conveniently forget their own mistakes or refuse to accept constructive criticism and are thus unable to make the changes required to be more effective.

7. Withdrawal. Shy people, those with something to hide, or others who seek to avoid conflicts will sometimes physically or emotionally withdraw or pull away from others as a protective mechanism. This defensive behavior is apparent in people who are excessively quiet, who refuse to become socially involved, or who act as though a conflict does not exist.

Defensive reactions are motivated, goal-directed behaviors with the goal being self-preservation and maintaining self-esteem. At one time or another everyone will use a defensive reaction. When defensive reactions are not used excessively or for a prolonged period of time, they can be helpful in achieving short-term need satisfaction. Long-term use of any defensive reaction results in abusive behavior.

Abnormal Behavior   Continual difficulty in adjusting to ordinary situations, such as coming to work on time every day, is one of the recognized unhealthy behavior signs. Being defensive and overly suspicious, using illogical thinking, and overcompensating are other common unhealthy behaviors. What psychologists label as **abnormal behavior** is an exaggeration or extension of so-called normal behavior. It is an inability to adjust to everyday situations, typically resulting in an overreaction to routine matters.

People who develop abnormal behavior because of a chronic inability to adjust can become mentally ill in their desperate attempts to find themselves acceptable and worthy. While it is a difficult task (not recommended for the lay person) to diagnose abnormalities, professional psychologists and psychiatrists are able to detect certain syndromes of unhealthy behaviors, which they classify as types of neurosis or psychosis.

A **neurosis** is a mild personality disorder. Neurotics are seldom hospitalized and are often found in the work environment. For example, neurotics include people who are overly anxious, have phobias, or are preoccupied with imaginary illnesses, as well as those who are perfectionists, are given to excessive worrying, or are mildly depressed.

A **psychosis,** on the other hand, is a severe personality disorder resulting from an individual being so extremely defensive that he or she loses touch with reality, often suffering from hallucinations, delusions, and extreme withdrawal.

Because today only the worst cases of psychotic and neurotic behavior are hospitalized, many law office managers must now relate to large numbers of people who, except for their continued medication, might be considered totally incapacitated. People with personality disorders are problems for the law office manager who must deal with their chronic absenteeism and trouble-making behavior, their inability to consistently produce to standards, and their frequent complaints of personality conflicts with coworkers.

It is important to understand that motivation is a very individual matter. Neither a great leader nor anyone else motivates another person. Each of us, in the end, motivates ourselves. The best you can do toward motivating someone else is to determine that individual's needs and help him or her find a context within which those needs can be satisfied. So when you are asked, "How do you motivate others?", the answer is, "They have to do it themselves—with a little help from their friends."

9—4   Power and Its Impact

Leadership is defined earlier in this chapter as an *attempt* to influence others. But just how do you attempt to influence individuals or groups? Through personal and position power. **Power** is not an attempt to influence but the *ability* to influence others.

Despite its importance in the leadership role, power is a subject many people prefer to avoid simply because of its somewhat unsavory reputation. But power and its uses are real-world issues not to be underestimated or avoided. Effective leaders know how and when to use their position power and their personal power.

Position Power

Individuals who are able to influence others to do a certain job because of their position in the firm have **position power,** according to Paul Hersey and Kenneth H. Blanchard, authors of *Management of Organizational Behavior.* However, position alone does not create power, because someone else in the same or similar position may be more or less influential. So position power is merely a reflection of top management's willingness to delegate authority and responsibility. In other words, you might have the title of Office Manager, but without any authority to make decisions you will have very little position power or influence with your coworkers.

Even though position power tends to flow from the top down, this is not to say that leaders do not influence the amount of power they are given. You can acquire position power by winning the confidence and trust of those at the top with your outstanding performance and by asking for more authority and responsibility.

Position power allows you access to needed resources in order to meet objectives as well as the ability to carry out your responsibilities with relative autonomy. For some, position power represents an opportunity to exploit others and satisfy greed. But for most law office managers, having the resources available and the authority to make decisions regarding their use is enough position power.

Personal Power

Unlike position power, which comes from those at the top in the law firm, **personal power** is the extent to which followers are willing to follow a leader. Personal power thus comes from below. Followers must respect, feel good about, and be committed to their leader or no power will be attributed to that leader.

You can influence the amount of personal power you have by the way you treat others; but make a few mistakes and you will see that personal power can also be taken away. Unfortunately, personal power is a day-to-day phenomenon. One day you might have it and the next day you might not.

No doubt, the preferred situation for a leader occurs when there is both personal power and position power. It is not always possible, however, to build a relationship on both. The obvious question, then, is whether it is more important to have personal power or position power. Niccolò Machiavelli, in his classic 16th century treatise on political philosophy, *The Prince*, contends that if having both personal power and position power is not possible, relationships based on fear tend to last longer than those based on love alone.

Although position power and personal power are unique and distinct, they are interacting influence systems. Followers are affected by their perception of the leader's ability to influence those at the top of the firm, and the willingness of people at the top to delegate position power to you is often dependent on their perception of the followers' commitment to you. So it is not enough to have either position power or personal power—to be a leader you need to have both.

Office Politics

Leaders must engage in various types of power-oriented behavior to augment their official authority. While these activities can be described as "political," the use of that term does not refer to unethical conduct. Instead, **politics** describes the manner in which positions of power are established and influence is exerted in the administrative process. Any intentional action taken by a group or individual to promote or protect self-interest is considered political behavior. There is no implication in the word itself of the use of power for undesirable ends.

Political activities are not necessarily complex. Not embarrassing your boss and willingly accepting certain assignments are political acts, as are compromising or creating obligations by doing favors for others. Developing close relationships with others who have power or exploiting your technical skills and knowledge are other ways of using political behavior to build your power base. For example, a computer-literate, experienced, consistently dependable legal word processor with a great personality has an enormous amount of power and political clout in most law firms.

On the other hand, political activities can interfere with getting the work done if the "politicians" are more concerned with the advancement of personal interests than in meeting deadlines. Whether the political game-players are peers, bosses, or others in the firm, you must deal with them appropriately. Addison Steele, author of *Upward Mobility* (Alexandria, Va.: Time Books, 1978), writes from experience in the publishing field in warning against three types of organizational game-players who can also be found in the law office.

1. *Those who play power games to win.* Stay out of the way of these types, who are willing to do whatever it takes to get ahead, including chopping down anyone who gets in their way. When possible, let them know you are not a threat.

2. *Those who play politics for the sake of playing.* These are the most dangerous types because they are playing for the fun of it without clear goals and are therefore unpredictable. Let this type think you are the most naive person in the office. You hear nothing, see nothing, and repeat nothing. Never trust this type of game-player.

3. *Those who play politics convinced they will lose.* Take a kind, nurturing attitude toward these types, who see themselves as decent people in a hostile environment without any choice but to play politics, even though they do not expect to win. These players are very insecure and easily threatened, so do not count on them to support you when you need a political ally.

In addition to recognizing and handling basic types of game-players, Steele gives us a couple of suggestions for dealing with all the players.

1. *Avoid taking sides in power struggles.* Your goal is to be recognized as your own person and to gain a reputation for objectivity and fairness. You can be supportive of others where appropriate and still draw the line at fighting their battles for them.

2. *Keep social contacts constructive.* No matter at what level in the organization you might socialize, if you are part of a group that meets regularly for any reason, be aware of the "three Ps" — politics (is anyone using this group to build themselves up or tear others down?); pretense (are you free to be yourself and say whatever is on your mind, or must you always be aware of what others will think?); and pettiness (are these get-togethers vicious, and are you afraid people would talk about you if you were not there?).

Regardless of your personal views on the need to be political in your position as office manager, the fact remains that a certain degree of political astuteness is essential not only for survival but to form a power base in order to get things done.

SUMMARY

9–1

Leadership is an attempt to influence others to achieve specific objectives because they want to, not because they have to. As an intensely interpersonal process, your ability to lead is largely dependent upon your leadership style, or the patterns of behavior that are associated with you as a leader. These include your attitude, your ability to communicate, and your skill as a manager in being able to achieve goals. Three of the most common leadership styles include the autocratic leader, who leads by issuing direct orders; the developmental leader, who relies on staff participation in setting objectives and making decisions; and the situational leader, who adapts his or her style to fit the situation and the group or individual.

9–2

Your attitude toward yourself and others will greatly influence your ability to be a leader and your leadership style. Douglas McGregor noticed that leaders tend to have either a positive or a negative attitude toward those they lead. He labeled those with a pessimistic view as Theory X managers; they think most employees dislike work, need to be closely supervised, and are motivated by the threat of punishment. Theory Y managers hold a more optimistic view of workers; they think that work is as natural as rest or play, that workers like to be creative and prefer to work on their own when possible, and that recognition of their work is often reward enough to keep them motivated. Unfortunately, some leaders would like to be Theory Y leaders but have had bad experiences with this approach when others have either failed in their efforts to work without close supervision or took advantage of the situation. McGregor calls this the Derived X leadership attitude, or the I've-Been-Burned Theory.

9–3

Maslow's hierarchy of needs theory explains motivation in terms of a five-level hierarchy beginning at the bottom level with basic physiological needs and progressing upward to safety/security needs, social needs, self-esteem and ego needs, and culminating in the need to self-actualize, or achieve one's full potential. On the other hand, Herzberg's two-factor theory suggests that motivation, in part, is a function of job maintenance or hygiene factors, which must be present in order to attract and maintain employees but also tend to be dissatisfying; and motivation factors, which include recognition, authority, and responsibility, as well as the work itself. Today's managers are given the additional task of dealing with complex behavioral motivation problems, such as defensive reactions and abnormal behaviors, which include people with neurotic and psychotic personality disorders.

9–4

Power is not an attempt to influence but rather the ability to influence others. Position power reflects the ability to influence others to do a certain job based on position alone, while personal power indicates the extent to which followers are willing to follow a leader because they respect and feel good about the leader. Leaders need to engage in various types of power-oriented behavior, which can be described as political behavior, to augment their authority.

REVIEW

Key Terms

abnormal behavior
autocratic
contingency approach
defensive reaction
Derived X theory
developmental leader
leadership
leadership style
motivation
need theory
needs
neurosis
personal power
politics
position power
power
psychosis
self-fulfilling prophecy
situational style
Theory X
Theory Y
two-factor motivating theory

Questions for Review and Discussion

1. Define the terms *leadership* and *leadership style*.
2. What are three common leadership styles presented in this chapter and what are the primary characteristics of each style?
3. Describe the attitudes associated with Theory X and Theory Y.
4. What impact does attitude have on leadership style?
5. Describe how human needs affect motivation.
6. Discuss Maslow's need theory.
7. What is the underlying premise of Herzberg's two-factor theory?
8. Today's office managers are faced with difficult motivational problems not considered by Maslow or Herzberg. What are they and why are they occurring now?
9. Compare and contrast defensive behavior and abnormal behavior.
10. Explain the functions of power and politics in leadership.

Activities

1. Divide into groups of two. One member of each group will assume the role of office manager discussing a recurring behavioral problem with an extremely defensive employee. The purpose of this role play is to learn how to respond to defensive people and reach agreement on a solution to the problem. Then the group participants will switch roles until everyone has had the opportunity to be in the manager's role. Time required: 45–60 minutes.
2. Form groups of four or five people to identify motivational problems in their workplaces and formulate possible solutions using the theories of Maslow, Herzberg, and McGregor in discussing alternatives. If the problems are associated with defensive or abnormal behavior, ask for alternative courses of action. Time required: 45–60 minutes.

CHAPTER 10　Managing Groups

OUTLINE

10–1　The Nature of Groups
　　　　The Reason for Groups
　　　　Types of Groups
　　　　Group Characteristics
10–2　Group Conflicts
　　　　Group Goals and Individual Goals
　　　　Agendas
　　　　Groupthink
10–3　Resolving Conflicts
　　　　Managing Controversy
　　　　Managing Conflict of Interest
10–4　Solving Problems and Making Decisions
　　　　Problem-Solving Steps
10–5　Negotiating Effective Solutions
　　　　Negotiation Styles and Their Outcomes
　　　　Choosing a Negotiating Style

COMMENTARY

Lately you have been thinking that you could get much more accomplished if you worked entirely alone, without having to consider the opinions, needs, and goals of other people. Yet the reality is that most law firms are dependent not only upon the efforts of the individuals who work in it, but also upon the various groups within the firm—the lawyers, paralegals, secretaries, word processors, managers, and other members of the staff. All are essential to the success of the firm. However, from time to time one group will have trouble relating to another group within the firm and it takes a great deal of your time to smooth over ruffled feelings.

　　Last month, for example, when the secretaries decided to slow down their work production in a silent protest for being given too much work they considered paralegal duties, the managing attorney came to you to find a solution. The days you spent trying to reach a compromise turned into weeks of bad feelings, low morale, and an alarming increase in absenteeism. Although a solution was eventually reached, there is a nagging feeling in the back of your mind that it is only a matter of time before something else comes up that will once again test your leadership and negotiation skills.

OBJECTIVES

In Chapter 9 you learned that your leadership style, attitude, and power will determine your effectiveness as a leader. After studying this chapter you will be able to:

1. List the reasons why the formation of groups is a natural occurrence in any organization.
2. Identify the types of organizational groups.
3. Describe the common characteristics of all groups.
4. Discuss the reasons why conflicts arise in groups.
5. Define *groupthink*.
6. Explain the difference between controversy and conflict of interest.
7. Discuss how to manage conflict.
8. Outline the steps leading to logical problem solving.
9. Explain the three styles of negotiating and the probable outcome of each.
10. Discuss the differences between the win-win approach and the win-lose approach to negotiating.

10–1   The Nature of Groups

Since much of the work in a law firm is accomplished through group effort, an understanding of how groups function and their impact on both organizational and individual behavior is essential for you to be an effective manager and leader.

While the word *group* is often used to refer to any assembly of people—commuters on a train, a rock band, the people you "hang out" with—for our purposes, a **group** refers to two or more people who personally interact with each other in order to achieve a common goal.

The Reason for Groups

Remember Maslow's hierarchy of needs discussed in Chapter 9? The middle level on Maslow's hierarchy is the need for social interaction—a feeling of belonging, to be identified with one or more groups. While almost everyone has experienced the frustration of working with and being dependent upon other people, the reality is that few people like being alone or working in isolation for extended periods of time. To overcome feelings of isolation, most people will become part of a group for one, or all, of the following reasons.

Affiliation   Group companionship provides feelings of security, belonging, and friendship. As a general rule, people tend to voluntarily form strong affiliations with groups who share their interests and values. Whether the group is a professional association or a bowling team, the members of these social groups are more likely to become intimate friends over time than are coworkers due to the voluntary nature of the group affiliation. Most of us do not get to choose all the people with whom we must work, but we do get to choose those with whom we want to socialize after working hours.

Power   There is strength in numbers. Being a member of a group provides reassurance and support, often giving its members the courage to take a stand on an important issue which they might not do on their own. Labor unions, activist groups, and support networks are formed to take advantage of this strength-in-numbers power. Group membership increases your self-confidence and your likelihood of speaking out for your beliefs by reducing the fear, frustration, anxiety, and feeling of being a lone voice in the wilderness. Groups often succeed where an individual might fail.

Identity   Along with membership in a group comes an increased awareness of a personal identity—a sense of being somebody. Self-esteem is positively reinforced. Identification with a prestigious group, such as membership in a group known for its high scholastic achievements or a profession, is especially ego-enhancing.

Goal Accomplishment   In most situations a group will accomplish goals more effectively than any individual effort, due to the variety of skills and knowledge that are collectively provided. It is a well-known fact that the more brain power used to solve a problem, the better the chance for a successful resolution.

   Most people join a group or groups, then, for any or all of these reasons:

1. To affiliate with like-minded individuals
2. To increase their personal power
3. To enhance their personal identity
4. To accomplish goals

Types of Groups

Not only are groups a part of organizational life; they tend to have split personalities, so to speak, falling into two distinct categories.

Formal Groups   **Formal groups** are created by management for the purpose of attaining goals and objectives. Some formal groups are *problem-solving groups*, which combine the knowledge and resources of the group members to solve a problem or take advantage of an opportunity. *Committees*, a relatively permanent group of individuals who are responsible for specific assignments or activities, are one type of problem-solving group. For example, in the law office, an Executive Committee may be formed to take responsibility for the day-to-day operation of the firm and the Recruitment Committee is responsible for keeping the firm adequately staffed with attorneys and paralegals. A *task force* is a nonpermanent group assembled to deal with a nonroutine decision that affects all members of the organization—the annual holiday celebration, for example.

Informal Groups   By contrast, *informal groups* arise spontaneously throughout all levels of the firm. You can assume that whenever individuals associate on a fairly continuous basis, groups will form, with or without the approval of management, because the individual members receive a great deal of satisfaction from being part of the group. These are the people from the office who lunch together regularly or get together on the weekends. Informal groups are important to the firm. But they can have either a positive or a negative impact on the work itself and the work environment.

Group Characteristics

Whether the group is a formal one organized by management or an informal group formed spontaneously, all groups have three common characteristics: *norms*, *conformity*, and *cohesiveness*. You will gain a greater insight into how and why groups are formed by taking a closer look at these characteristics.

Norms Groups and the individuals in them have distinct needs, personalities, and beliefs about what constitutes normal behavior. But, sometimes surprisingly, individuals will undergo a kind of metamorphosis when they become members of a group. If being a member of the group is really important to them, they will change their personality, beliefs, and behavior to conform to the group. A **norm,** sometimes also referred to as a **social norm,** is a generally agreed-upon standard of behavior that every member of the group is expected to follow.

Group norms or standards have a very powerful influence over the member who wants to be accepted because, as we have already discussed, the group provides its members with feelings of security, power, and strength. People, as a group, will engage in activities that as individuals they would not think of doing.

Any group lacking strong standards of behavior is less stable and consequently less permanent than those with well-developed norms. Human nature compels most of us to gravitate toward groups of like-minded individuals with a strong identity.

Conformity Group pressure forces its members to **conform,** or comply, with the norms established by the group. Nonconformity threatens the group's standards, stability, and longevity, so the pressure placed on each member to conform is intense. Those who resist are rejected by other group members and eventually drop out, or are forced out, of the group.

Compliance is important because behavior is visible, and to succeed the group members must show they are united in their efforts. However, not all individuals conform to the same extent. The degree of conformity depends on the person's status in the group and level of self-confidence. Someone with a lower status in the group and little self-confidence is more likely to conform in order to be accepted by others than someone with a high status and more self-confidence. Willingness to conform also depends upon the extent to which the goals and values of the group are similar to those of the individual. There is no reason to belong to a group of people with whom you have little in common.

Cohesiveness Group **cohesiveness** is the emotional closeness that exists among the group members. In other words, cohesiveness depends upon how well the group "sticks together" and acts as a single unit instead of as a group of individuals. A cohesive group is attractive to its members, so the more they stick together, the more attractive group membership becomes.

On the other hand, group cohesiveness can be a problem if the group's goals are in conflict with the goals of other groups or with the goals of the firm. Before making any changes in the firm, you would be wise to pay attention to its various groups. You want to know what groups exist, how cohesive each group is, what norms they consider important, and how closely the individual members conform to those norms. If you attempt to change the group's structure or work methods and in the process inadvertently violate the group's norms, you will no doubt be faced with resistance to change, if not outright rebellion.

Groups can have both positive and negative effects on law firms. Unfortunately, there are still major gaps in understanding the reasons why some groups are effective and others turn out to be a source of continual difficulty for both group members and others in the firm. What we do know for certain is that groups are a part of every working environment and that effective leaders learn how to work with them to get results.

10-2   Group Conflicts

Group processes are not all smooth and cooperative. Conflicts can arise not only among members of a group but also between different groups within the same organization. These conflicts are often expressed by a lack of cooperation, withholding information, avoiding interaction, lack of trust, or outright revenge. To understand why conflicts arise, you need to look at the relationship between group goals and individual goals.

Group Goals and Individual Goals

Every formal organizational group exists to achieve some kind of goal. Most often these goals are defined as *tasks*, jobs to be done. The tasks performed by these formal groups are varied: getting a brief filed on time, assessing the financial condition of the firm, or meeting with office space planners to design new office space.

Informal groups, on the other hand, can have both task-oriented goals and *social* goals. For example, a group of secretaries stays after hours to help one of their members meet a deadline and then they go out to dinner to celebrate.

In addition to a group's goals, individual members also have their own goals. Sometimes an individual's goal in a group is nearly identical to the shared goal of the group. When a paralegal association decides to sponsor a welfare family to brighten their holidays, and an individual paralegal makes a contribution to the cause, both the group and the individual have a shared goal—a desire to help needy families. Having personal goals is not harmful to the group if they are compatible with the group's objectives.

When an individual's goals conflict with those of the group or the firm, however, problems will occur. For example, if two feuding members use meetings to disparage one another, their arguments could keep the group from getting much accomplished. Likewise, if one member of the group needs to make more money and takes on an extra job at night, the resulting decrease in productivity from exhaustion may be in direct conflict to the firm's goals of increasing output with fewer employees.

Agendas

When meetings are called for the purpose of providing information or for problem solving, the chairperson typically prepares and publishes a **planned agenda**—a program or list of items to be discussed or tasks to be done. Planned agendas are useful in keeping the group focused on a preset goal and are an invaluable time management tool.

However, even with a planned agenda, one of the potential pitfalls of any group interaction is the possibility that someone will be safeguarding a **hidden agenda,** personal goals not made public. Hidden agendas are comprised of the attitudes and feelings that an individual brings to the group. While often times "planned," hidden agendas can also arise spontaneously as a result of a disagreement with some idea expressed or with someone in the group. When there is a hidden agenda present, goal orientation shifts from the group to the individual so that the individual with the hidden agenda nearly always, either consciously or subconsciously, places obstacles in the path of the group's planned agenda.

Hidden agendas represent what an individual, or group, wants instead of what they say they want. While hidden agendas are neither better nor worse than planned agendas, they can interfere with the ability to focus and can block the progress of the group. If not recognized and understood, hidden agendas can waste a great deal of a group's energy and the firm's resources. Here are some ways to deal with hidden agendas.

1. Recognize that hidden agendas might be present. Individuals in the group could have personal goals that might be more important to them than the group's goals. This is not to imply that individual goals always take precedence over group goals, but that the possibility is always present.

2. Decide on the best way to handle a hidden agenda. Sometimes the best way is to bring the situation out in the open. For example, with feuding group members, it might be best for you to speak with them individually and work with them on resolving the problem. If the problem is a personal one, counseling might be recommended. The purpose for bringing any hidden agenda to the surface is not to create bad feelings or distrust, but to be able to talk about it, resolve it, and get back on track.

3. Do not scold or pressure the group because there are hidden agendas. They are a legitimate part of the group process, since each of us is constantly working out our individual needs in the group as well as the group needs. It is only natural that members of the group will see things differently and want different things accomplished.

4. Help the group work out ways to solve hidden agendas by acknowledging the problem, gathering data on it, exploring alternative solutions, and deciding on one. As the group deals with hidden agendas, it is easier to recognize with greater clarity what the group's goals really are as well as those of the individual members.

In summary, here are the ways you can help a group handle hidden agendas:

1. Recognize that a hidden agenda might be present when the group is having difficulty in reaching its goals.
2. Decide how to bring the hidden agenda to light.
3. Realize that a hidden agenda is a natural part of the group process because individual members have individual goals and needs.
4. Work toward finding a solution.

Groupthink

Another potential problem involved when working with groups is **groupthink,** which can be defined as the pressure on individual members of the group to stick together in their decisions and solutions to problems. The more cohesive the group, the more likely the individual members are to "agree not to disagree," especially when it comes to challenging the ideas of the group leader.

Groupthink can undermine the analytical process, legitimize ignorance, and reinforce biases because people do tend to be influenced by their peers. Therefore, some group members, particularly those with high status, can sway the entire group into pursuing an undesirable course of action. These groups are so "tight" that no one will dare risk questioning the leadership.

One example of groupthink in action occurred when the seniormost partners of a law firm wanted to merge their firm with another one and convinced the other partners the merger was a good idea. The merger took place, even though some partners with lesser status had doubts but did not express them. Although they did not agree with the merger, they went along with it, succumbing to pressure from the group.

Less extreme, but equally destructive, groupthink occurs most often at meetings where a decision has been made before the meeting even begins. The other members of the group are there merely to rubber-stamp the leader's choice. Silence on the part of participants is assumed to mean they consent to and agree to decisions made by the leader.

While a certain amount of groupthink can be expected from any group situation, there are some ways to minimize its occurrence, such as to diversify group membership to get different perspectives, provide opportunities and permission for open debate, clarify goals and purposes, and work toward developing the interpersonal skills of the group members. As individual members develop self-confidence and experience a "safe" forum for their ideas, they are more likely to express their ideas and opinions.

To determine how susceptible you are to groupthink, refer to the self-assessment form presented in Figure 10–1.

10–3 Resolving Conflicts

Conflict in groups and between individuals is not inevitably destructive. Because in most situations groups outperform individuals and tend to make better decisions than individuals, the trend in recent years has been toward managing rather than avoiding conflict.

Some amount of conflict is essential to the health of any law firm; otherwise, the working environment stagnates. On the other hand, too much conflict reduces both organizational and individual effectiveness. So the question is not how to get rid of conflict, but how to best manage conflict to enhance effectiveness.

As you might expect, managing conflict effectively depends on the situation and on the type of conflict involved. Generally speaking, conflict is considered to be appropriately managed when it does not interfere substantially with the *professional* relationship of the people involved.

To understand conflict situations further, consider the distinction between controversy and conflict of interest. **Controversy** is a difference of opinion that prevents or interferes with reaching a decision. This type of conflict is common in committee meetings. A **conflict of interest** occurs when an individual or a group intentionally interferes with or blocks the action of others in pursuit of special interests. These conflicts are common between groups or individuals in the firm desiring to pursue bigger budgets, more physical space, or more staff help.

Figure 10–1 How Susceptible Are You to Groupthink?

Following are several pairs of statements. For each pair, circle either the A or B statement, whichever is most characteristic of your behavior. In some cases, neither statement may be very typical of how you would respond, but select the response that you would be more likely to use.

1. A. There are times when I let others take responsibility for solving the problems.
   B. Rather than negotiate the things on which we disagree, I try to stress the things on which we both agree.

2. A. I try to find a compromise solution.
   B. I attempt to deal with everyone's concerns.

3. A. I am usually firm in pursuing my goals
   B. I might try to soothe the other person's feelings and preserve our relationship.

4. A. I try to find a compromise solution.
   B. I will sometimes sacrifice my own wishes for the wishes of the other person.

5. A. I consistently seek the other person's help in working out a solution.
   B. I try to do what is necessary to avoid useless tension.

6. A. I try to avoid creating unpleasantness for myself.
   B. I try to win my position.

7. A. I try to postpone the issue until I have had some time to think it over.
   B. I give up some points for others.

8. A. I am usually firm in pursuing my goals.
   B. I attempt to get all concerns and issues immediately out in the open.

9. A. I feel that differences are not always worth worrying about.
   B. I make some effort to get my way.

10. A. I am firm in pursuing my goals.
    B. I try to find a compromise solution.

11. A. I attempt to get all concerns and issues immediately out in the open.
    B. I might try to soothe the other person's feelings and preserve the relationship.

12. A. I sometimes avoid taking positions which would create controversy.
    B. I will let the other person have some of their positions if they let me have some of mine.

13. A. I propose a middle ground.
    B. I press to get my points made.

14. A. I tell my ideas and ask others for their ideas.
    B. I try to show others the logic and benefits of my position.

(continued)

Managing Controversy

Until recently, conflict in the office of any sort has been unwelcome—perhaps because we associate it with a lack of harmony, emotional pain, or destructive behavior. Or lack of experience in turning group conflicts into something more positive might have kept you from allowing them to surface.

But conflicts are now increasingly seen as useful tools in effective group problem solving. If managed carefully, conflicts can yield a number of benefits. For one thing, groups with dissenting members can accomplish more than those who suffer from groupthink; and when group leaders support disagreement, teamwork becomes more valued over competition, individual participation increases, and more ideas are presented and explored.

Mutual goal setting is another benefit of well-managed dissension. When group members "buy into" goals, there will be a stronger commitment to

Figure 10–1   *(continued)*

15. A. I might try to soothe the other person's feelings and preserve the relationship.
   B. I try to do what is necessary to avoid useless tension.

16. A. I try not to hurt the other person's feelings.
   B. I try to convince the other person of the merits of my position.

17. A. I am usually firm in pursuing my goals.
   B. I try to do what is necessary to avoid useless tensions.

18. A. If it makes the other person happy, I might agree with their views.
   B. I will let others have some of their positions if they will let me have some of mine.

19. A. I attempt to get all the concerns and issues immediately out in the open.
   B. I try to postpone the issue until I have had some time to think it over.

20. A. I attempt to immediately work through differences.
   B. I try to find a fair combination of gains and losses for everyone.

21. A. In approaching negotiations, I try to be considerate of the other person's wishes.
   B. I always lean toward a direct discussion of the problem.

22. A. I try to find a position that is intermediate between yours and mine.
   B. I assert my wishes.

23. A. I am very often concerned with satisfying everyone's wishes.
   B. There are times when I let others take responsibility for solving the problem.

24. A. If your position seems very important to you, I would try to meet your wishes.
   B. I try to get others to settle for a compromise.

25. A. I try to show others the logic and benefits of my position.
   B. In approaching negotiations, I try to be considerate of the other person's wishes.

26. A. I propose a middle ground.
   B. I am nearly always concerned with satisfying everyone's wishes.

27. A. I sometimes avoid taking positions that would create controversy.
   B. If it makes the other person happy, I might agree with their views.

28. A. I am usually firm in pursuing my goals.
   B. I usually seek the other person's help in working out a solution.

29. A. I propose a middle ground.
   B. I feel that differences are not always worth worrying about.

30. A. I try not to hurt the other person's feelings.
   B. I always share the problem with the other person so we can work it out.

(continued)

achieving them. This results in increased trust and cohesion among group members, and the decisions reached are more easily implemented with less resistance than in a no-conflict group.

Even though controversy can enhance problem solving, some group members will go to great lengths to avoid it, preferring to smooth over differences. When norms such as "don't rock the boat" or "be a team player" are evident, you can introduce controversy to get the group moving. One way to do this would be to divide the group into subgroups, giving each a different position to defend on the issue up for discussion. Another way is for you or another group member to be the "devil's advocate."

An important leadership function is to help group members learn that even though their ideas are disputed, their personal competence is not being questioned. Phrases such as "we are all in this together" and "let's find a solution that is good for everyone" indicate the appropriate attitude for the

Figure 10–1 *(continued)*

Scoring: Circle the letters below that you circled on each statement of the assessment.

	Competing (forcing)	Collaborating (problem solving)	Compromising (sharing)	Avoiding (withdrawal)	Accommodating (soothing)
1.				A	B
2.		B	A		
3.	A				B
4.			A		B
5.		A		B	
6.	B			A	
7.			B	A	
8.	A	B			
9.	B			A	
10.	A		B		
11.		A			B
12.			B	A	
13.	B		A		
14.	B	A			
15.				B	A
16.	B				A
17.	A			B	
18.			B		A
19.		A		B	
20.		A	B		
21.		B			A
22.	B		A		
23.		A		B	
24.			B		A
25.	A				B
26.		B	A		
27.				A	B
28.	A	B			
29.			A	B	
30.		B			A

Total number of items circled in each column:

Competing _____   Avoiding _____

Collaborating _____   Accommodating _____

Compromising _____

Interpretation:

Competing
High score: You can be seen as being unconcerned regarding others.
Low score: People do not know where you are coming from; you are unwilling to let others know where you are on issues and concerns.

Collaborating
High score: You may be seen as willing to look at all the inputs and outputs, which requires a lot of work.
Low score: You are overlooking ideas for creative, innovative solutions. You may be seen as impatient, impulsive and willing to pull out.

Compromising
High score: Your attitude is I'll take half and you take half.
Low score: Do you recognize when you must share even though the solution is not perfect?

Avoiding
High score: How is your comfort level with conflict? Do you hang in there?
Low score: Do you recognize when you must share even though the solution is not perfect?

Accommodating
High score: You may be seen as a needless person.
Low score: You sometimes fail to recognize your needs are less important than others.

group, rather than "I'm right and you're wrong." Group members should be looking for shared successes and rewards—as well as shared responsibility for failures—not individual recognition.

Managing Conflict of Interest

You know that a conflict of interest occurs when the goals of an individual or a group interfere with or block the actions of others who are also pursuing their own interests. These are some of the usual ways of managing a conflict of interest.

Authority Decision Managing a conflict of interest between two persons or two groups is often done by *appealing to a higher authority* for a decision. However, if you give orders to stop arguing or you settle a dispute by creating winners and losers, you may temporarily have peace and quiet but you will have done nothing toward addressing the root cause of the conflict and it will surface again.

Negotiation and Bargaining Another common conflict management technique is negotiation and bargaining, during which the parties attempt to reach a *compromise* resolution. A notable characteristic of compromise settlements is that both parties lose something and there is no obvious winner. Sometimes the compromise settlement process is facilitated by a person of higher authority.

Win-Win Outcomes When you can bring the conflicting parties together to discuss the issues face to face, you are using a powerful conflict management technique known as **integration**. Because the parties themselves talk through their disagreements and then commence developing a mutually agreeable solution, integration works to resolve the real cause of the conflict and, in the process, reduces tension between the parties.

Integration is a *win-win* method, instead of a *win-lose* or *lose-lose* method. In a win-win situation, all parties walk away with something gained by using their imagination to work out a mutually satisfactory solution. The major advantage of integration is the shared commitment of all parties to find a solution. Once having shared this commitment a strong foundation exists for further collaboration and resolution of future conflicts.

Here are some ways you can make the group you are working with more effective:

1. Avoid arguing for your own viewpoint. Instead, state your point as clearly and concisely as you can and listen to others.
2. If the discussion reaches an impasse, do not assume that someone must win and someone must lose. Look for a new option that is the next-best alternative to everyone.
3. Never change your mind just to avoid an argument.
4. If an agreement comes too quickly, take another look. Different interpretations of what was agreed to may be hiding underlying differences. Make sure that everyone fully understands the intent and content of the agreement.
5. Do not give way to other viewpoints unless you feel they have reasonable merit.

6. Avoid using conflict-reducing tricks to reach agreements, such as the majority vote, calculating an average, flipping a coin, and bargaining.
7. Encourage differences of opinion.
8. Make sure that every member of the group contributes.

10-4 Solving Problems and Making Decisions

Solving problems and making decisions are important management functions. Yet some people have difficulty making decisions—usually because they are afraid they will make the wrong choice. Figure 10–2 demonstrates why decision making and problem solving are both difficult and risky. You will not be correct 100 percent of the time. The best you can hope for is that your decision will have the least negative impact on the least number of people.

Problem-Solving Steps

Whether you are using a committee or taking sole responsibility, there are many ways to approach problem solving. The steps that follow represent one problem-solving approach.

Step One: Define the Problem An old maxim says "A problem well-defined is a problem half-solved." This maxim has truth, since defining a problem accurately requires objectivity—the ability to see things as they *are*, not as we *think* they might be. Often when the real problem is discovered, the solution is obvious.

In defining the problem care must be taken to be sure you are getting to the root of it. Sometimes, what seems to be the problem is often just the symptom, and to work on curing the symptom and not the root cause of the problem is a waste of time. For example, there is one employee in your firm who seems to continually have a cold, the flu, or any other current virus. These are symptoms of a root problem—not enough rest, too much stress, disinterest in the job, a conflict with the boss, or a combination of these and other factors. To treat only the symptom will provide a temporary solution, but the root cause still exists and will erupt again and again until it is recognized and handled. Likewise, docking the pay of a habitually tardy employee may be a temporary solution, but

Figure 10–2 Problem-Solving Obstacles

- Employees are afraid to criticize bosses.
- People are self-protective of their positions.
- Technical expertise is intimidating to those with less knowledge.
- Personal conflicts interfere with constructive problem solving.
- People see problems from their own viewpoint rather than the broader organizational perspective.

Source: Adapted from *What Managers Need to Know*, Roger Fritz (Naperville, Ill.: Organizational Development Consultants, 1988). Reprinted with permission.

until attention is given to the root cause—personal problems at home, job boredom, or lack of direction—the problem will continue to recur.

Keep your emotions in check during this phase of problem solving and do not be too eager to come up with a definition, especially before gathering enough facts. The tendency among problem solvers is to become an instant expert in psychology and spend too much time analyzing the situation without getting enough facts.

Step Two: Gather and Analyze Information   Before jumping to conclusions, it is best to gather as much relevant information as possible to help determine whether your assessment of the root cause of the problem is accurate, who is involved in the problem and will be affected by a solution, and what resources are available to assist in the process.

Many decision makers get stuck at this point in the process. Because of the overwhelming amount of information now available on any subject, we can easily burn out from information overload. While gathering information is an important step in problem solving, it is equally important to weigh the cost and time required to gather information against its value in contributing toward a better decision. The higher the stakes, the more information required. For example, you will spend more time and money gathering information on buying a new computer system than on the purchase of a typewriter.

Some decision makers use lack of information as an excuse to not make a decision. Mark H. McCormack notes, in his book *What They Don't Teach You at Harvard Business School* (New York: Bantam Books, 1985), that "Facts are a decision maker's tools, but (1) they won't take the place of intuition, (2) they won't make the decision for you, and (3) they are only as useful as your ability to interpret them."

Step Three: Develop Alternative Solutions   Group involvement is often useful in the problem-solving process at this point. Good decisions are the result of having a number of creative alternatives from which to choose. Often it is not until several alternative recommendations have been presented that your second or third solution appears to be the best.

When working with others to develop alternative solutions, the process is greatly helped if everyone keeps an open mind and is willing to explore all the possibilities, even those that might appear ridiculous. Everyone must be committed to keep working on the problem until a satisfactory solution is found. Don't stop when you have one or two possible solutions. Keep asking, "What else would work?" Write down all possibilities no matter how wild they may seem, and only when all brains have been drained begin discussing the merits of each alternative.

Step Four: Analyze the Implications of Selected Alternatives   Before proceeding to carry out any recommendations, the group should consider the likely results of each alternative. Since any decision will no doubt affect many other people, you would be wise to try to anticipate the affect of your selected alternatives before going ahead with implementing a solution. You might inadvertently be creating more problems instead of solving one.

During this phase of problem solving remind yourself and the group (1) why you want to solve this problem, (2) what goal you want to achieve, and (3) what facts are relevant.

Step Five: Select the "Best" Alternative Since you will rarely find the "perfect" solution, the best alternative is the one that will accomplish your desired objectives and have the least negative impact on others.

Decision making requires that you take calculated risks. Holding out for the perfect solution is one of the decision-making traps to avoid. You will find in some situations that no one solution stands out as being better than the rest. At this point you will have to rely heavily on your own judgment and intuition in reaching a decision. In some cases there may be no "good" decision. Then you must select the option that is "least worst," and that may be to stick with the way things are. After exploring all the alternatives, if you firmly believe that no change is best, have the courage of your convictions and make that decision.

Timing is an important factor in decision making. Once it is time to make a decision, do it! Then commit yourself to making the decision work and do not look back. Many decision makers drive themselves crazy with 20/20 hindsight. The reason you spend time and money to gather information is to be able to make the best possible decision with the information that is available at that time.

Step Six: Implement Your Decision After you have firmly committed to your decision, the next step is to communicate and sell it to others. You need the support of all who are going to be affected to ensure success. Announce your decision to the group as a whole when possible. This helps to minimize false rumors and chitchat on the grapevine. Then follow up with individual meetings and written instructions, if required.

When communicating your decision, either in writing or verbally, you will gain more cooperation if you cover these points: (1) the objectives to be achieved, (2) the plan of action, (3) time targets for the plan, (4) changes that will take place—where and when, (5) how the plan will be carried out, (6) who will be affected, and (7) why this course of action was selected to solve the problem.

The "why" of any decision is important to gaining cooperation, yet it is often overlooked. This is unfortunate because most people will not be committed to the solution unless they understand how it was reached, why a particular plan was selected, and how it affects them. By pointing out the benefits and advantages, as well as the expected side effects, you will allow those involved to feel more secure about the process and the result.

Step Seven: Evaluate and Modify To make sure that your decision accomplishes the objectives, consistent and routine follow-up is required to find out how well the plan is going. If during the evaluation process you find that the objectives are not being accomplished or that time lines are not being met, minor modifications or adjustments might be in order. Any major modification should be treated just as you would a new problem. In other words, a major modification would require that you go back to Step One and start all over again.

In summary, here are the steps to follow to solve a problem or reach a decision:

1. Define the problem.
2. Gather and analyze pertinent information.
3. Develop alternative solutions.
4. Analyze the implications of selected alternatives.
5. Select the best alternative.
6. Implement your decision.
7. Evaluate and modify, if required.

Typically, if the steps to problem solving and decision making are followed, the result is a logical and satisfactory approach to reaching decisions that are comfortable and easy to live with for everyone.

10-5 Negotiating Effective Solutions

Working with groups of people presents many opportunities to use your problem-solving, decision-making, and conflict resolution skills. But perhaps no managerial skill is as important as your ability to negotiate. Identifying a problem and finding a viable solution to it are only the beginning steps in a process that does not end until everyone who has a vested interest in the outcome is satisfied.

Even being a skilled communicator and problem solver does not guarantee a positive outcome. Whenever the parties do not initially agree about an issue, they have three choices.

One choice is to stop trying to find a solution. "I've tried talking to her, but it doesn't work. There's nothing more I can do." "We can't reach agreement, so the deal's off."

Another choice is to impose a solution. "I'll decide how we are going to get this job done." "Either you meet my demands, or I'll see you in court."

The preferred choice is to reach an agreement by negotiating. "Let's figure out something we can both live with." "We have already agreed we both want this deal. Let's see how we can work out the terms."

Negotiation is the process of reaching a mutually acceptable agreement between individuals or groups. Negotiating is a part of life. It is the way we routinely settle conflicts and conduct our daily business. "If you will go to the cleaners, I'll go to the market." "I'll help you finish this project today, if you will help me tomorrow." "I'll be happy to take on more responsibility, if you will give me a bigger budget and a secretary."

There is nothing magic about negotiation. But if it is poorly handled the problem can be worse than before, with all parties feeling they have been taken advantage of. However, when the negotiation is skillfully handled, the positions of all the parties will improve.

Negotiation Styles and Their Outcomes

There are three types of negotiation styles, each of which produces a very different result.

The Win-Lose Style The win-lose negotiating style assumes that one side will win by achieving its goals and the other side will lose. Game theorists call win-lose results a zero-sum outcome since the winner's gain is exactly equal to the loser's loss. One example of a zero-sum outcome is spousal support or child support. Every dollar the payee can negotiate comes out of the payor's pocket.

When engaging in a win-lose negotiation, the person with the most information is in the most powerful position. For example, when negotiating salary with a potential employer, imagine how much stronger your position would be if you knew the answers to such key questions as: How much do they want you? Who else are they considering for the position? What salary are they willing to pay? What are others in similar positions being paid?

A win-lose approach to negotiations is sometimes obvious and appropriate, while at other times it is less apparent and destructive. For example, groups often set themselves up for win-lose outcomes by following the principle of majority rule—if 51 percent of the group votes one way then 49 percent are losers.

Another example of the win-lose approach occurs when the parties start the negotiation process by stating the specific outcomes they want to see. For example, a paralegal wants to spend more time with his child. He comes to you and asks that his workday be shortened to five hours. The stage is now set for a win-lose outcome. Either the paralegal will win and get the time he wants with his child while you will lose billable hours, or you will prevail and the paralegal will have to settle for the current schedule or quit.

The Lose-Lose Style Lose-lose outcomes are common when one party attempts to win at the expense of the other. While it is difficult to imagine that anyone would deliberately seek a lose-lose outcome, that is often the outcome of a win-lose negotiation. Consider the example of the paralegal who insists on a five-hour working day. If he forces the issue, he may wind up not only having his request denied but then being fired or asked to resign as a result of his nonnegotiable demand. If that happens everyone loses—the firm loses a talented worker and the paralegal's career and bank balance will suffer.

Lose-lose outcomes also occur on larger issues as well. In the past decade, unreasonable union demands have forced more than one airline into bankruptcy, and a few employers have been known to destroy the effectiveness of their workers by taking advantage of them. Mutually destructive outcomes can also arise from personal disputes among employees. For example, feuding coworkers may destroy their own careers by acquiring a reputation of ''being difficult to work with'' or ''not being team players.''

Compromise can sometimes seem better than fighting a win-lose battle and risking a lose-lose outcome. When resources are scarce or limited, compromise may indeed be the best solution. For example, if two attorneys each need a full-time secretary but budget restrictions make this impossible, they may have to compromise by sharing one secretary.

While compromise may be necessary in some cases, by definition the outcome of a compromise is a partial lose-lose situation, since both parties must give up at least some of what they were seeking. In the case of the paralegal who wants a shorter workday, if you were to offer a compromise and reduce his workday from eight hours to six hours instead of the requested five-hour day, that would not be of much help to either party. That would not give him much additional time to spend with his child, and the firm would still lose billable hours.

The Win-Win Style Win-win negotiators *assume* that a solution can be reached that will satisfy the needs of all parties. Instead of looking at their opponent as an adversary to be defeated, win-win negotiators see them as an ally in their search for a satisfactory solution.

In most situations the needs of the negotiating parties are not incompatible. They are just different. And win-win outcomes are nearly always possible. By focusing on the end result instead of the means of getting there, win-win solutions can be found using the same kinds of problem-solving steps described in this chapter. For example, in the case of the paralegal who is seeking a reduced work schedule, the employee really needs extra time to care for his child before and after school. The firm needs to have a certain amount of billable hours. These needs do conflict, but they are not mutually exclusive: both parties

Figure 10-3 Negotiation Style Assessment

Answer yes or no to each of the following questions:

	Yes	No
1. Do you feel that decision making should be a group activity with input from staff, peers, or family?	___	___
2. Do you feel that others' personal lives are as important as their responsibilities to their jobs?	___	___
3. Do you feel that it is unfair to use attacks in negotiations?	___	___
4. Do you keep personal confidences that others have shared with you rather than use the information against people?	___	___
5. Do you get pleasure from recognizing the achievements of others?	___	___
6. Do you think it is important to get the opinions of others at meetings?	___	___
7. In approaching a new situation, do you listen and observe before jumping in to voice an opinion or take charge?	___	___
8. Do you avoid making decisions in the heat of anger?	___	___
9. In making decisions, do you consider the impact they will have on others?	___	___
10. Do you explore the perceptions of others in order to negotiate more effectively?	___	___

Scoring: If you have answered yes to five of the above ten questions, congratulations! You have strong Win-Win Negotiator tendencies. A yes answer to six or more questions means that you are probably perceived by your family and colleagues as a Win-Win Negotiator.

Source: *Winning by Negotiation*, Tessa Albert Warschaw (New York: McGraw-Hill, 1980). Reprinted with permission.

want to continue the working relationship and both want the relationship to be a happy one. Once the root problem is brought to the surface, the process of finding a win-win solution can begin.

Compatible goals almost always guarantee a win-win outcome. In this case a number of win-win solutions are possible. For example, you could let the paralegal work the additional hours at home; or perhaps he could share the position with another worker who wants to work a three-hour day, giving the firm the hours they need and the employee more free time. Another solution might be that the firm could help all its employees who are parents locate reliable sources of child care or offer on-site child care as an employee benefit.

The assessment form presented in Figure 10-3 will help you determine your approach to negotiating a workable solution to similar problems that arise in your firm.

Choosing a Negotiating Style

Since no rational person would purposely seek a lose-lose outcome, and compromise is a second choice when it is possible to win everything you want, negotiators are left with the decision of whether to adopt a win-win approach or to use win-lose tactics. How do you decide which negotiating style to use? Here are some general guidelines.

Table 10–1 Negotiation Style Comparison

Win-Win Style		Win-Lose Style
Cooperation	vs.	Competition
Trust	vs.	Power
Open communication	vs.	Distorted communication
Mutual concern	vs.	Self-centeredness

Use the win-win style when:	*Use the win-lose style when:*
You have common interests.	The other party takes a win-lose approach.
Power is approximately equal, or you are in a weak position.	You have a clear conflict of interests.
A continuing, harmonious relationship is desired.	You are in a much more powerful position.
The other party takes a win-win approach.	You are not concerned about a long-term relationship.

The win-win style and the win-lose style are basically incompatible because the behaviors that enable one style to work make the other one impossible. The differences in these two incompatible styles are more apparent when they are categorized as in Table 10–1.

Win-win negotiators cooperate; win-lose negotiators see each other as competitors or adversaries. Your attitude about whether the other party is friend or foe can be a self-fulfilling prophecy. In other words, if you treat someone like an enemy, they are likely to behave that way. Or, if your attitude is one of cooperation, chances are you will get cooperation in return.

In a win-lose contest, power is the name of the game. With justification, the parties fear that the other side will take advantage of any weaknesses. In win-win situations power is replaced by trust and the parties do not take advantage of each other.

While it pays to distort or withhold information when using the win-lose negotiating style as well as to exaggerate and bluff—"This is absolutely my final offer"—the problem solving cannot succeed without open communication when you are going for a win-win outcome. In fact, nothing will destroy the chances of a win-win outcome faster than dishonesty.

Finally, in win-lose negotiating each party is focused on its own goal and will only give up ground when forced to. In the win-win approach, not only do the parties engage in active listening and attempt to understand the other's position; they work to help each other achieve a mutually satisfactory outcome.

SUMMARY

10–1

The formation of groups is a natural part of organizational life because most people prefer the feelings of security, friendship, power, and identity that result from group affiliation to isolation. Whether the group is a formal one created by management for specific tasks or emerges spontaneously and informally, all groups have norms, emphasize conformity, and display differing degrees of cohesiveness.

10–2

Conflicts arise in groups when group goals and individual goals are incompatible and when group members have a hidden agenda. Groupthink can also be a problem when the pressure to conform and stick together is the norm rather than the expression of individual ideas and opinions.

10–3

Both controversy and conflicts are to be expected in work groups. Effectively managing controversy by forming subgroups or selecting someone to play devil's advocate can stimulate group discussions and creative thinking. Conflict of interest, or having incompatible goals, is often resolved through problem solving and negotiation.

10–4

Solving problems and making decisions in logical sequential steps help ensure that all alternative solutions are considered and that the best one selected will produce the desired results with the least negative impact.

10–5

Of the three approaches to negotiating, no one willingly chooses the lose-lose style, although that is often the outcome when the parties attempt to win at the others' expense. The win-lose style may be appropriate when there is a conflict of interest and no long-term relationship is involved. However, the win-win style, where everyone walks away having gained something, is usually the preferred approach to resolving differences.

REVIEW

Key Terms

cohesiveness
compromise
conflict of interest
conform
controversy
formal groups
group
groupthink
hidden agenda
informal groups
integration
negotiation
norm
planned agenda
social norm

Questions for Review and Discussion

1. It has been said that the formation of groups is a natural occurrence in organizations. Why?
2. What types of groups are found in law firms?
3. All groups have three characteristics in common. What are they?
4. Given your answer to question 3, why do conflicts arise?
5. What is groupthink?
6. Is there a difference between controversy and conflict of interest? Explain.
7. What are some ways to effectively manage a conflict of interest?

8. List the steps involved in problem solving.
9. There are three approaches to negotiating. What are they? What is the probable outcome of each?
10. When is the win-lose style of negotiating appropriate?
11. When would you choose the win-win approach?

Activities

1. Assess two groups of which you are a member. Identify whether they are formal or informal work groups, a social group, or a family group. What is the purpose for each group and why did you become a member? List the group's norms. To what degree (on a scale from 1 [low] to 10 [high]) is there pressure to conform? What happens to members who do not conform? To what degree (on a scale of 1 to 10) is the group cohesive? How is this cohesiveness, or lack of it, displayed?

2. Assemble three to five individuals to role play members of a task group. They need to research, draft, edit, rewrite, assemble, and perform any other tasks required to have 75 copies of a 110-page document ready for a court hearing scheduled for 1:30 Monday afternoon. It is now the Friday morning before the Monday deadline. The word processor has a "hot" date on the weekend. She is giving all kinds of excuses for not being able to work on the weekend, blaming the attorneys for not getting their work done on time, and so on. Other task group members also have commitments they must fulfill. The group must identify the problems, resolve the issues, and come to agreement on a solution. Time required: 20–50 minutes.

3. Form groups of three to five individuals. Ask each member of the group to present a problem they are experiencing that could benefit from the group's input. Each group will select one or more of the problems presented. Then, following the problem-solving steps outlined in this chapter, have each group define the problem, propose several alternative solutions, and choose the best one.

GLOSSARY

Abnormal behavior: An exaggeration or extension of so-called normal behavior.

Accountability: A system for assessing blame or credit for performance.

Accounting cycle: The process of recording information in the journal and ledger, closing the income and expense accounts, and preparing the income statement and balance sheet.

Accounting equation: Assets equal liabilities plus proprietorship plus income minus expenses (ALPIE).

Accounts payable: Monies owed by the firm to suppliers of goods and services.

Accounts receivable: A charge account owned by clients that the firm can collect.

Accounts receivable coverage: Provides insurance protection for loss due to the inability to collect monies owed when the records have been lost, destroyed, or damaged.

Action plans: Specific steps in the planning process.

Affirmative action: An attempt to correct past discriminatory employment practices by recruiting minority group members.

Age Discrimination in Employment Act (ADEA): Prohibits employers from discriminating against a person 40 years of age or older.

Assets: Anything of value owned by the firm. Also called property.

Aural privacy: Sounds that can be heard but are unintelligible.

Authority: The power to act or command others.

Autocratic: The autocratic, or authoritarian, leadership style relies on authority and the power of the position to get things done.

Average collection period: The average length of time between sending out a billing statement and the receipt of payment.

Backup: Data that is copied from the hard disk onto another disk to prevent loss.

Balance sheet: A financial statement wherein all property held is always equal to any claims against that property.

Base year: A method for calculating the tenant's pro rata share of any increase in the landlord's operating expenses using a preestablished date and actual accounting records.

Billable hours: Time spent working on a client's matter for which the client is billed.

Bit: Individual binary digits.

Bona fide occupational qualification (BFOQ):   The only exception to the Age Discrimination in Employment Act wherein an older person might reasonably be excluded from consideration because of a business necessity; a practice that is necessary for the safe and efficient operation of the business.

Bookkeeping: The process of recording and organizing each financial transaction.

Bottom line: The same as net profit or any monies remaining after all expenses have been paid, including taxes.

Bug: An unintentional flaw or mistake in the initial design of a software program.

Business interruption insurance: Provides for the loss of income due to a disaster.

Byte: Characters stored in memory cells; eight bits equal one byte.

Cancellable lease: Allows lessee to upgrade or add to the equipment covered by the lease or to get out of the contract before expiration without paying a penalty.

Case retainer: Fees paid prior to the commencement of legal action; may be the entire fee due for a client matter or may represent only part of the total fee.

Cash flow: The actual net cash that flows into or out of the firm during some specified period.

Central processing unit (CPU):   The brains of the microcomputer found on a single microcomputer chip which executes the program instructions to process data.

Civil Rights Act of 1964:   Federal legislation that prohibits discrimination in hiring, training, promotion, pay, fringe benefits, or other conditions of employment based on race, color, religion, sex, or national origin. This legislation was subsequently extended to include people with physical disabilities.

Closed: The end of the accounting period during which time no more transactions are recorded.

Closing the books: The process of giving zero balances to the income and expense accounts by transferring profit or loss to the proprietorship account.

Cohesiveness: The emotional closeness that exists among group members.

Communication: The transfer of information between two or more people.

Comparable worth: A compensation concept which purports that jobs requiring comparable knowledge, skills, and abilities should be paid at comparable levels.

Compensating balance: The minimum checking account balance some banks require to be maintained on deposit as compensation for their services.

Compromise: A settlement of differences in which each side makes some concessions.

Conflict of interest: A situation where regard for one duty or party leads to disregard of another. Also, the intentional interference with or blocking of actions of others in pursuit of one's own interests.

Conform: Compliance with the norms established by a group.

Consumer price index (CPI): A measure of the average change in prices over time based upon a fixed "market basket" of goods and services including food, clothing, shelter, fuel, transportation fares, and charges for medical services.

Context: Time and place.

Contingency approach: An approach to leadership developed by Fred Fiedler recognizing there is no one best way to influence people; leadership style is largely dependent upon the situation and the people involved.

Contingent fee: A fee arrangement which is conditional, that is, paid only when a legal matter has been successfully resolved.

Controlling: The management function of commanding and directing resources to achieve goals.

Controversy: A difference of opinion that prevents or interferes with reaching a decision.

Corporate culture: A set of basic assumptions held by the founders based upon their value systems.

Cost-of-living adjustments (COLA): An index that considers the rate of inflation and its impact on purchasing power based upon changes in the Consumer Price Index.

Culture: The behavior patterns and values of a society or social group.

Cumulative trauma disorder: A computer-related injury caused by the continuous repetition of hand and arm motions.

Current assets: Cash or property owned and expected to be changed into cash or used up within a year.

Current liabilities: Short-term debts that are to be paid in less than one year.

Current ratio: A measure of financial liquidity. Calculated by dividing current assets by current liabilities.

Cursor: A blinking arrow or other symbol on the computer screen which tells the user that the system is ready for input, or where characters will appear on the screen.

Debt: Claims of creditors against property owned by the firm.

Defensive reaction: A way of thinking that cushions the blow resulting from one's immediate inability to overcome an obstacle or barrier.

Delegating: Assigning work to others.

Depreciation: The practice of gradually writing off the cost of an asset as it is used up.

Derived X theory: Also known as the "I've-Been-Burned" theory, this leadership attitude applies when a manager provided job enriching responsibilities and opportunities for personal growth only to have others fail in their efforts or take advantage of the situation.

Developmental leader: This leadership style provides people with the opportunity and encouragement to excel in performance by seeking staff participation in setting objectives and in some decision making.

Directing: The management function of exchanging ideas, motivating, and leading others toward goals.

Diskettes: Thin, pliable, magnetically coated plastic disks on which data is stored; also known as floppy disks.

Double entry: A bookkeeping process requiring at least two entries for each accounting transaction.

Drug-Free Workplace Act: Requires employers who receive federal monies to establish a drug-free workplace.

Effective: Knowing how to use resources to get things done.

Efficient: Producing the desired results at minimum cost.

Electrified floors: A floor that has concrete poured over and around ducts containing telephone and power lines.

Electronic data processing equipment coverage: Insurance protection for all electronic data processing equipment, including computers, against physical loss.

Employment at will: A legal doctrine which holds that, in the absence of a collective bargaining agreement or other written contract, either the employer or employee has the right to terminate their relationship at any time without reason or cause.

Entity: Something that exists as a particular and discrete unit. Individuals and corporations are equivalent entities under the law.

Equal employment opportunity (EEO): The employment of individuals in a fair and nonbiased manner.

Equal Pay Act: Prohibits discrimination in pay, fringe benefits, and pensions based upon gender.

Expense: An accounting reflection that assets have been used up in the process of, or for the purpose of, earning income.

Expense stop: A method for calculating the tenant's pro rata share of any increase in the landlord's operating expenses based upon the landlord's projections.

Extra expense insurance: Protects against increased costs in finding and maintaining an alternate place for doing business while recovering from a disaster.

Feedback: The response which acknowledges that the message has been received.

File-server: A type of computer that allows information to be used by more than one person simultaneously.

Financial lease: Offers the option of purchasing the equipment at the end of the lease period for a predetermined fixed dollar amount.

Fiscal year: A twelve-month accounting period established for the purpose of more easily reporting and evaluating the financial activity of a business entity.

Fixed assets: Buildings, equipment, books, and other things of value owned by the firm and intended to be used for more than one year.

Fixed fee: Sometimes also called a flat fee; usually associated with routine services performed by the firm.

Fixed liabilities: Long-term debts which are to be paid in more than one year.

Flexible lease: Allows the option of changing equipment during the lease period.

Formal groups: Groups created by management for the purpose of attaining goals and objectives.

Full service gross lease: Amount paid by tenant as rent; includes all services.

Gigabyte: Equal to 1,024 megabytes, or about a billion characters of micro-computer storage capacity.

Goal: A specific target that you work toward achieving in the future.

Grapevine: The informal communication network.

Gross lease: Tenant pays rent only.

Gross profit: The difference between fee income and the costs of producing that income.

Group: Two or more people who personally interact with each other in order to achieve a common goal.

Groupthink: The pressure on individual group members to stick together in their decisions and solutions to problems.

Hard disk: Made from nonbending, rigid aluminum on which about 5,000 pages of data can be stored.

Hidden agenda: Personal goals not made public.

Hourly fee: Rate charged to a client for time spent on the client's legal work.

Income: Something of value received in return for services provided to clients.

Income statement: A financial statement that indicates income minus all expenses for the period covered by the statement and any profit or loss for the period.

Informal groups: Groups created spontaneously throughout the firm with or without the approval of management.

Intangible: Invisible, not readily discerned.

Integration: Bringing all the parts together to make a whole.

Job: A group of related activities and duties that are similar in nature.

Job description: A written compilation of the responsibilities, duties, and tasks for each job together with the position title and to whom the position reports.

Job design: The process of determining the responsibilities, duties, and tasks for each job and describing how these are to be performed.

Job enrichment: An approach to breaking job monotony by redesigning the job.

Journal: The book in which each financial transaction is written in chronological sequence.

Just-in-time: An inventory system that allows orders to be delivered just as a supply is about to run out.

K: The symbol for 1,000.

Kilobyte: Also called "K" in computer jargon; represents 1,024 bytes, or characters of information stored in memory of a microcomputer.

Leadership: An attempt to influence others to achieve specific objectives because they want to, not because they have to.

Leadership style: The patterns of behavior that are associated with you as a leader.

Ledger: The book in which each financial transaction is recorded by account name or number instead of by date.

Leveraging: Making a profit from the services performed by others.

Liabilities: Monies owed to creditors; debts.

Load factor: The tenant's pro rata percentage share for use of restrooms, corridors, elevators, and building services.

Management: The carefully planned use of an organization's resources to achieve goals. Management also refers collectively to the people who establish the goals of the organization and who are responsible for achieving them.

Management by objectives (MBO): An evaluation tool for translating organizational goals into specific, individual objectives, and a method for measuring the relative worth of an individual employee to the organization.

Megabyte: Equal to 1,024K, or about a million characters of microcomputer storage capacity.

Memory: Also called main storage, this is the area for storing programs and data.

Message: A conscious or unconscious act that conveys meaning.

Microchip: A wafer of silicon about one-fourth inch square and less than four thousandths of an inch thick that contains imprinted circuits through which electronic impulses travel.

Microfiche: A sheet of microfilm containing rows of images in a grid pattern.

Microfilm: A process in which paper documents are put on a roll film cartridge or jacket of film.

Mini-max inventory system: When a supply falls to a preestablished minimum level, an order is placed to bring that supply up to a preestablished maximum level.

Modem: A peripheral device that converts microcomputer-generated electrical digital signals into audio signals and transmits them via telephone lines over long distances.

Modified gross lease: In addition to a base rent, tenant pays for janitorial service and electricity.

Motivation: The process of energizing behavior toward need satisfaction.

Mouse: A microcomputer output device used to move the cursor on the screen.

Needs: The incentive or motivation to achieve goals or fill a void that results from feeling deprived or experiencing a lack of something.

Need theory: A motivation theory proposed by Abraham Maslow stating that all humans have levels of needs (illustrated in the form of a pyramid) and categorized as either physiological or psychological. Maslow believes that human motivation is based upon achieving individual needs.

Negotiation: The process of reaching a mutually acceptable agreement.

Net lease: Under these terms the tenant pays some or all of the real estate taxes in addition to the base rent.

Net profit: The difference between gross profit and any other expenses, such as taxes.

Net-net lease: The tenant pays a base rent, some or all of the real estate taxes, plus any agreed-upon insurance premiums.

Networks: Systems of person-to-person relationships through which information flows.

Neurosis: A mild personality disorder.

Nonverbal: Messages that are contained in the sender's eyes, face, body movement, positioning, physical appearance, tone of voice, and in the time and place of the communication.

Norm: A generally agreed-upon standard of behavior that every member of a group is expected to follow.

Occupational Safety and Health Act: A federal law, commonly known as OSHA, that requires the employer to provide a safe working environment for employees.

Operating account: An account used for day-to-day financial transactions.

Operating lease: Requires monthly payments over a fixed period of time.

Operating system: A software program that manages the operation of the microcomputer.

Operations management: Includes accounting functions, facilities management, support staff personnel management, information technology management.

Organizing: The process of coordinating the firm's resources to achieve goals.

Owners' interest: The owners' original capital contribution to start the firm plus any profits. Sometimes also known as owners' equity or capital.

Partnership: A business owned by two or more individuals.

Percentage lease: The tenant pays a percentage of gross income in excess of a predetermined minimum in addition to a base rent.

Peripherals: Input and output devices connected to the microcomputer.

Personal power: The extent to which followers are willing to follow a leader. This power comes from below.

Piracy: The unauthorized copying of computer software.

Planned agenda: A program or list of items to be discussed or tasks to be done.

Planning: The management function of establishing future goals and objectives.

Politics: The manner in which positions of power are established and influence is exerted in the administrative process.

Position: Different duties and responsibilities performed by only one employee.

Position power: The ability to influence others to do a certain job because of the leader's position.

Posting: The process of copying journal entries into the ledger.

Power: The ability to influence others.

Practice management: The mix of the number of cases and types of cases the firm will represent.

Precautionary balance: A reserve for unpredictable fluctuations in cash flow.

Pregnancy Discrimination Act: Amends the Civil Rights Act of 1964 by stating that pregnancy is a disability and that pregnent employees must be treated the same as any employee with a medical condition.

Privacy Act: Prohibits employers from releasing employee records without consent; allows employees access to their personnel file and allows any inaccurate information therein to be corrected, amended, or supplemented.

Professional corporation: A business practice owned by one or more members of the profession with special statutory protection for the owners against debt and some types of liabilities.

Profit: Excess of money earned over total expenses.

Profit margin on income: A percentage figure that indicates the amount of profit earned for every dollar generated in fees.

Property: Anything of value owned by the firm including cash, equipment, and buildings.

Psychosis: A severe personality disorder.

Pure retainer: Payment of a fee that binds the law firm to that particular client and prohibits the firm from representing certain other clients.

Quick ratio: A measure of financial liquidity. Calculated by deducting inventory from current assets and dividing the remainder by current liabilities.

RAM: Random access memory; data stored in the computer's internal memory that can be stored, removed, or lost when the power is turned off unless steps have been taken to save it.

Receiver: The person or persons to whom the sender directs the message.

Records management: The systematic storage of paper records for quick retrieval upon demand.

Rentable area: Refers to the entire floor, including restrooms, corridors, stairwells, elevator shafts, and interior columns.

Responsibility: Refers to a specific task and implies a duty to see that the task is performed.

Retainer: Fee paid by a client at the beginning of a specific matter, usually nonrefundable.

Retainer for general representation: A flat annual fee with services included and those excluded carefully spelled out in a written agreement.

ROM: Read only memory; data is fixed in the computer's internal memory and cannot be easily changed or destroyed.

Self-fulfilling prophecy: When one person's attitude or expectations can influence the behavior of others.

Sender: The initiator of a communication.

Sexual harassment: Any unwelcome advances, requests for sexual favors, and other verbal or physical conduct of a sexual nature used as a basis for employment conditions; any sexually oriented behavior that interferes with the employee's work performance or creates an intimidating, hostile, or offensive working environment.

Signage privileges: The right to have the firm's name prominently displayed on the building.

Site licensing agreement: Allows the duplication of a specified number of copies of a software program for use in one location.

Situational style: A leadership style that recognizes there is no one best way to influence others and that the technique used to lead others is largely dependent upon the situation and the people involved.

Social norm: See *Norm.*

Sole proprietorship: A business entity owned by one individual.

Speculative balance: A reserve to enable the firm to take advantage of bargain purchases.

Split screen: The ability to display a document in its original form on the left side of the screen while modifications are performed to a copy on the right side of the screen.

Staffing: The managerial function that deals with recruiting, placing, training, and developing members of the firm.

Statute of limitations: The time fixed by law within which parties must take judicial action to enforce their rights.

Statutory fee: Determined by state legislatures; varies from state to state.

Stereotyping: A bias resulting from cultural experiences that contribute to holding preconceived ideas about certain groups of people and events.

Synchronized cash flow: Cash inflows that coincide with outflows thereby allowing cash balances required for day-to-day operation to be kept to a minimum.

Tangible: Visible, measurable.

Theory X: A pessimistic leadership attitude identified by Douglas McGregor typified by the belief that most employees dislike work and will avoid it whenever possible; that employees must be closely supervised and threatened with punishment to get them to perform.

Theory Y: An optimistic leadership attitude identified by Douglas McGregor which holds the belief that most employees who are allowed to experience personal satisfaction in their work will not only like their work but will require little supervision and will do more than is expected of them.

Tickler: A reminder system of important dates, meetings, and deadlines.

Topology: A geometric configuration.

Transaction balance: Cash balance associated with routine payments and collections.

Trial balance: The process of testing the accounting equation to see that both sides are in balance.

Triple net lease: The tenant pays a base rent, some or all of the real estate taxes, any agreed-upon insurance premiums, plus agreed-upon repair and maintenance costs.

Trust account: An account set up for the purpose of depositing monies being held by one party for the benefit of another.

Turnkey clause: A clause in the office space lease which states that all improvements will be completed and everything will be in place when the tenant walks in to occupy the office.

Turnkey system: A computer system that is completely installed with all hardware, software, and database ready for immediate use.

Two-factor motivation theory: A motivation theory developed by Frederick Herzberg classifying job functions into one of two categories: either motivational and satisfying or maintenance-hygiene and dissatisfying.

Usable area: The square footage the tenant actually uses.

Valuable papers coverage: Provides replacement for loss, damage, or destruction of client files and office records.

Verbal: Messages consisting of words spoken or written.

Virus: An intentionally created program that replicates itself within the computer system using up available memory and destroying data and programs.

Vocalics: The manner in which words are spoken.

Workletter: That part of the lease that itemizes and assigns a dollar value to the tenant improvements provided by the landlord.

INDEX

Abnormal behavior, 214
Accountability, 4
Accounting. *See also* Budget preparation;
    Financial management
    basic principles of, 126–132
    cycle, 132–134
    PPOD principle, 127, 129–130
Accounts payable, 130, 145
Accounts receivable
    as assets, 129
    insurance coverage for, 94
    managing, 144–145
Action plans, 7–8
Affirmative action, 151
Age Discrimination in Employment Act of
    1967, 153–154
Agendas, 223–224
Aggression behavior, 213
AIDS (acquired immune deficiency
    syndrome), 157–158
ALA (Association of Legal Administrators),
    3, 165
Alphabetic filing system, 54
ALPIE accounts, 133
Altman & Weil, 3, 5
Americans with Disabilities Act of 1990, 154
Apple-DOS, 102
Arithmetic/logic unit (ALU), 100
Ashton-Tate, 118
Asset management ratios, 136–137
Assets, 129
Association of Legal Administrators (ALA),
    3, 165
AT&T (American Telephone & Telegraph
    Co.), 110, 112
Aural privacy, 81
Authority
    defined, 4
    and delegating, 15
Autocratic leadership, 201–202

Automation, office, 21. *See also* Computers;
    Equipment; Information management
Average collection period, 136–137

Backup, computer, 101, 115
Balance sheet, 128
Bar coding files, 55–56
Base year, 85
Billable hours
    and cash flow management, 144
    in fee setting formulas, 27–28
    importance of, 20
    tabulating for management, 39
Billing procedures. *See also* Financial
    management
    automated systems, 105, 106
    dos and don'ts, 39–40
    importance of, 38
    types of, 38–39
Bit, 100
Blanchard, Kenneth H., 191, 204, 215
Body language, 185–188. *See also*
    Communication
Bona fide occupational qualification, 153–
    154
Bookkeeping, 132, 133. *See also* Accounting
Bottom line, 128
Budget preparation. *See also* Accounting;
    Financial management
    automation of, 105
    cash flow, 142–143
    importance of, 138–139
    monthly budgets, 140–141
    net income budget, 141–142
    in planning, 8
Bug, software, 118
Build-to-suit-tenant clause, 83
Bus topology, 110, 111, 113
Business interruption insurance, 94
Byte, 100

Carpal tunnel syndrome, 121
Case retainer, 25
Cash accounting method, 131
Cash flow
  and billing procedures, 38
  in budget, 142–143
  defined, 143
  importance of, 5, 143
  management of, 143–145
  and office equipment, 66
  problems, 143–144
  synchronized, 145
Ceiling height, 80
Central processing unit (CPU), 100
Channels of communication, 182, 183–184
Civil Rights Act of 1964, 150, 152
Classified job ads, 153, 164
Cleaning service in building, 77, 78
Client database, 51
Closing the books, 133
Cohesiveness, in groups, 222
COLA (cost of living adjustments), 161
Color-coding file method, 59
Committees, 221. See also Groups
Communication. See also Feedback
  barriers, 182–184
  on billing practices, 39
  body language, 185–188
  channels, 182, 183–184
  effectiveness self-assessment, 189
  elements of, 181–182
  grapevine, 196
  listening techniques, 188, 190–191
  networks, 194–196
  stereotyping, 184
  verbal, 181
  vocalics, 183–184
Comparable worth, 153
Compensating balance, 143
Compensation, employee, 160–162
Compromise in negotiation, 234
COMPUSERVE Information Service Co., 65
Computers. See also Information
    management; Software
  bar coding systems, 55–56
  billing systems, 38–39
  components of, 99–102
  and health problems, 120–121, 157
  insurance for, 94
  for inventory systems, 69
  networks, 110–113
  on-line database information companies,
    65
  operating systems for, 102–103
  and optical disk storage, 60
  peripherals, 101–102
  power protection devices, 103
  scanners for, 113–114
  selection process, 109
  storage capacity, 100–101
  technology updates, staff input, 203–204

timekeeping systems, 32, 35
  vendor selection, 109
Confidentiality, client. See also Security
  aural privacy and, 81
  importance of, 49–50
  and voice mail, 48
Conflict of interest. See also Controversy
  in legal work, 51
  in groups, 223–225
  managing, 229–230
  negotiation, 233–236
  within staff, 225
  win-win outcomes, 229–230, 234–235
Conformity, in groups, 222
Consumer Price Index (CPI), 85, 161
Contingency approach to leadership, 204
Contingent fees, 25–26, 27
Controlling, 15
Controversy. See also Conflict of interest
  defined, 225
  managing, 226–227
Copiers. See Photocopiers
Copyright Act of 1980, 119
Corporate culture, 149–150
Cost-of-living adjustments (COLA), 161
Courier services, 37–38
CPI (consumer price index), 85, 161
CPU (central processing unit), 100
Criticism, 192
CRT (cathode ray tube), 102
Culture, defined, 149
Cumulative trauma disorder (CTD), 120–121
Current assets, 129, 135
Current liabilities, 130, 135
Current ratio, 135
Cursor, 101

Daily action sheet, 12
Deadline dates, 8
Debt, 126, 130
Decision making, 230–233
Defensive reaction, 213
Delegating
  defined, 12
  effectively, 14–15
  fear of, 13
  for time management, 11
Deposition process
  planning for, 6–8
  software for, 104, 116
Derived X leadership attitude, 206
Desktop publishing, 105
Developmental leadership, 202–204
Dialog Information Service, 65
Digital Equipment Corp. (DEC), 110
Directing, 12
Disabled persons, 154–155
Disasters, planning for, 93–95
Discrimination, job. See Equal employment
    opportunity (EEO)
Diskettes, 101

Disseminator of information role, 19
Disturbance handling role, 20
Doculiner software, 104
DOS (disk operating system), 102
Double entry bookkeeping, 133
Dow Jones News/Retrieval, 65
Drug-Free Workplace Act of 1988, 157

Earnings, 130
EasyLAN, 112
EEO (equal employment opportunity), 151–155
EEOC (Equal Employment Opportunity Commission), 152, 165, 166
Electrified floors, 80
Electronic data processing equipment insurance coverage, 94
Electronic typewriters, 114–115
Elevator service in building, 76–77
Emergency planning, 93–95
Employment at will doctrine, 150–151
Energy, peak time, 10
Entity, 127
Entrepreneur role, 20
Equal Employment Opportunity Commission (EEOC), 152, 165, 166
Equal employment opportunity (EEO), 151–155
Equal Pay Act of 1963, 153
Equipment. See also Supplies, office
  for bar code files, 55
  filing, 56–58
  micrographics, 60
  optical disk storage, 60
  paper shredders, 60, 62, 63
  purchasing of, 66–67
  renting and leasing, 67–68
  tax considerations, 68
Ethernet, 110
Ethical considerations
  and client confidentiality, 49–50
  conflicts of interest, 51
  expenses, 38
  and software usage, 119
Expense stop, 84, 85
Expenses. See also Financial management
  in accounting, 131–132
  overhead, 26–27
  tracking methods, 35–38
Extra expense insurance, 94

Facsimile (fax) machines
  charges, tracking of, 37
  personal use by employees, 70
Fair Labor Standards Act, 150, 153
Fantasizing behavior, 213
Fee structure, 25–27
Feedback
  barriers, 184
  defined, 182

negative, 192–194
positive, 191–192
Fiedler, Fred, 204
Figurehead role, 17
Files. See Records management
Filing cabinets, 56
Financial leases, 67
Financial management. See also Accounting; Budget preparation
  accounting principles, 126–132
  cash flow management, 143–145
  client billing procedures, 38–40
  costs and expenses, 35–38
  costs of practice, 21
  ethical considerations, 38
  fee setting formulas, 27–28
  fees, types of, 25–27
  financial statements, 134–137
  income budget, 139
  leveraging concept, 28
  PPOD principle, 127, 129–130
  ratio analysis, 135–137
  steps in, 139–143
Fire alarms, 79
Fiscal year, 128
Fixed assets, 129
Fixed fees, 26, 27
Fixed liabilities, 130
Flat fees, 26, 27
Flexible leases, 67
Flexible working hours (flextime), 175–176
Floor-load capacity, 80
Floppy disks, 101
Formal groups, 221
Formulas
  ALPIE accounts, 133
  average collection period, 136–137
  business mix, 29
  cash flow, 143
  current ratio, 136
  hourly fee setting, 27
  leveraging, 28
  quick ratio, 136
  rentable and usable area, 76
Four-day workweek, 175–176
Full service gross lease, 84

Garbage in, garbage out (GIGO), 121
Gigabyte, 100
Goals
  accomplishment of, 221
  defined, 6
  group and individual, 223
  and hidden agendas, 224
Grapevine, 196
Gross lease, 84
Gross profit, 128
Groups
  characteristics of, 222–223
  conflict resolution, 225–230
  conflicts in, 223–225

Groups (continued)
  formal and informal, 221
  groupthink in, 224–225, 226–228
  hidden agendas in, 224
  human need for, 220–221
  and problem solving, 231–232
  problem-solving, 221
Groupthink, 224–225, 226–228

Hanging file folders, 59
Hard disks, 101
Health issues
  AIDS, 157–158
  from computer work, 120–121
  drugs and alcohol, 157
  office hazards, 155–157
Heating, ventilating, and air conditioning
    (HVAC), 82
Hersey, Paul, 204, 215
Herzberg, Frederick, 211
Herzberg's two-factor theory, 211
Hidden agendas, 224
High-density mobile storage systems, 56, 57
Historical cost method of accounting, 129
Hourly fees, 26, 27–28
How to Get Control of Your Time and Your Life
    (Lakein), 10

IBM Corp., 110, 113, 118
IDEAshare, 112
IDEAssociate, 112
Image enhancement, 75
Impact printers, 101
Income, 130–131
Income statement, 128–129
Informal groups, 221
Information management. See also
    Computers; Software
  calendar software programs, 116–117
  document management software, 115–116
  electronic typewriters, 114–115
  end-user needs survey, 103–106
  hardware selection, 109
  litigation support software, 104, 116
  networks, 110–113
  and office automation, 21
  scanners, 113–114
  software ethics, 119
  software selection, 106–109
  and support staff, 119–120
  vendor selection, 109
  viruses and bugs, 118–119
Ink jet printers, 102
Innovation, importance of, 14
Insurance
  business policies, 94
  for equipment, 67, 94
Integration technique, 229–230
Intel Corp., 110
Interviews, job, 165–167

Intrapreneur role, 20
Inventory control, 69
I've-Been-Burned Theory of leadership, 206

JIT inventory system, 69
Job, defined, 163
Job description, 163, 164
Job design, 163
Job enrichment, 173
Job sharing, 175–176
Job stay-ons, 212
Job turn-ons, 211
Johnson, Spencer, 191
Journal, accounting, 132
Just-in-time (JIT) inventory system, 69

Kilobyte (K), 100

Lakein, Alan, 10
LAN (local area network), 110–113
LANLink, 112
Laser printers, 102, 105
Law library
  cataloging, 65
  floor-load capacity for, 80
  inventory system, 66
  management of, 62, 64
  moving, 91–92
  reference materials in, 65
Law office managers. See also Management
  backgrounds of, 3–4
  decisional roles, 19–20
  informational roles, 19
  intangible skills, 17–20
  interpersonal roles, 17–19
  need for, 21
  survey of, 3, 5–6
  tangible skills, 6
Leader role, 17
Leadership. See also Management;
    Motivation
  attitude assessment, 207
  autocratic, 201–202
  characteristics of leaders, 205
  defined, 201
  Derived X attitude, 206
  developmental, 202–204
  and maturity, 204–205
  office politics and, 215–216
  and power, 214–216
  situational, 204–205
  style, 201
  style assessment, 202–203
  Theory X attitude, 205–206, 207, 208
  Theory Y attitude, 206, 207, 208
Leases, office. See also Relocation
  checklist for, 85
  increases in, 85
  negotiable items, 83
  types of, 84
  workletter, 80–82

Leasing, of office equipment, 67
Ledger, 133
Legal administrators. *See* Law office
    managers
Legal Assistants Management Association,
    165
Letter quality printers, 101
Leveraging, 28
LEXIS, 65
Liabilities, 130
Liaison role, 17, 19
Lighting in law office, 82
Liquidity ratios, 135–136
Listening techniques, 188, 190–191
Load factor of building, 76
Lobseng, Norman, 192, 193
Local area network (LAN), 110–113
Lose-lose negotiating style, 234
Lotus 1–2–3, 107, 119
Lotus Development Corp., 119

Machiavelli, Niccolo, 215
Machine system for timekeeping, 32
Maintenance-hygiene factors of motivation,
    211
Management. *See also* Operations
    management; Practice management
  conflict resolution, 225–230
  definitions of, 4
  efficiency and effectiveness, 10
  of law practice, 5
  MBO program, 168–169
  negotiation styles, 233–236
  performance evaluation by employees, 169
  problem solving, 221, 230–233
Management by objectives (MBO), 168–169
Management of Organizational Behavior (Hersey
    and Blanchard), 205, 215
Maslow, Abraham, 208
Maslow's needs hierarchy, 208–210
MBO (management by objectives), 168–169
McCormack, Mark H., 231
McGregor, Douglas, 205–206
MEDIS, 65
Megabyte, 100
Mehrabian, Albert, 183, 185
Memory, computer, 100
Messenger services, 37–38
Microchip, 99–100
Microcomputers. *See* Computers
Microfilm and microfiche, 60
Micrographics, 60
Mini-max inventory system, 69
Mintzberg, Henry, 17
Mobile file systems, 56, 57
Modem, 102
Modified gross lease, 84
Monitor of information role, 19
Motivation. *See also* Leadership;
    Management

defined, 208
  Herzberg's two-factor theory, 211
  and Maslow's need theory, 208–210
  and personality disorders, 212–214
Mouse, 101
Moving. *See* Relocation
MS-DOS, 102

National Association of Legal Assistants, 165
Nature of Managerial Work, The (Mintzberg),
    17
Need theory, 208
Negotiation, 233–236
Negotiator role, 20
Net lease, 84
Net profit, 128
Net-net lease, 84
NetWare, 112
Networks
  communication, 194–196
  computer, 110–113
Neurosis, 214
New case memo set, 52
New case multipart set, 53
NEXIS, 65
Nobody's Perfect (Weisinger and Lobseng),
    192, 193
Nonimpact printers, 102
Nonverbal communication. *See also* Body
    language; Communication
  decoding, 187–188
  defined, 181
  and listening, 190
Norms, in groups, 222
Novell Corp., 112
Numeric filing system, 54

Occupational Safety and Health Act of 1970
    (OSHA), 155–156
OCR (optical character recognition), 113–114
Office environment, 86
Office politics, 215–216
Office Supply Order Systems, 70
One-Minute Manager, The (Blanchard and
    Johnson), 191–192
"One-write" system for timekeeping, 32
Open-shelf filing systems, 56
Operating account, 131
Operating leases, 67
Operating system, 102–103
Operations management. *See also* Personnel
    management; Staffing
  controlling function, 15–17
  defined, 5
  directing function, 12–15
  law library, 62, 64–66, 91–92
  office consumables, 68–70
  office equipment, 66–68
  organizing function, 10–11
  planning function, 6–10

Operations management (continued)
reception staff, 48–50
staffing function, 11–12
Optical character recognition (OCR), 113–114
Optical disk storage technology, 60
Organizational resources, defined, 4
Organizing
active files, 59
defined, 10
time management and, 10–11
OSHA (Occupational Safety and Health Act of 1970), 155–156
Overhead expenses, 26–27
Overnight mail couriers, 37–38
Owners' interest, 126, 129–130

Paper shredders, 60, 62, 63
Paralegals
hourly billing rate, 28
importance of, 21
as information source, 196
legal research duties, 65
as managers, 3
technology impact on, 120
Parking facilities, 79–80, 83
Partitions in law office, 81–82, 89–91
Partnership, 127
PC-DOS, 102
Peak energy time, 10
Percentage lease, 84
Performance measurement
appraisal form, 170–171
comparison process, 16
importance of, 14
methods of, 167–169
qualitative vs. quantitative, 16
staff evaluation form, 172–173
upward evaluation form, 174–175
Performance standards, 15–16
Peripherals, computer, 101–102
Personal power, 215
Personnel management. See also Performance measurement; Staffing
and corporate culture, 149–150
employee compensation, 160–162
federal legislation affecting, 151–158
health issues, 120–121, 155–158
hiring guidelines, 163–167
interviews, 165–167
job satisfaction, increasing, 169, 173, 175–176
and new technology, 119–120
policies manual, 158–160
sexual harassment issues, 155, 156
work schedules, 175–176
Photocopier expenses, tracking, 37, 105
Pilferage problem, 70
Piracy, software, 119
Planned agenda, 223–224

Planning
action plan, 7–8
budget preparation, 8
contingencies, 8
data collection, 6–7
defined, 6
for disasters, 93–95
follow-up, 8
goal setting in, 6
implementation, 8
methodology of project, 7
office space, 87–91
skills self-assessment, 7
worksheet for, 9
Politics, office, 215–216
Position, defined, 163
Position power, 215
Posting, 133
Power
and groups, 220–221
and leadership, 214–216
PPOD (profits, property, owners' interest, and debt), 127, 129–130
Practice management. See also Management
business mix formula, 28–29
cash flow and, 145
computerized programs for, 39
defined, 5
fees and billing practices, 27–29
leveraging concept, 28
Precautionary balance, 143
Pregnancy Discrimination Act of 1978, 154
Prince, The (Machiavelli), 215
Principle of truth and balance (TAB), 131
Printers, 101–102
Privacy Act of 1974, 158
Problem solving, 221, 230–233
Professional corporation, 128
Profit, 126, 128, 129
Profit margin on income, 137
Profitability ratios, 137
Projection behavior, 213
ProNet, 112
Property, 126, 129
Proteon Corp., 112
Psychosis, 214
Pure retainer, 25

Quick ratio, 136
Qwerty keyboard, 101

RAM (random access memory), 100
Rationalization behavior, 213
Real estate broker, commercial, 85–86
Reception staff, 48–50
Records management
active file organization, 59
defined, 50
emergency planning, 94
file creation, 50

Records management *(continued)*
  filing equipment, 56–58
  filing systems, 53–56
  inactive files, 59–62
  on-line form file, 66
  and productivity, 58
  retention guidelines, 60, 61
Relocation
  building assessment, 75–80
  leases, 83–86
  location assessment, 75
  moving company selection, 91–92
  moving costs, 92
  needs assessment, 87
  reasons for, 74–75
  standard workletter, 80–82
Rentable area of building, 76
Renting, of office equipment, 67
Repression behavior, 213
Resource allocation role, 20
Responsibility
  defined, 4
  and delegating, 15
Retainer fees
  defined, 25
  determining, 27
  trust account for, 131
  types of, 25
Retainer for general representation, 25
Revenues, 130
Ring topologies, 110
Rixon Incorporated, 119
Robert Morris Associates, 135
ROM (read only memory), 100
Roosevelt, Franklin D., 152

Safety. *See also* Security
  coordinator for emergencies, 93
  features for buildings, 77, 79
  in work environment, 155–156
Salaries, 160–162
Sales, 130
Scanners, 113–114
Scapegoating behavior, 213
Screen-based electronic typewriter (SBET),
    114
Secretaries
  as information source, 196
  as managers, 3
  technology impact on, 119–120
Security. *See also* Safety
  for building, 79
  of client files, 57
  paper shredders for, 62
  of staff, 50
Self-fulfilling prophecy, 206
Server Technology, 112
Sexual harassment, 155, 156
Sholes, Christopher, 101
Signage privileges, 83

Site licensing agreements, 119
Situational leadership, 204–205
Smoke detection systems, 79
Smoking, in office, 157
Social norm, 222
Software. *See also* Computers; Information
    management
  for billing, 39
  calendar, 116–117
  client database, 51
  DocuLiner, 104
  document management, 115–116
  litigation management, 104, 116
  piracy problems, 119
  selection process, 106–109
  for timekeeping, 32, 35
  vendor selection, 109
  viruses and bugs, 118–119
  for word processing, 109
Software Link, The, 112
Sole proprietorship, 127
Space planning, 87–91
Speculative balance, 143
Split-screen technology, 60
Spokesperson role, 19
Sprinkler systems, 79
Staffing. *See also* Personnel management
  defined, 11
  reception staff, 48–50
  and security, 50
Standards. *See* Performance standards
Star topology, 110, 112, 113
StarLAN, 110, 112
Statute of limitations, 116
Statutory fees, 26, 27
Steele, Addison, 216
Stereotyping, 184
Subject filing system, 54–55
Supplies, office, 68–70. *See also* Equipment
  employee pilferage, 70
Surge suppressors, 103
Survey of legal administrators, 3, 5–6
Synchronized cash flows, 145

TAB (principle of truth and balance), 130
Task force, 221
Taxes, and office equipment, 68
Telephone systems
  evaluating and choosing, 45–47
  modems for, 102
  and voice mail, 47–48
Telephone usage
  costs of, 46
  expense tracking, 35–37, 105
  personal long-distance calls, 70
  for reception staff, 49–50
Theory of Leadership Effectiveness, A (Fiedler),
    204
Theory X leadership attitude, 205–206, 207,
    208

Theory Y leadership attitude, 206, 207, 208
Thermal printers, 102
Tickler file, 116
Time management, 10–11
Time planning system, 30–32
Timekeeping
    and client billing, 38–39
    importance of, 29–30
    record form, 33–34
    systems, 30–35
To Do list, 11, 12
Today's Office magazine, 86
Token ring network, 110
Topology (network), 110–112
Transaction balance, 143
Trial balance, 133
Triple net lease, 84
Trust account, 131
Turnkey clause in lease, 83
Turnkey system, 109
Typesetting, 105
Typewriters, electronic, 114–115

UNIX, 102
Upward Mobility (Steele), 216
Usable area of building, 75–76

Valuable papers coverage, 94
Verbal communication. *See under*
    Communication
Video monitor, 102, 157
Virus, computer, 118–119
Vocalics, 183–184
Voice mail, 47–48

Wang Laboratories, 113
Weisinger, Hendrie, 192, 193
WESTLAW, 65
*What They Don't Teach You at Harvard
    Business School* (McCormack), 231
Win-lose negotiating style, 233–234
Win-win negotiating style, 229–230, 234–
    235
Withdrawal behavior, 213
Word processing, 103, 106–107, 109, 114
WordPerfect, 109
Work and the Nature of Man (Herzberg), 211
Workletter in lease, 80–82
Workstations, 89–91

Xerox, 110